NEGOTIATING CONFLICT

NEGOTIATING CONFLICT

INSIGHTS AND SKILLS
FOR NEGOTIATORS AND PEACEMAKERS

MARK ANSTEY

Director of the Industrial Relations Unit,
University of Port Elizabeth

1991
JUTA & CO, LTD

First published in 1991

Copyright © Juta & Co, Ltd
PO Box 14373, Kenwyn 7790

ISBN 0 7021 2612 8

Printed and bound by Shepherds Press, Retreat, Cape Town.

The book gives an insight into his array of skills. It draws together much of the modern thinking on conflict and negotiation.

Negotiation and indeed mediation are skills learned by experience. Short of direct exposure there is no better teaching method than reference to well constructed case studies and practical examples, and this book has a number of these.

It demonstrates that conflict is capable of effective management, if not resolution, by means other than coercion and force. That is a lesson we need to learn in South Africa if there is to be a prospect of lasting peace. This book is therefore most welcome at this time, and we may well have cause to reflect in the future how important its contribution really was.

Charles Nupen

ACKNOWLEDGEMENTS

This book reflects some years of research, training and practice in the fields of negotiation and mediation. While its final compilation was a solitary task, its structure and content are the product of interaction with many people.

Academic and professional colleagues helped me shape ideas, provided information, reviewed pieces of the work, pinpointed salient gaps in the book and suggested how they might be filled. Here special appreciation is expressed to Martheanne Finnemore, Judy Parfitt, Louis Kamfer, Derek de Villiers, Adriaan Van der Walt, Charles Nupen, and Chris Baker, all of whom took time out to read either the whole work or parts of it, and to share with me their ideas or commentary. However, the book's contents reflect learning and ideas which have their source across a far wider spectrum of persons over the years — students, trade unionists, managers, and community workers; and my colleagues in the social work profession, in the Independent Mediation Service of South Africa and in industrial relations practice. Parties who privileged me by asking me to assist them in settling disputes or facilitate a new approach to their relationship gave me experiences to assist others' learning.

The bibliography reveals how heavily I have leaned on the work of other theorists and writers, but the practical contributions of all these other persons have given my understanding of theory life — and I hope that this is what is shared in return — a living, usable document for people in conflict situations.

Cynthia Hopkins' professional and patient assistance with some of the typing was invaluable. Appreciation on this score goes beyond the technical; it extends to her capacity to reduce my frustration at critical moments when the intricacies of word processors threatened my ability to get on with the job.

Finally, the compilation of a book takes time. It requires the back-up of a family which unselfishly gives time. My family offered more than this. To Irene who read through the manuscript providing that unique blend of professionalism and support which only a wife can give; and to Jessica and David who have shared so much learning with me, who applied some of their early reading skills in grappling with pieces of this work, and who have showed such interest in its production — thank you.

Mark Anstey

PREFACE

The purpose of this book is to provide an understanding of conflict and an introduction to the skills of negotiation and problem solving. It does not attempt another analysis of the South African situation, but seeks rather to acquaint the reader with some core tools for grasping conflict process across a broad range of situations, and if negotiation is the alternative of choice for dealing with tensions, to provide an outline of various approaches which might be utilised.

My own experience of negotiation is rooted in labour-management relations and many of the examples and anecdotes used to illustrate points refer to industrial relations situations. However, this is not a work directed at labour negotiators alone. Examples are also drawn from studies in international relations, community conflicts and interpersonal exchanges.

Chapter One provides an introduction to the nature of conflict and problems in its analysis. A conceptual framework is presented which addresses causes of conflict and a range of aggravators/moderators which mediate its expression. Scarce resources, structural problems, communal tensions, information problems, ambiguity during periods of social change, and differences arising out of the identification and coordination of strategies for change are discussed as central sources of conflict. Conflicts are expressed in a variety of ways, ranging from violent efforts to coerce opposition through to negotiation and problem solving. Attention is given therefore to factors which aggravate or moderate the expression of conflict — the history of relations, aspirations and perceptions, constituent pressures, the use of strategies, tolerance, internal coherence, the availability of acceptable procedures and forums for dispute handling, balances of power, and shared group conflict limiting norms.

Chapter Two outlines factors which contribute to the escalation and de-escalation of conflict. The conflict escalation process typically involves changes in the nature of demands and issues, communications between parties, their perceptions of each other, and their use of tactics. In addition important changes occur within groups engaged in conflictual exchange, which heighten tensions and often lock them into further efforts to inflict damage on each other. Typically processes of gratification, entrapment, provocation, and internal group changes contribute to escalating conflict. Not uncommonly as relations change, violence occurs. Attention is given to the debate surrounding the use of violence and factors contributing to its use. A large case study outlining the escalation of conflict and consequent violence in the SATS strike of 1987 is provided to illustrate the theoretical points raised in this discussion.

Finally, factors contributing to stalemate and conflict de-escalation are discussed — the failure of contentious tactics, loss of social support, unacceptable costs, organisational conservatism, third party intervention and internal changes in groups.

Chapter Three points out that negotiation is not the only option for parties involved in conflictual relations. It occurs when the parties decide to use it in place of, or in conjunction with other methods of conflict resolution which may include coercive, disruptive or insurrectionist tactics. In other words negotiation is a consequence of conscious strategic choices. Certain ideological commitments may preclude negotiation or acknowledge its usefulness only in terms of tactical or holding functions in the face of a stronger opposition. Pluralism is the belief system which most facilitates negotiation with its acknowledgement of diversity of interests in society, of rights to associate freely and establish pressure groups, and its systems of formal bargaining and dispute resolution. Pluralism is not premised solely on concepts of compromise and power balance but acknowledges that not all principles, values or goods may be compromised and that pluralist societies are certainly not characterised by power balance between all interest groups as such. However they do allow room to operate for interest groups, and they are characterised by negotiation and cooperation (institutionalised forms of conflict regulation) rather than coercion and insurrection. A wealth base, mutual tolerance and a prevailing desire to see the system continue seem to be important elements in the ongoing stability of these systems. It is far harder to establish a viable democracy in poverty stricken countries.

Various approaches to negotiation and problem solving are available to those wishing to pursue this route. The choice of which to use depends on such factors as power relativities, needs of the parties, perceived outcomes and rewards in using the process as opposed to other tactics, ideological commitment, mutual accordance of legitimacy, constituencies, and available mechanisms to facilitate the process.

Chapter Four describes the distributive or positional approach to negotiation, its phases and tactics. The work of several authors is reviewed and basic techniques and skills of preparation, opening, signalling, proposing, packaging and bargaining, and closing negotiations are discussed. The emphasis is not on providing endless lists of tactical ploys — constructive tactics have only one function, that is to facilitate the achievement of an agreement or settlement. If planning is centred on tactics alone, rather than the issues for which the meeting is to be held, then they may well become obstacles to progress as parties lose sight of their purpose and concentrate on visionless tactical exchanges.

Chapter Five outlines a range of creative alternatives to positional bargaining. The techniques associated with joint problem solving, and more importantly the pre-requisites for the approach to be viable are discussed. Burton's approach to resolving deep-rooted conflicts is outlined and the 'bargaining on the merits' approach of Fisher and Ury, and Fisher and Brown are synthesised and described. These authors have relied heavily on existing social science knowledge and research but offer a creative alternative to traditional approaches to negotiation. Finally the work of de Bono in the field is touched on. While it seems that most bargaining devolves down to the traditional distributive approach it is proposed here that greater effort to move to an interest based negotiation approach might be helpful in many situations.

Chapter Six investigates the basics of communication and attitude change in the recognition that negotiation is essentially a persuasive communication. The nature and complexities of communication are outlined before moving to some discussion of techniques to improve skills of establishing a listening environment, improve the negotiation climate, improve message transmission and listening and observation, and understand communication networks. The usefulness of the question is addressed before discussion of the process of persuasion and attitude change.

Chapter Seven is devoted to the skills of mediation. Several key issues are debated — the acceptability of mediators, timing of entry to disputes, the evaluation of effectiveness of an intervention, and mediator power and assertiveness. An inventory of mediator strategies and tactics is provided and a contingency approach to the use of these discussed on the basis of understanding the conflict dynamic. Differences between labour and community conflicts are outlined and some hints for community mediators provided. A community mediation is discussed to highlight some of the points made. Finally a new approach to assisting fractured labour-management relationships is presented — the Relationships by Objectives (RBO) programme.

Chapter Eight, the final chapter, does not attempt a conclusion as such, but provides a synopsis of the content of the book by way of a usable framework of key issues which negotiators and mediators might use to assess the conflicts in which they are engaged, the use of tactics by the parties involved, the nature of the negotiation process, and obstacles to effective negotiation. It is hoped that this will be of practical use to those involved in processes of negotiation and peacemaking, and allow this book to be a little more than just interesting reading.

CONTENTS

APPENDICES

1
CONFLICT AND STABILITY

Conflict is endemic in South African society. Between 1986 and 1990 an estimated 8 500 people lost their lives through political violence, over 3 500 of these during 1990 alone. By comparison, 2 724 people died in the Northern Ireland conflict in the twenty years between 1969 and 1988 (Gallagher 1989). Since 1960 approximately 73 000 detentions under security or emergency legislation have taken place (Human Rights Commission 1990). Three and a half million people have been forcibly removed from their homes under apartheid legislation. The law enforcement, justice and prisons systems have been overburdened with the criminal prosecution of people simply seeking work. In an effort to stem the urbanisation process on a racial basis the apartheid system gave rise to 17 million pass law convictions (Riordan 1990).

ANC guerilla actions increased from 4 in 1976 to 203 in 1986 and 183 in 1987, totalling 715 incidents over this period (Indicator 1988). Between 1988 and 1990 over 65 rightwing attacks on individuals and property were recorded (SA Barometer 1990). Mass action against city council structures has witnessed the widespread breakdown of local government structures perceived as the product of the apartheid system.

Between 1984 and 1990 more than 120 attacks on the homes of councillors were carried out, and over 20 councillors killed. Nearly a third of the Transvaal's 82 Councils collapsed during 1990, with mass resignations giving rise to 235 vacancies out of the 692 seats in the Province. (Star 24/10/90; The Democrat Dec 1990). Rent, school, and consumer boycotts have seriously eroded the viability of the social system.

Between 1985 and 1989 at least 11 million, but more probably as many as 15 million mandays were lost to the economy through strike action, twice as many as the cumulative total of the preceding 75 years. Political stayaways lose the economy millions of mandays each year (Anstey 1990).

In a tabloid of South African conflict since 1818, Frescura (1988) writes:

> . . . since 1811 we have seen 24 major conflicts and over two score smaller localised conflagrations (in South Africa). This means that on average one major rebellion, war, or uprising has taken place every third year in this country over the last 176 years. (p 129)

The dimensions of South African conflict are many — racial domination, ethnic intolerance, ideological division, class stratification and poverty associated with inequitable wealth distribution, authoritarian rule and subversive 'third forces' anxious to destabilise peace processes have been commonly cited as causes of ongoing tensions and violence. There is probably substance to all these — the situation is not one dimensional. This chapter does not attempt yet another analysis of the South African conflict. While referring to it at points, its central objective is to assist an understanding of conflict generally, and to this end many situations and debates will be touched upon.

CONFLICT DEFINED

Coser's (1956) early definition of conflict sees it as:

> . . . a struggle over values and claims to scarce status, power and resources in which the aims of the opponents are to neutralise, injure or eliminate their rivals. (p 8)

This definition sees conflict as

- ❏ a struggle over *values or scarcity*; and
- ❏ *goal directed* in that the parties seek to neutralise or injure each other in their efforts to obtain their objectives.

Himes (1980) defines conflict as follows:

> Social conflict refers to purposeful struggles between collective actors who use social power to defeat or remove opponents and to gain status, power resources and other scarce values (p 14)

In terms of this approach social conflict:

❏ is *purposeful behaviour* involving planning as to how to attain scarce values and overcome resistance (this does not mean it is always logical or efficient);

❏ takes place in a *social structure* which qualifies the situation in various ways;

❏ involves the *use of power* to neutralise or remove obstructing groups or resistance;

❏ is associated with *collective action* of a *strategic nature* designed to reduce resistance by an opponent who is led to understand that relief from pressure can be achieved only by concessions or capitulation;

❏ centres around the acquisition of *scarce resources and values.*

Writing from a sociological perspective, Himes's emphasis on collective action is not surprising, but it is limiting. Although this work is primarily concerned with the interaction between collectivities, this should not preclude an understanding that conflict can occur also at interpersonal or intra-individual levels.

Kriesberg (1973) states:

> Social conflict is a relationship between two or more parties who (or whose spokesmen) believe they have incompatible goals (p 17)

This definition centres on conflict as

❏ a *relationship;* and importantly

❏ that conflict is rooted in people's *beliefs* about goals, as opposed to objective facts.

This focus on people's beliefs is carried through in Pruitt & Rubin's (1986) definition:

> ... conflict means perceived divergence of interest, or a belief that the parties current aspirations cannot be achieved simultaneously (p 14)

Utilising these contributions conflict is defined as follows:

The first part of this definition addresses the causes of conflict, the second its expression.

DEFINITION OF SOCIAL CONFLICT

Conflict exists in a relationship when parties *believe* that their aspirations cannot be achieved simultaneously, or *perceive* a divergence in their values, needs or interests (latent conflict)

and

purposefully employ their power in an effort to defeat, neutralise or eliminate each other to protect or further their interests in the interaction (manifest conflict).

Box 1.1

SOME DIMENSIONS OF CONFLICT

The legitimacy of conflict

Himes (1980) addresses the issue of conflict as a legitimised process, pointing out that all societies struggle with tensions between conflict and cooperation in an ongoing way over time. Over time norms are established which limit the expression of conflict behaviour and sanction deviations from this standard. This tends to not be a rigid standard but shifts in society over time. While most societies accept a level of conflict expression as inevitable none tolerate it in all its forms or levels. High intensity, violent forms are threatening to the survival of a system and are generally not tolerated. Some societies allow wide latitude for non-violent protest and disruptive tactics, seeing in their manifestation important symptoms of a healthy democracy, and perceiving conflict to have important functional qualities for societal health and adaptability. In other more rigid structures there is little latitude for such expression which is perceived as a fundamental threat to survival of the system (Clegg 1975).

Himes writes:

> Conflicts may be defined as legitimate when they are required, endorsed, or permitted by the universalistic norms of an inclusive social system, for instance, that of a society or community . . . conflicts that exceed the limits imposed by societal consensus . . . are defined as nonlegitimate (p 18–19)

This raises problems in defining acceptable behaviour in societies in transition — when is a guerilla a terrorist, when does a freedom fighter become a criminal? By what criteria are such judgements to be made — a few universal standards, or simple majoritarianism, or dominant group standards even if espoused by a minority in a society? The legitimacy question is a vexed one complicated by shifting norms, cul-

tural variation, means-ends debates, and questions of justice
and morality. Himes (1980) comments:

> ... it seems evident that the demarcations of legitimate and
> nonlegitimate conflict reflect self-interests of inclusive so-
> cial systems (p 21)

Legitimacy, he argues, stems from tradition, collective policy
and political authority. These are interrelated and in stable
societies probably self-reinforcing. In societies in transition,
or in crisis, all these sources may be called into question — a
normative crisis emerges confounding moral judgement in
periods of uncertainty.

Functional and dysfunctional conflict

Social views on conflict have shifted over time. Coser (1956)
observes several changes in position, early sociologists such
as Cooley seeing conflict as a positive vehicle for progressive
social change, later ones such as Parsons and Lundberg assuming a more conservative view of conflict as being a primarily disruptive, dysfunctional phenomenon. This latter
view was also held by Elton Mayo, the theorist whose ideas
spawned the humanist approach to management as a means
of conflict avoidance. Coser (1956) criticises Mayo's work as
failing to acknowledge that actual conflict of interests may
exist rather than mere differences in attitudes or 'logics'.
Mayo's work was biased toward a view of organisations as
essentially stable, harmonious and integrative in character.
Coser's (1956–1957) work represented a break from these
views. Returning to the work of George Simmel he developed
a set of propositions regarding the functions of conflict which
are regarded as of major significance to this day (see box 1.2).
His basic starting point was the perspective that

> ... no group can be entirely harmonious, for it would then
> be devoid of process and structure. Groups require dishar-
> mony as well as harmony, dissociation as well as associ-
> ation; and conflicts within them are by no means altogether

> disruptive factors. Group formation is the result of both types of processes. The belief that one process tears down what the other buildsup, so that what finally remains is the result of subtracting one from the other, is based on a misconception. On the contrary, both 'positive'and 'negative' facts build group relations. Conflict as well as co-operation has social functions. Far from being necessarily dysfunctional, a certain degree of conflict is an essential element in group formation and the persistence of group life. (p 31)

Having acknowledged that conflict and cooperation are concurrent and necessary processes in group life, it must be acknowledged that both can be dysfunctional as well as positive in consequence. The struggle for health in group life may be seen as centred in its efforts to achieve a viable balance in the ongoing tension between these processes so that it enjoys sufficient cooperation to achieve goals of survival and growth for its participants but also sufficient divergence to generate the creativity and energy required for this same purpose.

Deutsch (1973) distinguishes between *destructive* and *productive* conflict. In the former, processes of conflict escalation result in mutual attacks and efforts to destroy each other, misjudgements and misperceptions and situational entrapment in which the conflict becomes magnified. In such a process a group's capacity to achieve its goals or even survive may be seriously jeopardised. Productive conflict on the other hand witnesses the arousal of a problem-solving motivation, triggers creativity and innovation, stimulates new ways of interacting and promotes interparty relations in terms of communications, trust, sensitivity and understanding. From this perspective it is not the conflict *per se* that is regarded as functional or dysfunctional but how it is handled (Deutsch 1973; King 1981).

COSER'S PROPOSITIONS
ON THE LATENT FUNCTIONS OF CONFLICT

1 A group binding function

Conflict establishes and maintains the identity and boundary lines of groups and societies by conserving social divisions and stratification systems.

2 A group-preservation function

Conflict may act to maintain a social relationship freeing feelings of hostility rather than allowing them to accumulate. Social systems provide specific safety-valve institutions to drain off hostile and aggressive sentiments, but this has the cost of reducing pressure for system modification to meet changing conditions, as well as contributing to individual frustration.

3 Realistic and Non-realistic conflict

Realistic conflicts are instrumental, goal seeking and external, arising when people clash in pursuit of aims over scarce resources such as power, resources or status. Non-realistic conflicts have a tension releasing, self-rewarding character. They are not viewed as a means toward the achievement of realistic ends, but are an expression of displaced aggression.

4 Conflict and hostile impulses

Aggressive or hostile impulses are not sufficient to explain social conflict. They are states of feeling or attitudes which predispose toward conflict, but a conflict is centred in an interaction between parties. In realistic conflict there may be no hostility although usually these feelings are present acting to strengthen the capacity of parties for action.

5 Hostility in close social relationships

Close social relationships usually have an overall unitary character, but contain an ambivalent inter-twining of positive and negative cathexes.

BOX 1.2

6 The closer the relationship, the more intense the conflict

Dissidents who do not cross over to the enemy but establish rival groups threaten group unity and identity. Conflict in such situations tends to be more radical and passionate in quality, though not more frequent than in distant relationships.

7 The impact and function of conflict in group structures

Conflicts that do not contradict basic core values may serve to remove dissidents and reestablish group unit. 'Loosely structured groups and open societies, by allowing conflicts, institute safeguards against the type of conflict which would endanger basic consensus and thereby minimise the danger of divergences touching core values' (Coser 1987 p 80). A social system is 'sewn together' through the interdependence of antagonistic groups and a 'crisscrossing' of conflicts which act to cancel each other out thus preventing disintegration 'along one primary line of cleavage' (p 80).

8 Conflict as an index of stability of relationships

Stable, close relationships may be characterised by frequent conflicts. If these are 'realistic' rather than based on accumulated hostility and ambivalence (nonrealistic) and they do not threaten basic consensus, then they may be seen as an index of stability in a relationship.

9 Conflict with out-groups increases internal cohesion

In groups where a high degree of consensus exists prior to the conflict, the energies of members are mobilised increasing group cohesion. In groups where existing consensus/ solidarity is low, they may be threatened with disintegration owing to inner divergences. 'Despotism... is required for carrying out hostilities where there is insufficient group solidarity to mobilise energies of group members' (p 95)

BOX 1.2
(Continued)

10 Conflict with another group defines group structure and consequent reaction to internal conflict

Groups engaged in continued external conflict tend to be internally intolerant, assuming a sect-like character and remaining limited in size. 'Their social cohesion depends upon total sharing of all aspects of group life and is reinforced by the assertion of group unity against the dissenter' (p 103). Ideologically tolerant groups tend to be large and 'contain' conflict through flexible structures.

11 The search for enemies

Rigidly organised struggle groups may search for enemies to maintain unity and cohesion — imaginary threat has the same function as real threat. A threatened internal cohesion may evoke the search for an external enemy or an internal dissenter, particularly in groups in which realistic conflict is inhibited within.

12 Ideology and conflict

Where participants in a conflict perceive themselves as representatives of collectivities, fighting for group rather than personal ends, they are likely to be more 'radical and merciless' in behaviour. 'Strict ideological alignments are more likely to occur in rigid than in flexible adjustive structures' (p 119).

13 Conflict - the unifier

Conflict may stimulate the establishment of new rules, norms and institutions serving as an agent of socialisation for both contending parties, intensifying participation in social life and facilitating change and readjustment.

14 Interest in the unity of the enemy

Where a rough balance of power exists between two parties, they tend to prefer unity within the other. This facilitates joint control/regulation of the struggle, institutionalising its expression and forms of exchange i.e. rendering it more predictable and controllable for both.

BOX 1.2
(Continued)

15 Conflict establishes and maintains a balance of power

Conflict allows disputing parties to assess each other's relative strength and to seek ways of avoiding disequilibrium. Thus conflict may act to stabilise and balance a society through the creation and modification of norms, an institutionalisation of preferred means of exchange and adjustment of relative power.

16 Conflict creates associations and coalitions

In rigid societies suppressed conflicts tend to be more intense and ideological in character than in flexible structures. In these conflict may promote organisation, bringing together unrelated groups 'into temporary coalitions and associations around pragmatic interests within flexible inclusive systems'. (Himes 1980 p. 131). 'Coalitions and associations give structure to an individualistic society and prevent it from disintegrating through atomisation' (Coser 1956 p 149).

17 Change within social systems

Conflict prevents rigidity and facilitates adoptive internal reorganisation.

18 Change of social systems

Conflict promotes social transformation by modifying major structures, values and institutions.

BOX 1.2

UNDERSTANDING CONFLICT: A FRAMEWORK

Thomas (1976) distinguishes between two conflict models, both of which focus on the conflict handling behaviour of the parties involved — a structural model and a process model.

The *structural* model

> ... attempts to understand conflict phenomena by studying how underlying conditions shape events . . . to identify parameters which influence conflict behaviour and to specify the form of that influence. Because these conditions or parameters are relatively fixed or slow changing . . . they are seen as structural in nature. (p 893)

Typically the structural model focuses on such factors as personal predispositions, social pressures, negotiation procedures and rules, incentives and their influence on conflict behaviour.

The *process* model on the other hand focuses on the internal dynamics of conflict episodes, studying events and their effects on succeeding events in conflict episodes. Thomas proposes that while the two approaches can be conceptually separated they are in reality strongly interrelated:

> ... the two models complement each other. The structural model tends to be useful for suggesting systemic changes, while the process model tends to be helpful in managing an ongoing system. The structural model suggests long run improvements in relationships, while the process model helps one cope with crises. . . . Both models and the tactics which they suggest are necessary for effective conflicy management. . . . In reality they fit together into one larger view of conflict structure and process. The structural variables constrain and shape the process dynamics, while knowledge of the process dynamics helps one predict the effects of structural variables. (p 894)

A full understanding of any conflict must then give attention to both structural and process aspects of a relationship, and how they influence each other. Sources of conflict, conflict behaviour and the perceptions and feelings of the parties involved require attention.

In a review of conflict models, Dessler (1980) proposes a general conflict model of his own which seeks to integrate the contributions of Pondy (1967), Walton and Dutton (1969), Schmidt and Kochan (1972) and Ruble and Thomas (1976). In much simplified form this may be presented in the form below.

Most theorists agree that conflict *antecedents* may be classified into such groupings as scarce resources, differing goals, drives for autonomy, power/authority imbalances, ambiguity or interdependence. Conflict *behaviour* may take a variety of forms which can be categorised into Ruble and Thomas's (1976) competing, avoiding, accommodating, compromising, or collaborating. The form the conflict behaviour eventually assumes is the product of numerous *moderating influences* that determine the extent to which the conflict is perceived or felt, and how the parties approach the issue in the context of their wider relationship.

Using Dessler's (1980) conceptual framework as a base and integrating the more recent contributions of such authors as Moore (1985) and Pruitt and Rubin (1986), the following framework is proposed (figure 1.1).

SOURCES OF CONFLICT

Differing goals

The most obvious source of conflict is differing goals between parties, especially where there is an *interdependence* in their relationship and there is a *scarce resource* for which they are

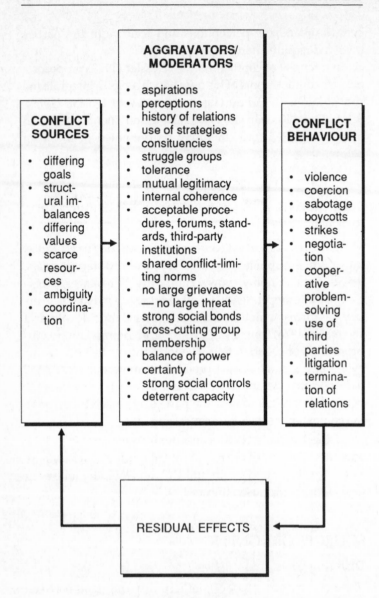

Figure 1.1
A conceptual framework for understanding conflict

competing. The interdependence factor means that neither party can achieve its objectives without at least some cooperation from the other party. For instance there is proposed to be an interdependence in the labour–management relationship. While they may have differing goals in as far as management seeks always to reduce costs of production, and workers to maximise returns from their investment of labour, they have a mutual need for the production process to continue if they are to achieve their goals at least partially. Their interdependence produces an inherent and ongoing conflict — neither can afford to destroy the relationship although objectives of each are different. The scarce resource factor obliges a conflictual engagement between parties. They are not able to meet their needs elsewhere, but must seek to satisfy them in interaction with the other.

Differing goals are readily evidenced in the proposals of liberal and social democrats for structuring a future economy for South Africa which will allow for growth and redistribution (box 1.3). While both schools have as their objectives a growth economy, fairer redistribution of wealth and a democratic polity their differences reflect more than a divergence over strategy or problems over coordination of effort to achieve the same end — they reveal fundamentally different objectives as far as ownership of the means of production, control over the economy, and the role of the state are concerned if they are adopted as positions. Positions such as these tend to produce entrenched stances in the well-worn capitalist–socialist debate. From an alternative bargaining perspective these goals could be seen as merely two sets of proposals for a future economy, and as having importance as an expression of the key interests and needs of different groups in society. Rather than ends in their own right they could be seen as possible routes to meeting these diverse interests and needs. A more constructive approach might be

LIBERAL DEMOCRATIC PROPOSALS

- universal franchise
- devolution of power to decentralised regional government
- minority safeguards in legislative bodies
- removal of discrimination and segregation
- independent judiciary and rule of law
- 'democratisation' of business
- free and independent trade union movement
- improved access for blacks to land and capital
- extension of ownership and control in the economy
- deregulation and privatisation
- possible 'compensation' for victims of apartheid
- provision of venture capital/small business development
- informal sector development to provide housing and social services
- obliged social spending by financial institutions and private sector involvement in community development
- educational reform
- agricultural training and cooperative development for rural populations

BOX 1.3(*a*)
Liberal democratic proposals
for a future South African economy

DEMOCRATIC SOCIALIST PROPOSALS

- universal franchise
- centralised government
- socioeconomic reconstruction for purposes of income and wealth redistribution
- market economy but under overall state supervision
- state projects on housing, employment and social service
- state controls over the banking sector
- state production services to meet demands of rapid urbanisation and employment requirements
- decentralisation/dismemberment of monopolies/conglomerates
- attraction of employment creating foreign investment
- greater levels of social control through worker councils and local and state planning
- a free and independent trade union movement and greater industrial democracy
- promotion of collective ownership schemes
- promotion of small-scale enterprises land redistribution and major rural development programmes

BOX 1.3(*b*)
Democratic socialist proposals
for a future South African economy

to list core needs of the various interest groupings, e.g. return on investment, job creation, a welfare net, education, housing. Then to identify what might facilitate the attainment of these — a growth economy, foreign investment, wealth redistribution, job creating investment, trained teachers and builders etc. Then proposals might be put forward directed at the identified needs and centred in planning ways to achieve the mechanisms necessary to allow progress. Too often individuals and groups start with positions and fight over these before identifying what the real problems are, and using techniques to seek joint solutions. The problem is, of course, that redistribution programmes are likely to cost some parties and benefit others, at least initially. However much work is done in identifying needs and interests, and looking for common ground and ways of resolving differences to the benefit of all, limited resources are likely to produce competition at some point. Unless owners of wealth and power perceive their interests to be preserved through restructuring, and 'have nots' perceive their interests to be served by providing some guarantees to property owners, cooperation is unlikely. Here again though, there may be differences between short- and long-term goals — 'enlightened self interest' may recognise a route which would see the protection of long-term interests to lie in certain short-term costs or sacrifices. The gap between approaching such issues along competitive or problem-solving lines is elucidated in chapters 4 and 5.

While scarce resources may limit the extent to which joint problem solving might be used, it is too often neglected in instances where it could be employed.

Structural imbalances: class conflict

Structural imbalances occur in cases where there is actual or perceived inequality of control of resources, ownership and resource distribution. Thus issues of power and authority are of central concern, dominant groups using their capacity for control to entrench their position of privilege.

Developing the example above, whites in South Africa, in attempting to protect their identity and privilege, introduced a complex network of laws which served to structure people's opportunities in terms of education and business, removed freedoms of choice in the areas of worship, recreation, residence and association, and constrained access to capital and land. As a consequence serious structural imbalances emerged, confusing class and race as issues of social stratification, and giving rise to a highly conflictual society.

The classic argument for structural imbalances lies in the Marxist critique of capitalism. More recently it is apparent in the critique of state bureaucracies in the Eastern bloc, which developed as a consequence of efforts to find an alternative to capitalism in the form of planned economies along Marxist–Leninist lines. Bureaucratic power elites emerged, failing to achieve either economic growth or political democracy. A very brief account of some of the major threads of this debate as it has evolved over the last century is provided here.

Marx argued that labour is the source of all value. Labour is, however, paid in wages only to the extent of its own value, this being the amount required to train and maintain the life of the labourer. Capitalists employ labourers for more hours than needed to for this purpose, thus securing a surplus value which they collect as profit. This exploitation of labour is seen not so much as arising from any malicious intent on the part of individual employers but a consequence of the capitalist system which obliges a continued drive for accumulated capital in the form of profits (surplus value). Capital is accumulated in two forms: variable capital in the form of hired labour and constant capital in the form of raw materials, tools and machinery. Accumulation of constant capital increases the capacity for production but causes technological unemployment. As the reserve army of the unemployed grows so wages are kept down as workers are obliged to compete amongst themselves for jobs.

As a consequence of this process ownership and wealth, and thus *power* is concentrated increasingly in the hands of a few, leading eventually and inevitably to the development of monopoly capitalism. Those without property are obliged to sell their labour to survive, their work being reduced to the level of any other commodity in the production process. With the shift to constant capital, each worker's efforts to secure a job, or improve his or her wages or work environment is resisted by the capitalist as a cost. As Hyman (1975) observes:

> . . . within capitalist industry, workers are treated less as men and women with distinctive needs and aspirations than as dehumanised factors of production . . . the capacity to work is thus bought and sold, rather like fruit and vegetables. (p 20)

As increasing wealth accumulates in the hands of a few capitalists, so does their power over political, education, public and legal institutions. The lot of the working class is one of increasing immiseration, powerlessness and insecurity both in the workplace and in the wider society.

The capitalists use their control over the means of production to seek further profits to live from the labour of others. The inequitable distribution of wealth in South Africa, coupled with the clear concentration of wealth in the hands of a few conglomerates allows easy application of this analysis to the South African situation. Savage (1985, 1987) reports that 6 groups of companies control 84,3 % of total market capitalisation on the Johannesburg Stock Exchange, with Anglo American alone accounting for over 53 %. Decisionmaking regarding the concentrated wealth in the private sector lies in the hands of 2 676 directors of companies. Of these, 27,6 % control 59,1 % of directorships of public companies through systems of interlocking directorships. In 1980 nearly 60 % of the country's personal income was received by only 10 % of the population, largely white. On the other hand there is a housing shortage of over 800 000 units, 56 % of households live in poverty (largely black) and there is a rapidly growing unemployment, health and welfare crisis.

In the longer term the capitalist process is seen as self defeating with falling rates of profit for capitalists as the proportion of variable capital (the only source of surplus value) declines against that of constant capital. Marxists proposed that mass unemployment and a crisis in capitalism would ensue, with the consequence of mass mobilisation, revolution and a radical restructuring of the economy.

Capitalism from this perspective then is inherently flawed, producing structural imbalances which would see its inevitable demise as it peaked in the form of monopoly capitalism and mass unemployment. (Grossman 1967; Hyman 1975)

The Communist Manifesto proposes that capitalism has simplified the class antagonisms into two great groups facing each other — the bourgeoisie and the proletariat — the consequence of a long series of revolutions in the modes of production in which the bourgeoisie emerged victorious. To survive they have to continually revolutionise the means of production and thereby the relations of production and thus of society as a whole. Industrialisation, urbanisation and capitalist imperialism are inevitable consequences. As a consequence of unceasing exploitation and conflict the working class would form trades unions. Their failure to stop exploitation would see the mobilisation of the wider working class, and as the crisis deepens a split in the bourgeoisie as a small group leaves its ranks to join the proletariat. Unlike previous movements which were all essentially minorities the proletariat would be a self conscious majority working for the interests of the majority. In essence the requirement for large numbers of workers would allow the mobilisation and organisation of the working class, the bourgeoisie thus producing its own demise by its needs for profit. The revolutionary process would be led by the Communist Party acting in the interests of the working class as a whole to destroy the private ownership of property and thus the social power of the ruling class. National differences would diminish with the expansion of capitalism and disappear with the victory of communism. To prevent future exploitation the proletariat would vest control of all modes of production in the state, as well as control over the means of economic exchange.

Lenin proposed that it would not be sufficient to wait for workers to develop a political class consciousness — it would have to be brought to them in order for them to move beyond the narrow confines of an economic awareness of the struggle. Professional revolutionaries would be required for this task and to lead and organise the revolution. The Communist Party was seen as the body for this task acting on behalf of the proletariat as a whole, and bringing revolutionary political theory and organisation to the masses. It would be the vanguard of the revolution establishing a dictatorship of the proletariat under the hegemony of the Party to lead the working classes through the process of radical change. In the transition to a socialist society, the state would carry the tasks of crushing resistance of the exploiting class, defending the gains of the revolution, introducing socialist changes, improving the living conditions of the people, guiding the masses into socialism, and extending the struggle to liberation movements internationally (Sabirov 1987). Lenin supplanted the historical determinism of Marx with a pro-active theory of revolution under the guidance and control of the Party, and in so doing, eroded concepts of democracy and liberty both in the transition process to a socialist state and in government.

Marx's economic analysis of severe structural imbalances in society was thus developed progressively into a theory of revolution, and beyond that a plan of action to put this into effect on an international footing. Thus imperialism became an important issue of debate. Lenin saw imperialism as the process of capital accumulation on a world scale during the period of peak capitalism. The export of capital by capitalist monopolies would extend their control over the world's raw materials, enabling the extraction of super-profits by the exploitation of labour in developing countries. The definition and meaning of imperialism produced early difference between Lenin and Kautsky, and continues to be the subject of heated debate today in Marxist circles. Suffice it here to state that from a revolutionary perspective the weakest link of capitalism was seen to be in underdeveloped countries where the bourgeoisie would be weak but there would be sufficient industrialisation to create a class conscious proletariat. The capacity of the richer countries' ruling classes to placate the demands of the proletariat through material upgrading would be absent. Mobilisation of both the peasantry and the workers would be necessary for this process. Socialist victory in the Third World would expose the contradictions of capitalism in the First World leading to world revolution for consummation of the socialist struggle. (Bottomore 1983; Buzuev 1987)

The neatness of this theory of structural conflict as an inevitable consequence of the capitalist system did not go unchallenged from within the socialist movement, however. Nor was the developing theory of revolution without vigorous dissent between socialist leaders. As early as 1899 revisionists such as Bernstein disputed Marx's predictions regarding increasing industrial concentration, recurrent economic crises and increasing immiseration of the masses. He argued for an evolutionary socialism within a democratic

process of reform rather than revolution or political catastrophe. He proposed that the extension of political rights to
the working classes would lead progressively to a stable and
wealthy social democracy. In such instances, he argued, revolution and a 'dictatorship by the classes' would be not only
counterproductive but a reversion to political atavism and a
rise in unwanted violence. (Bottomore 1983; McLellan 1988)
Bernstein's revisionism attracted a sharp response from such
figures as Rosa Luxemburg who discredited it as reactionary
and suggestive of a *reform* of capitalism rather than its *replace-
ment* by socialism.

Luxemburg had her own differences with the Leninists
however, being a vigorous critic of the concept of the vanguard party as likely to result in the enslavement of the young
labour movement by a power hungry intellectual elite. She
saw the heart of the revolution as being spontaneous action
by the mass movement arising naturally out of social conditions — an inevitable rather than an artificially organised
process. A Central Committee would endanger this natural
process and subvert the revolution, replacing it with bureaucracy and a dictatorship by a minority party rather than the
working class.

Another opponent to the dictatorship of the proletariat
was Kautsky who was committed to working class revolutionary action but also supported universal suffrage and
parliamentary democracy. He was a strong proponent of the
idea that the proletariat needed a democracy before and after
the revolution, in a form which would allow both rule of the
majority and protection of minorities. He warned against
confusing class with party, and the dangers of totalitarian
control:

> Protection of minorities is an indispensable condition for
> democratic development, and no less important than the
> rule of the majority (in McLellan 1988 p 92).

He proposed that the more advanced a country was in capitalism and democracy, the closer it was to socialism -these would be the elements that would see a future growth economy and sustainable democracy for the benefit of all. Needless to point out this drew considerable anger from Lenin the major proponent of the idea of the dictatorship of the proletariat under party control.

Trotsky's concept of the 'permanent revolution' suggested that not all countries would have to proceed through the stages to advanced capitalism before socialist revolution could take place. Thus in developing countries revolution could be achieved by a strong proletariat leading lower orders of a post-feudal society, this in turn contributing to the spread of revolution in more resistant industrialised countries. Trotsky saw socialism as having to improve on productivity and standards of living achieved via capitalism and argued that it would therefore have to be achieved at the pinnacle of capitalist development in advanced countries. His view that Soviet society under Stalin as a degenerated workers' state would require further revolutions to achieve socialism, and his criticisms of the party as having betrayed the revolution by establishing a parasitic bureaucracy and building it in one country to the neglect of the international requirement, saw him eventually assassinated by an agent of Stalin. (Bottomore 1983; McLennan 1988)

Lenin's 'socialist state' was founded on a process of organised terror, mass executions and a rapidly growing state apparatus of control centred around the Cheka which was established to fight counter-revolutionary tendencies. Parliamentary democracy was destroyed and a wide range of individual freedoms lost to a system of state control. This laid the base for Stalin's state totalitarianism, a regime of unprecedented oppression and brutality. As Lenin's critics feared, the degeneration of socialist ideals through control from above (the dictatorship of the party) took place. Purges of dissidents saw millions ruthlessly slaughtered or forcibly removed to work camps (Gulags). (Johnson 1983) Successive regimes under Kruschev, Breshnev and Andropov proved less oppressive but witnessed a period of foreign aggression and the prolonged 'cold war' with Western powers. Few insights into Soviet life were possible until the recent move to power of Gorbachev.

The economic and political crisis in Soviet Russia demanded a new vision. This new approach is reflected in Gorbachev's Perestroika (1987), in which he refers glowingly to the teachings of Lenin (rather than Milton Friedman as some would lead us to believe!). The collapse of Eastern European communism and the rise of the Soviet satellites against central control have provided a crisis for socialism (Slovo 1990) and prompted one political scientist to suggest that the 'end of history' has arrived with the death of great ideas conflicts being the consequence of the victory of liberal democratic ideals over all others (Fukuyama 1989). Socialists argue this is premature, seeing the current situation as a collapse of state dictatorships, a temporary loss of direction and espousing adherence to the vision of a socialist order for the future as the most just and viable option in the long run (Slovo 1990; Gorbachev 1989). They argue that socialism has not failed — it has never been tried — a bureaucratic authoritarian leadership having hijacked worker democracies. They point out that the market reforms of perestroika have not been successful in reversing the economic crisis of the USSR, and propose a consolidation of socialist forces as the way forward (Habib and Andrews 1990). Von Holdt (1990) acknowledges that Marx did not develop a theory of state and politics in his critique of capitalism, and nor did Lenin in his theory of revolutionary struggle which was 'dangerously empty' in its conception of democracy. Burawoy (1990) argues that these weaknesses in interaction with others led to dogma and despotism, but that the collapse of state socialism opens the way for a creative search for alternative models of socialism based in a radical rather than a bourgeois democracy.

Despite the optimism of some modern socialists, major failures are evident in the economic, political and human rights spheres of socialism as it has been practised, and while the Marxist analysis may provide some insights into the failings of capitalism, it has yet to produce a workable model of its own. On the political front decades of repression including genocide failed to remove, tame or find an accord with resistance. Nor has socialism dealt effectively with ethnic or communal conflicts within its states.

Within the Soviet bloc 1989 proved a year of fundamental change: Hungary declared itself an independent republic ousting Kadar and shedding communism; Poland achieved its first non-communist Prime Minister and Solidarity achieved an overwhelming election victory; East Germans started a mass exodus for freedom through Hungary eventually obliging the removal of the Berlin Wall, bringing about a crisis in government and a reunification drive with West Germany; Rumania's dictator Ceausescu was toppled and executed leading to the dissolution of the Communist Party and plans for free elections; Czechoslavakia witnessed the resignation of its politburo and a return to democratic process after over twenty years of party control; and in Bulgaria reformist moves were initiated. The dramatic shifts in these satellite states were continued closer to home for the Soviets in the form of strong secessionist drives in Lithuania, the legalisation of non-communist parties in Latvia, drives for independence in Estonia, and pushes in Moldavia for a return to Rumania after Ceausescu's demise. In addition Azerbaijan experienced serious internal division and nationalist uprising, Georgia experienced growing calls for independence following Soviet repression as recently as 1989, and Albania experienced popular unrest. These states are themselves riven in many instances with internal division of an ethnic nature producing regional crises in control. Discussion of communal conflict is undertaken in the next section.

Critics of socialism argue that whatever the accuracy of the Marxist critique in analysing the exploitative nature of capitalism and the inherent structural conflict it produces, its adherents have failed to produce governments of greater equity or growth economies to match those of the liberal democracies of the West. Berger (1986) in acknowledging the human costs exacted in the early phases of capitalism proposes that advanced capitalism has generated the most productive economies and highest standards of living for large masses of people in human history. He argues that industrial capitalism is more likely to maintain openness in the stratification system of a country and that capitalism is a necessary but not sufficient precondition of democracy under modern conditions. In sum, capitalist oriented countries have performed better in the fields of economic growth, standards of living for all their citizens, human rights ratings, political liberties for all their citizens and individual freedoms (Berger 1986). As a consequence it might be argued that their forms of government, essentially liberal democracies, with either majoritarian or consociational dispensations are more stable and less prone to revolutionary change having institutionalised conflict regulation. Having made these observations a cautionary note must however be sounded. The state dictatorships and centralised economies of the Soviet bloc failed, but multi-party democracies and market economies have yet to succeed in the conditions which prevail in these countries!

Threat to important values: communal conflict

Where cleavages between groups are sharply defined in rigid societal structures, the capacity to contain conflict is reduced. Groups may develop different ways of life, culture, ideologies and religions — their very difference may be the means through which they develop an internal coherence identity and unity. Intergroup conflict may actually act to strengthen this (Coser 1956).

South Africa's social system based on racial classification has sharply divided groups on the basis of colour, with a dominant white minority having retained a position of privilege through a process of active social engineering. Apartheid effectively confined black people to working class status, a system of social stratification by race being vigorously enforced through an extensive network of laws entrenching the ideology of racial separatism. As white people actively sought to retain their identity, culture and language through division, so this practice has actively escalated processes of intergroup conflict themselves seriously threatening 'white identity'.

Hanf (1989) distinguishes between conflicts of a class nature, and those of a communal character. In the latter parties define their conflict in terms of cultural rather than economic terms, such factors as religion, language, origin, and skin colour being central to determining social relations. Causes of conflict are *relative deprivation* where some groupings may perceive themselves as being exploited by others, or as lacking equal opportunities or rights for purposes of fair competition; and *symbolic deprivation* where a dominant group attempts to enforce its own symbols, culture and language over others in a heterogenous society. The applicability of these conflict sources is readily evident in South African society.

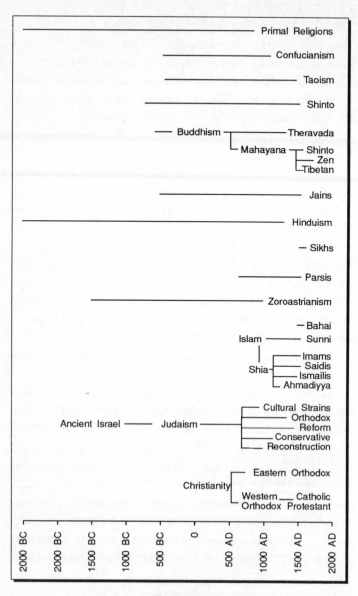

Figure 1.2
Religious diversity across the globe
(Source: Lion Publishing 1982)

Racial conflicts are evident accross the globe, but have been centrally identified as issues of colonial Africa, and particularly in South Africa's system of racial domination. South Africans' intense preoccupation with race may, however, act to cloud the fact that communal conflicts may have their roots in other issues as well — tribalism and religion for instance. Figure 1.2 reflects (very superficially) some of the diversity of religions in the world. Religious wars and inter-denominational disputes are communal in nature (although they may also have economic features).

Conflict between Hindus and Moslems in India and Pakistan reflects communal rather than class differences. Long-standing tensions between groups such as Shonas and Matabeles in Zimbabwe; Xhosas and Zulus in South Africa; Tutsis and Hutus in Rwanda; Eritreans, Somalis and Ethiopians; Africans and Arabs in Tanzania and Chad; Tamils and Sinhalese in Sri Lanka; Armenians and Azerbaijanis, Serbs, Albanians and Croats, Czechs and Slovaks in Eastern Europe; Jews and Arabs in the Middle East are rooted in tribal factors. The extermination of 6 million Jews by Nazis during World War 2 was driven by convictions of ethnic superiority.

Many societies are horizontally stratified by class as well as vertically cleaved by communal differences. Thus Hanf argues that it is not sufficient to analyse conflicts in purely one-dimensional terms. He proposes that any analysis should consider whether a society contains both classes and communities as self conscious groups, and then whether these are incorporated on an equal or an unequal basis.

In culturally homogenous societies conflict tends to erupt after periods of economic progress for the lower classes when expectations for further improvements are frustrated. In multi-communal societies when groups are incorporated on an equal basis conflict is less frequent. However, in cases of unequal incorporation when a community that has enjoyed class privilege faces the threat of losing it, conflict is likely to be apparent. Since President De Klerk's dramatic moves of releasing Mandela, unbanning the ANC, the SACP and the PAC, and entering into discussions with the ANC and SACP to clear the road for negotiations for a nonracial future dispensation, conservative white groups have responded angrily as their claims to self determination and privilege are threatened.

Hanf suggests that conflict is often expressed in communal rather than class terms because it is easier to mobilise around communal markers than class arguments which require a capacity to transcend community and an insight into economic relations, because the lower strata of privileged groups identify themselves with the group as a whole rather than their economic status, and because of symbolic deprivation where people feel themselves despised on account of their race or religion (for instance), regardless of their economic status.

He proposes that communal conflicts are more complex than class conflicts, and more difficult to regulate. Renner and Bauer suggested that the appropriate approach would be to depoliticise communal conflicts as far as possible by institutionalising cultural rights for all groups and by creating as much equality of economic opportunity as possible. In a survey of 32 cases of communal conflict Hanf (1989) concluded that negotiated compromise outcomes occurred in the minority of cases, were mostly preceded by violent struggle and in more than half of cases were resolved by way of partition when both parties recognised that peaceful coexistence was impossible (box 1.4).

Stable domination
- Burundi
- Egypt
- Turkey

Unstable domination
- Cameroon
- Chad
- German Empire
- Jordan
- Palestine
- Syria

Ongoing war or violence
- Ethiopia
- Sudan
- Uganda
- Burma
- Phillipines
- Sri Lanka
- Northern Ireland
- Iraq
- Lebanon

Partition after violence
- India
- Cyprus

Pre-emptive partition
- Mali Federation
- Malaysia
- United Kingdom of the netherlands
- Sweden

One-way accepted accommodation
- Rwanda
- Indonesia

Accommodation after violence
- Austria
- Holy Roman Empire
- Yugoslavia
- Switzerland

Pre-emptive accommodation
- Belgium
- Netherlands

NOTES:

Negotiated solutions in fewer than 50 % of cases, and in 50 % of these partition occurred — a mutual recognition that peaceful co-existence was impossible.

Most cases of coexistence preceded by violent struggle. 25 % of all cases unresolved and continue in violent struggle.

One-way domination is costly and often violent in character.

Box 1.4
Hanf's examples of conflict regulation in multi-communal societies

Hanf (1989) distinguishes three different ideological approaches to communal conflicts, which determine approaches used in seeking their regulation:

❏ *Jacobinism* which seeks to level all differences in class, culture and language for the creation of one, indivisible nation. It is usually used as a means for existing states to build nations by act of wilful elimination of all obstacles to political equality and unity.

❏ *Ethnic nationalism* which tends to be used as an opposition ideology, having been used as the driving force for anti-colonial liberation movements. In effect it is the rallying call of disaffected peoples — as Hanf writes: ' Whereas Jacobinism seeks nations for existing states, ethnic nationalism seeks states. (p 97)

❏ *Syncretistic nationalism* which also seeks to build nations, but recognises existing group differences and seeks to use them as building blocks for this purpose. It insists on neither unity nor diversity at all costs but rather unity in diversity. Typically it seeks either to institutionalise communities in a consociational effort to harness divergence for nation building, or to depoliticise communalism.

Where stable domination is evident and in cases of unstable domination, ruling groups tend to insist on national homogeneity, denying community differences. Violent confrontation ensues between Jacobins and ethnic nationalists. Partition solutions indicate that both domination and coexistence are possible. Where negotiated or one-way accommodation is achieved syncretistic nationalisms are in evidence, and communalism tends to be institutionalised in instances where accommodation has been preceded by violent exchange (Hanf 1989).

In an acknowledgement of South Africa's communal character Giliomee and Schlemmer (1989) propose an approach to resolving its conflict through a syncretistic nationalism.

Commenting on African conflicts, Sandbrook (1985) suggests that they are essentially communal in nature. Colonial rule produced peasant rather than capitalist societies.

> Ethnicity is often of greater political saliency than class. Tribalism is not, as some have assumed, a transitory phenomenon, soon to be replaced by class solidarities. Ethnic conflicts, sometimes coupled with religious divisions, will continue to undermine a sense of national purpose. Patriotism fails to unite sectional interests in defence of a broad national vision. Societies with such characteristics are hard to govern. The stage is set for a strongman to play the central integrating role. He overcomes political schisms and builds his personal rule by distributing material benefits, capitalising on personal loyalties and coercing recalcitrants. Appeals on a class or patriotic basis are unsuccessful. (Sandbrook 1985, pp 63–4)

In developing countries it is natural that the state should play a central role in the economy (Sandbrook 1985), but this also means that the state becomes the vehicle for access to material gains and power for a dominant group whose first priority in an unstable situation is to secure a constituency that will help it stay in power. In non-democratic regimes the opportunity for corruption is readily evident -checks and balances are absent, and demands on a small resource base are inevitably responded to first for a backing constituency rather than the wider population or competing power interests.

Scarce resources

Some space has been devoted to discussing three sources of conflict — structural imbalances, communal differences and differing goals. The expression of all these approaches is evidenced in analyses of the South African situation, Marxists citing the problem to be structural in the form of racial capitalism, white rulers historically preferring a communal analysis. A further source of conflict, it is argued here, serves not to clarify which of these analyses is the more accurate but to deepen problems in utilising either of them. It is the issue of scarce resources.

Hague and Harrop (1987) state that First-World countries comprise 15 % of the world's population but account for 63 % of its GNP, and Second-World countries 33 % of world population and 19 % of its wealth. Third-World nations comprise 52 % of the world's population but only 18 % of its wealth. This critical shortage of wealth underpins major obstacles to the achievement of democratic governments, and has been aggravated by the growth of a massive debt problem.

Between 1982 and 1987 international debt grew in Asia from $174 bn to $287 bn, in Latin America and the Caribbean from $332 bn to $431 bn, and in sub-Saharan Africa from $69 to $123 bn (*Time* 10/10/88). By the end of 1990 Africa's foreign debt stood at about $240 bn (*Evening Post* 15/1/91). In Latin America the debt had risen to $400 bn by 1989 and most countries were battling to meet interest payments on the sums owed let alone reduce capital. The size of the debt is indicated in the following estimates of foreign debt burden as a percentage of gross domestic product: Chile (113 %), Ecuador (103 %), Bolivia (89 %), Argentina (79 %), Uruguay (79 %), Mexico (76 %), Venezuela (73 %), Peru (49 %), Colombia (47 %), Brazil (37 %). Crippling debt has rendered the achievement of stable government in many of these countries very difficult. The United Nations Childrens' Fund ascribes lowered standards of living of almost 900 million people to the debt crisis, and it has been estimated that it will cause the death of 18 million children by the end of the century. (*Time* 9/1/89).

While problems in food distribution have been cited as the major reasons for starvation across the globe over the past 20 years, the effects of global warming on agriculture coupled with world population growth could produce an absolute food shortage in the near future. This could see the starvation of up to a billion people over the next twenty years according to Daily and Ehrlich of Stanford University (*EP Herald* 4/1/91). Scarcity of this sort is likely to exacerbate conflict between groups as they struggle for survival in already poorly resourced Third-World countries.

Sub-Saharan African economies are with few exceptions very poor, development being hindered by a scarcity of arable land, tropical disease, tiny markets, severe skills shortages, a reliance on single commodities, scarce mineral resources and ongoing political crises. Burgeoning population growth and increasingly onerous foreign debt are additional complexities (Sandbrook 1985). No real democracies exist on the continent in the liberal democratic sense, the range of orders varying from military rule to single person rule to single party rule, or a form of confined democracy for an economic elite as exists in South Africa. The period of colonialism witnessed the balkanisation of Africa in the scramble for territory and the departure of the powers left other major problems: inappropriate and unwieldy constitutions, inexperienced administrations, a skills exodus and new systems overburdened with social problems. Tribal division and corrupt political practices based on extractive political tendencies are salient features of many systems, and coups are the most regular form of change of government (Hodder-Williams 1984). Post-liberation Africa has experienced more than 100 coups but no changes of government through election (HSRC 1990).

The instability of regimes in the Second and Third World which are characterised by centralised and often authoritarian governments is rooted in and exacerbated by a poverty in resources. In communal conflicts where there is sharp competition between groups over scarce resources, political control is the means to economic power. Membership of a dominant or privileged group rather than ability determines access to wealth and opportunity (Hanf 1989). Thus cultural

differences rapidly translate into economic conflicts. In the
South African situation race and class became confused —
apartheid determined white privilege and black subordina-
tion. In a change process members of the lower strata of the
privileged group find their position of privilege most threatened. Paradoxically, as attempts are made to unwind privilege through group membership for purposes of equity, so
group membership and mobilisation is critical to upwardly
aspirant and dominated groups to secure a place in the sun
for themselves in a future dispensation. Conflict is then entrenched as those members of the dominant group most
threatened by change face loss of privilege, power and be-
longing just as the previously subordinated groups drive for
these is most militant.

South Africa, while having a better developed economy
than any other in Africa, is not a rich country and desperately
requires a growth economy if it is to meet the needs of its
burgeoning population. The conflict is not simply a communal one or a class one, but one over scarce resources. The
following synopsis is illustrative.

The population of the country, including the TBVC states
stood at about 29 million in 1980 including about 4,5 million
whites. This is projected to rise to over 50 million by the year
2010, of whom whites will comprise only about 5,5 million.
The white fertility rate is about 2,08 compared with the average black rate of 5,38, a far higher figure applying in rural than
urban areas (Simkins 1990).

White life expectancy for a male is 66,6, and for females
73,9 — for blacks it is only 53,9 and 59,8 respectively. However, these figures are distorted by an equally disturbing
infant mortality rate: 13,5 per 1 000 births for whites, and 80
per 1 000 births for blacks. While the white population shows
the distribution of an aging First-World concommitent with
its lifestyle, over 50 % of blacks are under 15 years of age and

about to make a massive appearance on the job market as young adults.

Current unemployment estimates are around 4 million which at current economic growth rates could rise to 10 million by the year 2000. A 5 % annual growth rate is required merely to maintain the estimated one third of the workforce in the informal or unemployed ranks steady over the next ten years. Current economic growth hovers at less than 1 % per annum.

To accommodate the rise in the black population and urban drift it is estimated that the equivalent of 10 to 15 new cities the size of Soweto will be required to be built in the next ten years. It is thought that there is a current housing backlog of over 800 000 family homes. To meet the demand for education it is projected that 300 schools a year must be built for the next ten years (one every working day) and that 8 000 teachers must be trained per annum. About 40 % of adult blacks are totally illiterate (Joyce 1988; Van den Berg 1989; HSRC 1985; Wilson and Ramaphele 1989)

The white population has dominated access to resources for the entire history of the country and has made a vigorous effort to entrench this domination through over forty years of apartheid. This has resulted in enormous imbalances in the distribution of wealth in the society on a racial basis with a clear distinction between white 'haves' and black 'have-nots'. South Africa has the highest gini coefficient in the world reflecting this inequitable distribution (0,65).

Communication/information issues

Information is an important source of power in intergroup situations. Control over the national media and suppression of the opposition press has been an important component of government strategy in recent years in South Africa. Likewise, companies are generally resistant to sharing information of a strategic nature with trade unions. This of course is not only related to the security of the business against competition, but just as vitally to power relations between employers and organised labour.

Lack of shared, legitimated information then gives rise to power struggles and contributes to rising levels of mistrust in relations. Over and above this it reduces the parties' capacities to understand each other's positions contributing to chances of misreading each other's circumstances and power realities. Instead of matters being worked out on the basis of a common data base, they are fought out on the basis of position and principle based on guesswork and assumption.

Ambiguity

During processes of social change uncertainty as to the boundaries of acceptable behaviour usually emerges, becoming not only the consequence but also the cause of conflict. Previous modes of interaction may be no longer acceptable, traditional methods of exercising authority may be rejected, people may be unwilling to continue to relate in a subservient way — and just as it is clear that old ways of doing things are no longer desireable or possible, so is there an absence of clarity on appropriate behavioural alternatives. The result is often a prolonged process of testing new boundaries in authority relations, upwardly mobile groups challenging the outside limits of previously acceptable behaviour, those under threat seeking new ways of retaining at least some of their old authority.

Thus, even in fairly enlightened management circles, there was some panic when the newly established industrial court ordered the reinstatement of employees it determined to have been unfairly dismissed in the early eighties. What would the boundaries be? What constituted a fair dismissal? Would management lose its rights on the hiring-firing front to militant unions and the industrial court? On the other side new hope inspired trade unions to challenge a wide range of managerial actions as they sought to establish the extent of their new powers and the sympathy of the court.

Riordan (1991) highlights some of the contradictory messages the government sent during 1990 — on the one hand that apartheid would soon be dead, separate group areas finished and in effect that mixed schools would eventuate, on the other hand that closed schools would be acceptable if parents so chose. While indicating that the Group Areas Act would soon be repealed, permits for purchase of a home in a white area were refused to people of colour. This, Riordan argues, caused uncertainty both in black and in white circles, and promoted suspicion of government integrity and political polarisation as people sought parties that promised greater certainty.

In transitions from authoritarian rule to democracy it has been observed that the rules of the political game are not clearly defined, but fluctuate and are vigorously contested. The process is usually initiated as a consequence of division in the ruling group between hardliners (authoritarians) and softliners who believe that some form of electoral legitimation will be required for government in the long term. It is given expression first by liberalisation of the system, which extends rights to individuals and groups for protection from arbitrary state action. This creates 'political space' which is exploited by advocates for change, and witnesses a massive escalation in popular mobilisation. This may invoke a right-wing coup to prevent the process from continuing in the face of a dangerous level of mobilisation and destabilisation. If the softliners perceive their interests to lie in the continuation of the process, and the bourgeois lend weight to the change, then transition to some form of democracy may be possible. Right- and left-wing militance make for a treacherous passage, and demands for retribution for past misdeeds by an authoritarian regime make for increased uncertainty. Thus transition is essentially a period of major ambiguity in societies attempting to reshape themselves, and is often accompanied as a consequence by heightened levels of militance, destabilisation and the possibilities of a right-wing backlash. Where there is a degree of coherence within various powerful interest groupings, the formation of temporary pacts of a military, economic and military nature may act to stabilise the process until the establishment of a wider democracy (a civil society) can take place (O'Donnell and Schmitter 1986).

Coordination

Conflicts also arise within and between groups when, despite sharing common objectives, they differ as to the appropriate strategy or the importance of various tasks in achieving these. Thus, production and maintenance units develop tensions as the one seeks output as a priority, the other the long term 'health' of machinery for production purposes. Both are concerned about organisational performance but view it from different perspectives. Other organisational tensions arise between sales and production in terms of raising business and capacity to meet demand, and between finance and industrial relations as to the timing of release of annual results and how these impinge on wage negotiations and shareholder confidence.

Similarly major differences have emerged between groups otherwise united in the struggle against apartheid. Questions of ideology, strategy, exclusion or inclusion of whites, the use of violence, sanctions, forms of engagement with government and acceptable conditions for this, and possible structure of future government have produced deep and acrimonious division in the forces opposed to apartheid. This has spawned a 'if you are not with us you are against us' way of thinking between these groups, with each accusing the other of either collaborating with the system or bolstering it through ill-conceived tactics. These problems of coordination weaken organisations and dilute their effectiveness.

AGGRAVATORS AND MODERATORS

Several causes of conflict may be apparent in a relationship, but the expression of this depends on the presence and influence of various intervening variables which serve to aggravate or moderate the actions of the parties involved.

Where parties have *high aspirations* which are in competition with each other, conflict ensues. High aspirations may be rooted in *perceptions of legitimacy and feasibility*. Thus when a party believes that it has a moral right to certain resources or opportunities, it is more likely to employ its resources to achieve these. Further, if it believes that these are attainable, this will reinforce its willingness to pursue them, if necessary through contentious methods. Thus in the unrest of 1984 struggle groups in South Africa seemed not only to perceive the moral imperative to be theirs, but also to believe that the government would accede to the wide ranging use of pressure tactics they employed. This latter belief was shattered by the declaration of a State of Emergency, the banning of various organisations and the mass detention of leaders of struggle groups. While the South African government had (and has) the capacity to temper its opponents' perceptions of their power (feasibility), it has not succeeded in altering their perceptions about the legitimacy of their struggle. If anything the tactics used to suppress opposition enhanced their perceptions of being victims of a gross injustice.

Other factors contributing to high aspiration levels are *invidious comparison*, and *past achievement*. Labour negotiators will be well acquainted with the invidious comparison — both employers and trade unionists seem to manage to find examples of poorer or better payers in their industries, and to use these for pressure purposes in negotiation. The use of comparisons obviously affects the parties' feelings of entitlement to certain rewards and thus their aspiration levels.

Trade unionists sometimes face real problems with their constituencies following a dramatic achievement in a particular year. If you have managed to procure a 70 % wage increase in last year's negotiations, how satisfied will your members he with a mere inflationary increase this year? Several employers have made such adjustments in their minimum wages following negotiation and (quite often) industrial action. Having done so they feel that the wage gap has been remedied, that they are on firmer moral ground as regards their conditions of employment, and usually expect union demands and action to be 'more reasonable' in the next round. Not uncommonly they find these expectations shattered. Union members' experience of the process may be quite different — the legitimacy of demands and the feasibility of achieving them have been strengthened, and if industrial action was seen to be the effective instrument then its usage will have been reinforced. Union leaders, once the euphoria of a dramatic victory has worn off, may find themselves representing a constituency with raised levels of hope and militancy rather than a satisfied and grateful group. All the parties find themselves in a 'crisis of expectations' conflict spiral.

Other factors which contribute to high aspirations include the formation of *struggle groups* and *perceptions of power*.

As struggle groups are mobilised in a conflict situation, so their perceptions of actual power relativities may be distorted. Aspiration levels may not be tempered by appropriate reality appraisal. The processes contributing to such distortions are outlined in the section on conflict escalation. Where a society or specific relationship is in a phase of transition, *traditional norms* are commonly weakened giving rise to greater aspiration levels on the part of groups hoping for dramatic improvements in their status, power or access to scarce resources.

The *history of relations* between parties is often an aggravating factor in conflicts. In a mediation in a wage dispute in a chicken farm, managers gave a lengthy explanation of their financial pressures. The shop stewards responded by stating that the reason for this parlous position was that the factory manager was stealing chickens and selling them in an outlet of his own. Not surprisingly this evoked an angry response from the management team, and this was exacerbated only when head office, anxious to be seen to be acting fairly, instituted an independent inquiry into the allegation. Needless to point out, management was not particularly inclined from this point to give warm consideration to improving its wage offer.

Some investigation revealed that although other chicken farms in the same group and same area settled on wages annually, this farm was afflicted with disputes and industrial action.

Annually negotiations were protracted and bitter, strikes and lockouts were employed — and the previous year management had accused shop stewards of stealing chickens during a strike!

The union had simply waited a year to reciprocate.

There is a distinctly different feel to negotiations where relationships have deteriorated to the point where the parties have become more interested in damaging each other than in settling the issues overtly in dispute. In stable relationships the parties are able to focus their energies on the dispute itself — in poor relationships, mistrust, strong emotions, misperceptions, poor communications, and desires to punish assume precedence. Parties dig in on issues of principle and tactics are used for purposes of mutual attack rather than settlement searches.

Where parties cannot see any alternatives (*zero sum perceptions*)to resolve the conflict, confrontation is likely. Disputes over scarce resources may result in parties developing all-or-nothing perceptions on the issues inhibiting flexible, creative approaches and compromise.

The indicators for *social stability* lie in understanding the causes and aggravators of conflict. Two main areas can be identified: factors allowing for effective *conflict regulation*, and those allowing for a *stabilisation of relations*.

The term *conflict regulation* is an acknowledgement that in many instances conflict may not be resolvable. For example it is argued that the goals of capital (efficiency, cost reduction, profit) and the goals of labour (security, higher standards of living) render their relationship inherently conflictual. This basic contradiction of goals does not allow for conflict resolution as such, but the dependency both have on continued production, to meet their needs, obliges them to seek jointly acceptable means of regulating the expression of their conflict. This means that the parties search for means other than blunt ongoing confrontation to settle their differences — normally through procedural agreements that facilitate the settlement of periodic or individual disputes and grievances, and time specific substantive agreements in which the parties agree to confine their use of pressure over conflicts of interest to certain times eg annual wage negotiations. Several elements can be identified as facilitating effective conflict regulation.

First, it is important that parties assign each other *legitimacy* in the relationship. When one party refuses to acknowledge the other as a player or representative in a conflict, then it dooms the exchange to one of confrontation.

It prohibits meaningful problem solving or negotiation because the parties cannot come to the table. The one that is not accorded legitimacy must use power tactics to oblige his recognition by the other. The effects of this are clearly illustrated in the SATS case in chapter 2. According a party legitimacy as a partner at a bargaining table does not imply acceptance of its demands, or its behaviour, it merely recognises the rights of that party to make demands and to negotiate on them. It is simply an acknowledgement that that party as a contributor to the conflictual relationship, has a right also to be participant in seeking ways to resolve or regulate differences.

The second requirement is for each of the parties to have an *internal coherence*. If parties to a conflict are riven with internal factions, then they will not be effective in achieving or implementing agreements. Constituencies will provide conflicting mandates, negotiators will be neutralised as they direct their energies to holding their own teams together rather than settling differences across the table and cautioned by the ever present threat that they may lose significant elements of their constituencies or be replaced if they become too ambitious in seeking accords with an opposition. Negotiators must be able to deliver the other side and their own in the dealmaking process.

Finally, effective conflict regulation requires *jointly acceptable forums, procedures, standards and third party institutions*. The presence of laws, rules, regulations and procedures is insufficient — they must be widely acceptable in their origin and their implementation if they are to be experienced as vehicles for justice rather then oppression. A major obstacle to effective conflict regulation in South Africa has centred around perceptions of the law as a vehicle for order and justice. Whites have an experience of the law as a system of protection wherein both public and private rights may be protected and advanced. Blacks on the other hand have an experience of the law as a instrument of oppression. Laws promulgated in a parliament in which they had no voice progressively removed their voting rights, and sharply circumscribed their rights of movement, ownership of property, their access to business, education and welfare, and freedom of relations, association and protest. As Edmund Burke stated:

> People crushed by laws have no hope but by power. If laws are their enemies, they will be enemies to laws; and those who have much to hope and nothing to lose, will always be dangerous, more or less.

In effect as blacks were denied legitimacy in the law making machinery so they became its victims, and in turn, denied the legitimacy of the parliaments, the courts and the law enforcement bodies which in 'normalised' countries act to cement and order social relations.

Conflict regulation mechanisms contribute to peaceful engagement between parties, but other factors are also important in *stabilising relations.* Conflict regulation mechanisms are seldom in their own right sufficient to ensure peace and stability. Other elements help to grease the procedural machine. It greatly helps, for instance, if competing interest groups have developed *shared conflict limiting norms.* If all parties in a relationship have a direct concern over containing conflict, and vested interests in not allowing conflicts to escalate, then stability is enhanced. As soon as a party perceives that its interests might be better served through escalating rather than containing conflict, then regulatory mechanisms are jeopardised. Of course, procedural systems are established precisely for the purpose of allowing the expression of disatisfaction with a system in order that it might be modified to allow ongoing equilibrium. The intention is not only to facilitate the expression of disatisfaction within the procedures of a system, but also with the system itself. However, if a party perceives the system as 'rigged' so that it is allowed expression but never has its grievances attended to then it may well lose faith in the efficacy of that system. In many senses this is where the differences lie between the pluralists and the radical change theorists — the former assess democracy by the equity of available procedures for competing interest groups, the latter by the outcomes of the use of these for those 'at the bottom of the pile'.

Stability is also more likely in situations where there are *no large grievances and no large threats* felt by parties. In South Africa this is obviously a major obstacle to change -blacks with a long history of oppression behind them have numerous large grievances which they want redressed as a matter of right, whites see this process as carrying direct threats for their identity, culture, language, authority, rights and standards of living.

A wide diversity of *cross-cutting group memberships* allows a spreading of allegiances within a community reducing 'us-them' perceptions. Antagonists in the workplace, may be allies in a place of common worship; opponents in a commercial litigation may share an interest in a community or conservation concern. The tragedy of South Africa is that its rigidly enforced social cleavages on the basis of race did not allow the development of crosscutting group memberships -it became a situation of white bosses, black workers; white education and black education; white worship and black worship. Race and class conflicts became confused entrenching perceptions of difference rather than diffusing them across a range of social criteria. As a consequence no sense of common nationhood was allowed to develop, thus eroding motivation to build a common future as interest groupings expended their energies in confrontational exchanges. This process has been the consequence of the absence of another important stabilising element — a norm of *tolerance and understanding* between groups.

Finally the absence of a *balance of power* in intergroup relations ensured that disempowered groups became locked into struggles for recognition and participation over long periods. Whites in power sought to use their own power to coerce these groups into subservient relationships. Again energies expended in fighting over legitimacy rather than solving problems of common concern.

Where the elements listed above are absent, there is a tendency to achieve stability by exercising coercive power. If government by consent cannot be achieved, or is seen to be undesireable, there is a tendency to resort to *strong social controls and acts of deterrence.* Efforts to govern by means other than broad social consent in South Africa gave rise to authoritarian legislation, the growth of a large security apparatus, states of emergency, and the emergence of security based 'hit-squads'. Between 1965 and 1989 about 73 000 detentions under various emergency and security laws were carried out — the vast majority of these never coming to trial. This produced an inherent instability — to quote Burke again:

> The use of force alone is but temporary. It may subdue for a moment; but it does not remove the necessity of subduing again: and a nation is not governed, which is perpetually to be conquered.

Once the energies of players in a system are directed at attacking each other rather than common problems then the stability required to build competitive nations or organisations is jeopardised.

2
CONFLICT:
ESCALATION AND DE-ESCALATION

Where there is an absence of conflict regulation mechanisms or factors contributing to the stabilisation of relations, or in cases where these are insufficient to countervail the influence of aggravators, conflicts may be expected to grow in intensity and size. When this occurs marked changes are evidenced in the perceptions opposing parties hold of themselves and each other, their tactics change, the nature of demands is modified and the internal dynamics of each side are fundamentally altered.

Pruitt & Rubin (1986) propose three models of conflict escalation:

❏ *The aggressor–defender model* describes situations wherein one party is active in pursuing its ends, escalating its use of contentious tactics progressively as its efforts are frustrated. The other party only reacts, increasing levels of response in accordance with the activities of the aggressor. The escalation continues until the aggressor desists or wins.

❏ *The conflict spiral model* proposes that escalation is the consequence of a self-reinforcing circle of action and reaction between the parties. This spiral may be retaliatory (punitive) or defensive (self-protective) in character, and unlike the one-way flow of the aggressor–defender model this process has a two-way causation model, each party reacting to the actions of the other.

❏ *The structural change model* builds on the conflict spiral model, arguing that conflictual tactics produce residual

changes in the parties, and this encourages further contentious behaviour. 'Thus escalated conflict is both antece-
dent and consequent of structural changes' (Pruitt &
Rubin 1986, p 92). These authors propose three types of
structural change in conflict situations: psychological,
group and community changes. These are enlarged on in
this section.

THE CONFLICT ESCALATION PROCESS

The conflict escalation process and its consequences in terms
of intra- and intergroup relations is well explicated in the
literature (Coser 1956 and 1967; Deutsch 1973; Schein 1980;
Pruitt & Rubin 1986).

In distinguishing between *destructive and constructive conflict* Deutsch (1973) observed that the former has a tendency
to expand and escalate as the parties assume increasingly
competitive stances, commit their resources to the conflict
process and misjudge the situation on a variety of levels.

Figure 2.1 summarises the key elements of the conflict
escalation process.

Issues and demands

As the conflict grows, so the number of issues in contention
between the parties tends to proliferate. In a strike which took
place over wages, the dispute was finally settled after a
six-week mediation. The wage issue was settled after one
week, and the next five weeks were spent seeking resolution
of the issues which had arisen during the strike: dismissals,
violence and intimidation. The agreed arbitration process on
these issues then continued for a further year.

Pruitt & Rubin (1986) observe that concrete specific demands often develop during the escalation process into grandiose, all encompassing ones of a generalised nature. These
are obviously far more difficult to respond to once trans-

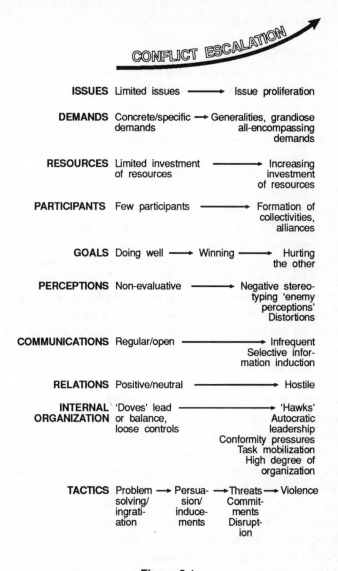

Figure 2.1
Key elements of the conflict escalation process

formed in this way, and the wider interactional context which emerges as a consequence of the conflict.

Communications

Deutsch (1973) states that in the process of destructive conflict communications become unreliable and impoverished, because available communication channels are either ignored or used to abuse the other party. The parties come to rely on 'spying' information rather than direct exchange, and poor communication enhances the possibilities of error, misjudgement and misperception in the relationship.

Mutual perceptions

Schein (1980) observes that as hostilities between groups increase and communications decrease, so it becomes easier to develop and maintain negative stereotypes. Each group experiences distortions of perception, selectively seeing only the worst aspects of the other party and only the best of itself. Concurrently each tends to deny both its own weaknesses, and the strengths of the other party, thus obstructing its capacity to assess objectively the situation, the problem, power realities, and options and opportunities for settlement.

Pruitt & Rubin (1986), in discussing the psychological aspects of processes that produce conflict escalation, give attention to this area, pointing out that 'like all structural changes, negative attitudes and perceptions are both cause and effect of the use of contentious tactics' (p 99). Conflicting parties tend to perceive each other as deficient in moral virtue, dishonest, warlike, untrusworthy and hostile.

In some situations a separation may be evidenced in perceptions of leaders and ordinary group members, the latter being seen as neutral or even positive in attitude but as being misled or in the grip of 'evil' leaders. This process is regularly evidenced in statements by political leaders assuring themselves and their constituents of the view that rebellions are really the consequence of a few subversives rather than mass commitment; and in the views of managers facing strike action that this is the influence of a few 'agitators' rather than the genuine will of 'their workers'.

Pruitt & Rubin (1986) point out that adversaries often fail to understand that the feelings they have for one another are reciprocal. This inhibits a capacity to acknowledge fear rather than aggression as a behavioural motivator, further feeding perceptions of the other's malice and destructive intentions. These authors ascribe seven contributors to conflict escalation to negative attitudes and perceptions:

❏ They encourage a tendency to blame the other for any unpleasant experiences.
❏ Any ambiguous behaviour is immediately interpreted as threatening.
❏ Inhibitions on aggression are diminished.
❏ Communications are interfered with.
❏ It becomes difficult to empathise with the other party.
❏ Zero-sum/all or nothing thinking is fostered.
❏ Enemy perceptions are developed and promoted.

A related process to that of negative attitudes and perceptions is *deindividuation*, whereby a person is seen as merely a member of another group or category rather than as an individual. Pruitt & Rubin (1986) argue that as the perception has no valence it is not a negative attitude or perception, but that it has the consequence of removing inhibitions against aggressive behaviour. Efforts to 'reindividuate' conflicts to reduce aggresive acts may even be resisted by the parties as they act to demobilise, caution the use of contentious tactics, and demand a recognition of the human realities of confrontation. It is much easier to deal with numbers, mobs and stereotypes.

Shifts in tactics

Deutsch (1973) notes that as conflict escalates, so there is a shift away from problem solving, persuasion and conciliation toward an increased reliance on strategies of power and the utilisation of tactics of coercion, threat and deception. A belief emerges that the solution to the conflict is only attainable via superior force or trickery.

Likewise he links the raised level of intensity of negative attitudes toward the other side to lowered norms regarding moral conduct towards them. Owing to the win–lose belief that develops through the conflict escalation process, the parties focus their efforts on maximising their own power while trying to minimise that of the other. Concurrently usual norms of intergroup conduct come to be regarded as inapplicable, and moral norms are lowered in terms of the adversarial interaction. This gives rise to what Deutsch (1973) terms a steady increase in behaviour considered 'morally outrageous' by the other.

Pruitt & Rubin (1986) attribute this process to an important psychological change in the parties which is strengthened as the conflict grows, namely a desire to punish or aggress against the other. Parties are likely to punish each other (and escalate the conflict) when they perceive the other's behaviour as arbitrary, that is, as a direct choice with no extenuating factors. Thus if there is an unpleasant consequence for a party which is seen to arise from an arbitrarily malicious act on the part of the other, then blameworthiness is more easily ascribed, and the desire to punish evoked.

The use of contentious or aggressive tactics is further increased when the parties are emotionally aroused (angry, frustrated). Again, aggressive acts are more likely if the usual social inhibitions on their expression are diminished or removed. Where there are strong protections or inhibitions against punishing the actual source of frustration, it may be displaced finding expression in acts against more vulnerable and accessible targets.

Group changes

Schein (1980) states that *within* competing groups there is greater bonding and loyalty and that members close ranks and bury internal differences to an extent. However, there are boundaries to this — it is not only a voluntary process but one which the group demands. Solidarity requires loyalty and conformity, and tolerance of deviants may be sharply circumscribed (Coser 1967; Pruitt & Rubin 1986). 'Enhanced cohesiveness is still another mechanism that results from and encourages conflict escalation.' (Pruitt & Rubin 1986, p 107) In addition the group becomes more task oriented, leadership patterns shift from democratic to autocratic and the group becomes more highly structured and organised as it mobilises to engage with an adversary.

Pruitt & Rubin (1986) propose that as a consequence of the polarisation which conflict engenders between groups, individual members become more hostile and extreme in their attitudes and perceptions. This would be partly the consequence of solidarity and conformity demands from the group and partly the product of its progressively inward-looking orientation, and selective information induction processes. Pruitt & Rubin suggest that in social conflict situations hostility and distrust are magnified in group contexts. Conflict escalation is promoted by 'runaway norms' which strengthen polarisation, communication breakdowns, distrust and zero sum thinking, and group goals come to centre around the defeat or destruction of the other party.

In addition to the above changes, groups involved in heavy conflict assume a more militant leadership, centring around individuals who hold strong adversarial attitudes and skills.

Democratic style leadership is often displaced in such scenarios, leaving groups in conflict with leaders who have a greater proclivity to fight than negotiate. Finally, Pruitt & Rubin suggest that new, more militant subgroupings may emerge within a collectivity engaged in an escalating conflict — 'a committee or department to deal with the emerging struggle' (p 107).

Relations *between* groups in conflict are characterised by the emergence of enemy perceptions, increased hostility and distrust, breakdowns in communication and selective information induction (Schein 1980). As already discussed moral norms are lowered and usual codes of conduct in terms of tactics come to be regarded as inapplicable giving rise to increasingly contentious exchanges of pressure tactics. Pruitt & Rubin (1986) note that often when two groups engage in heavy conflict it is difficult for other groups in the wider community to remain uninvolved contributing to a process of *community polarisation*. This acts to remove moderating influences and render nugatory crosscutting bonds which may have developed in a society and which act to stabilise it. In a recent strike in a brewery, strikers rallied youth group support and the community to pressurise taverners and she-beeners not to sell beer in an effort to extend pressure tactics. Taverners found themselves having to choose between support for the company or its labour on a domestic dispute.

PROCESSES PROMOTING CONFLICT ESCALATION

Several processes are proposed in the literature as promoting conflict escalation (Pruitt & Rubin 1986; Kriesberg 1973). These are closely linked to the changes associated with the escalation process reflecting its self-reinforcing character.

Gratification

Conflicting parties may achieve a sense of gratification from their use of coercive tactics, the sense of group solidarity, the excitement and challenge, and the feeling of 'meaningful' involvement in a cause (Kriesberg 1973). It must also be recognised that some groups' identities are rooted in their adversarial roles. Shifts to cooperative endeavour imply also a loss of identity, loss of leadership roles for some, and changed organisational goals and structures which may carry little diminished gratification opportunities. This may well act to lock parties into ongoing conflictual behaviour. Writing on national liberation movements in Africa, Zartman (1985) observes:

> . . . national liberation movements have their own logic in regard to escalation. They have nothing to lose by fighting and nothing to do but fight. They have none of the problems of responsibility of a state, and their combat activities help them to build political solidarity and control their followers. So unlike a state they can be defeated only by being destroyed, a very difficult task. And unlike a state, they cannot merely be persuaded to reorient their goals in regard to the conflict, for to change goals is to remove their reason for being. (p 13)

Entrapment

Kriesberg proposes that once extreme coercive acts have been carried out they tend to be justified by the actors. They also may evoke a strong counteraction from the other side.

Pruitt & Rubin (1986) describe a process of entrapment which encapsulates this phenomenon. It is 'a special form of escalation in which the parties expend more of their time, energy, money, or other resources in the conflict than seems appropriate or justifiable by external standards' (p 122).

The more severe or violent the action of one side, the more likely it is that escalation will occur as grievances and calls for retribution increase. Iraq's invasion of Kuwait in 1990 evoked strong condemnation from the United Nations. These rapidly took the form of threats, ultimatums and deadlines. These in turn required a show of force to indicate serious intent. Once the sanctions option was perceived to be ineffective, international forces lined up 600 000 troops, over 900 planes, 150 ships and 1 500 tanks to face down Iraq's forces, and the parties were entrapped. Saddam Hussein would lose face and probably power if he complied with demands to withdraw from Kuwait in the face of such a threat, and the allied forces could hardly leave without seeing him do so. The process of a shift in tactics from diplomacy to confrontation is readily evident. The increased investment of resources and a move to violence was accompanied by observations to the effect that Saddam Hussein was 'a man without pity', while he on the other hand mobilised around the call to a 'Holy War'. These statements in classic fashion served to lower inhibitions about the onslaught on Iraq, and also about the tactics to be used to resist the attack, further locking the parties into the use of strongarm tactics to resolve the matter — saturation bombing, 'human shields', and oil leaks. Each of these in its own way entrapped the parties further, ensuring each of plenty of ammunition as regards the morally reprehensible behaviour of the other and the justice or at least necessity of its own acts.

Provocation

Where conflict is regulated and institutionalised it lessens the likelihood of conflict escalation as mutual behaviour becomes more predictable, and less likely to be misunderstood. Kriesberg (1973) suggests that shared understandings about ways of pursuing conflicting goals may, however, be the basis for conflict escalation. One side may provoke the other into escalation to make it behave in a 'reprehensible' manner. In this way it might gain internally and in terms of external relations as a consequence of the conflict process.

In the Algerian conflict the strategy of the FLN, according to Johnson (1983), was not to win a military engagement but to provoke the French authorities by acts of violence to take reprisal action. This would alienate the population who would resist, requiring further repression which would steadily unite the masses against the government. In this way the country would be rendered politically ungovernable and require military control — a losing situation in the longer term for the current power holders.

The crossing of boundaries of acceptable behaviour may release parties from normal constraints producing unrestrained attack behaviour. Once a party breaches rules a little, it may unleash a torrent of contentious exchange at a new level. For example, once one adversary uses a chemical or nuclear weapon it opens the possibilities of unlimited use of such weapons as each side attempts to ensure dominance at this new level of exchange. In the Algerian crisis the savagery of attacks by the Arabs and the ensuing French reprisals in 1945 locked the parties into a longer term conflict and in 1955 the parties unleashed their forces on each other without restraint. When news of French atrocities reached France, liberal opinion turned against the war, and produced the crisis that returned De Gaulle to power in 1958. The conflict escalated, and white terrorism (OAS) wreaked a toll of 12 000 civilians and 500 security officials in the year after De Gaulle offered Algeria its freedom following a referendum in January 1961. A full-scale military operation was required to suppress this opposition to change, and was followed by a massive exodus to France in the realisation that relations were too damaged to build a joint future for the country. About 1,3 million of the French left. Muslim officials were not so fortunate — the FLN slaughtered tens of thousands of them (between 30 000 and 150 000) in an orgy of post liberation violence. (Johnson 1983).

Saddam Hussein's invasion and occupation of Kuwait in 1990 unleashed a powerful military response from international forces, a level of exchange quite different from that which might have been incurred if diplomatic claims to the territory had been pursued. These of course, would have been unlikely to succeed. He was thus left to weigh the strength of his desire for Kuwait against the risks of the international response it might invoke. Having taken Kuwait by force he provoked a military response, action and reaction entrapping all in a costly win–lose exchange. Once the war had started he pursued a clear strategy of seeking to provoke Israel into an armed response by bombing its cities, attempting to escalate the issues off the question of Kuwait to include the whole Middle East turmoil and particularly the issue of Israel and the Palestinians. This would have taken some of the focus off Iraq and probably acted to split the Allies, particularly the Arab countries involved in the conflict. In this sense efforts to provoke conflict escalation might well have had positive functional consequences for Iraq.

Leadership and control structures

Leaders who are secure from constituency challenges are freer to escalate (and de-escalate) conflicts. Also, groups not in direct control of highest decision makers are more likely to escalate conflict. Thus totalitarian leaders may lead their unwilling populations into wars, but so may undisciplined populaces drag their weak or insecure leaders into growing strife.

> In many struggles the people in direct confrontation are not under effective control of their presumed superiors. . . inability to control or coordinate action makes it difficult to de-escalate. (Kriesberg 1973, p 182)

The apparent inability of ANC and Inkatha leaders to stop factional violence in South Africa is illustrative of this point. Those in direct confrontation in the streets of the community live out motives of aggression and retribution in contradiction to calls by their leaders to cease hostilities. These same people may continue to proclaim allegiance to political parties and factions as they carry out acts of aggression at a far more personalised level. They may believe in the wider call for peace but fail to see it as applicable to their 'unique' situation, or perceive their own acts of violence as merely reactive necessities in the face of aggression by others. The use of a party banner acts to mobilise and cohere a side, and provides it with a broader and more acceptable rationale and identity, but it also acts to discredit the banner and others who act under its colours. Conflict escalates as leaders and parties calling unsuccessfully for an end to violence ascribe their failure to each other's subversive intentions and acts of aggression. This may be true of course, but equally it allows leaders unable to control their people a face-saving explanation of the situation, turning failure into an opportunity to maintain internal unity against external aggressors. It also makes for a situation wherein leaders realising their limitations in calling for a cessation of hostilities, may refuse to continue doing so in the recognition that they might jeopardise their standing with a militant constituency.

It has been argued, in line with some of the functional aspects of conflict outlined by Coser (Chapter 2), that some leaders require ongoing conflict with external forces to maintain internal control and unity. Barber (1991) proposes about Iraq's Saddam Hussein

War is the condition that ensures his regime's survival. It enables him to manipulate the minds and energies of his population entirely to his own ends. As far as he and his ruling caste are concerned, therefore, the key is not to win or lose in the accepted senses of those words, but to perpetuate the conflict for its own sake. That, in itself, is victory enough.. . . If this line of reasoning has any merit, it would follow that his immediate goal is neither to hold onto Kuwait nor to avoid hostilities. It is to achieve protracted crisis.. . . Like all totalitarians he needs conflict in the same way as a bicyclist needs forward motion to stay upright.

Group changes

The group changes already outlined in describing conflict escalation — decreased communications, stereotyping, selective information induction, internal mobilisation — contribute to lowered capacities to read behaviour signalling a desire to de-escalate the process.

Pruitt & Rubin (1986) suggest that conflict escalation is associated with desires to punish each other, where the parties blame or are angry with each other and there is social approval for aggressive acts. Parties become locked into perceptions of their own moral superiority, projecting images of threatening behaviour and 'enemy' characteristics onto the other as they polarise. In so doing structural changes in the groups act to bond them into the conflict spiral.

CONFLICT AND VIOLENCE

Himes (1980) points out how widespread and common violent conflict is in modern and modernising societies, and that it is strongly reflected in the history of most nations. However, a longstanding ethic of assimilation in societies has evolved which has led to a tendency to regard violence as alien and nonlegitimate despite its pervasive character. Thus, contrary to the verbal tradition which stresses peace, order and regulated competition, he notes that the active tradition is strongly oriented toward violence.

The reasons for a negative assessment of violence are obvious — by definition it involves behaviour designed to inflict physical injury to property or persons. Himes (1980) defines violent conflict as the

> intentional struggle between collective actors that involves the application of significant social power for the purpose of injuring, disrupting, or destroying human beings, human psyches, material property and/or sociocultural structures. (p 104)

Within this definition fall a variety of categories of action including assassinations, terrorist attacks, wars, riots, lynchings, vigilantism and violence by state authorities. Looting, injuries, deaths and destruction, breakdowns of social systems, consumption of resources and lives to destructive ends and residual hostilities are some of the negative aspects of violence.

Van der Merwe (1989) observes that the spiral of violence in South Africa acts as a major stumbling block to negotiations. Politicians argue that violence is justifiable under certain circumstances — whether in government or in opposition, violence is seen as a final option to achieve one's ends when other means fail. Thus the violent insurrectionists of yesterday may easily be the oppressors of tomorrow if they believe justice to be on their side — and depending on the moral and political bent of churchleaders, they may find theological support for their actions.

Referring to Kaunda (1980), Van der Merwe (1989) distinguishes between *institutional* violence involving physical force by agents of the state, *structural* violence whereby defined groups are deprived or denigrated, and *psychological* violence. McKendrick and Hoffmann (1990) differentiate between *legitimate* and *illegitimate* violence. The former grouping include legally sanctioned acts of violence in childrearing practices, family life, initiation rituals, law enforcement, and war. The latter grouping includes acts of violence which are punishable under law such as murder, assault, rape, robbery, burglary, child abuse, faction fighting, assassinations, and international terrorism/freedom fighting. These authors propose that all forms of violence are damaging and disruptive of the quality of life. In an analysis of the impact of violence they point out that it injures and destroys, restricts lifestyles, evokes fear, damages relationships, dehumanises, alienates, causes psychological disruption and leads to moral atrophy.

Coser (1967) however, suggests that violence has functional as well as dysfunctional qualities and proposes that an overly moralistic negative assessment based on its short term consequences may act to preclude an objective evaluation of its longer term beneficial functions. He suggests three positive functions of violence. In the first instance it may provide groups barred from legitimate access to opportunities in society an alternative means of establishing an identity, and act to symbolise commitment to a given cause (there is no going back after an act of violence). In other words it provides a means for a group to acquire *a sense of achievement* and commitment where more peaceful alternatives are absent. Secondly it performs the function of a *danger signal* to a society, its manifestation sensitising more privileged groups of the need for social reconstruction. Thirdly it may act as *a catalyst*, arousing new levels of solidarity in a community as it seeks to campaign against a crime wave, or implement new controls on government authorities abusing their power.

Himes (1980) points out that *achievement of intended ends* is a functional aspect of violence, for example, political liberation through guerilla warfare. It may also have a *unifying effect* on oppressed groups. It acts in some senses as a *regenerative*, reintegrating force in the wider society as a whole as it seeks to achieve more flexibility to accomodate diverse interest groupings. To these may be added the fact that it may *energise* a negotiation process, concentrating the efforts of parties to reach a settlement in the face of the appalling consequences of failing to do so. This last point is very debatable though —

violence may also escalate conflicts and leave residues of bitterness which confound long-term peace agreements. In this sense the use of violence may become a self-defeating tactic, acting also to lose a party social support and the moral high ground in a conflict.

Several theories have been advanced as to the causes of violent behaviour — alienation, the influence of electronic mass media, exploitative relations between owners of capital and the working class, value incompatabilities and dysfunctional institutions, frustration and aggression, and social learning theory have been advanced as explanatory concepts.

Deutsch (1973) suggests that defensiveness and resistance by a dominant group is:

> conducive to a sense of frustration and desperation in the group seeking a change and may propel it to employ pressure tactics that are perceived to be illegitimate and that have the effect of further alienating the already defensive dominant group. . . in such circumstances the development of an escalating spiral of force and counterforce is not uncommon. (p 113)

Deutsch proposes that unless an acceptable third party can intervene, this conflict spiral will continue until one of the sides is defeated, both become too exhausted, or the costs become intolerable to continue the conflict. Alternatively, the escalation of violence can be averted if the dominant group is sufficiently secure and unthreatened by acts of violence to respond flexibly and creatively to introduce changes in response to the message of desperation and urgency such acts convey, rather than to use counterforce.

Pruitt & Rubin (1986) suggest that people 'take the law into their own hands' where there is an absence of trusted forums or third-party institutions using extreme tactics and often escalating the conflict as a consequence. The endorsement of violence as a means to social justice is more likely in situations where average citizens feel they have no means to influence government decisions.

In summary, it would seem that these authors agree that violence is likely in situations where:

❑ high levels of discontent on the part of a subordinate group;

❑ evoke high levels of threat and defensiveness on the part of the dominant group; and

❑ there are no alternative legitimised processes, forums or institutions available to the parties through which the conflict might be resolved.

In such situations high discontent produces high pressures for change, evoking high defensiveness and high levels of frustration on the part of the dominant and subordinate groups respectively. This process is vividly illustrated in the case study which follows in this chapter.

Himes (1980) suggests that in certain situations a violent approach is formalised in group ideologies. An example would be the ideology of the ANC which moved to strategies of violence in the 1960s following disillusionment with the efficacy of negotiation. Further he suggests that an orientation toward violence is especially prevalent in societies with a dominant military hegemony, leading to forms of socialisation which have a greater acceptance of violence. Interestingly, Himes also suggests that violence is the product of poor social controls which are most in evidence in developing societies with rapid rates of urbanisation and cultural change leading to normative uncertainty. Arguably, as such situations reach intolerable levels, the use of the military for purposes of control is necessitated, further compounding the crisis and entrenching violence as a means of social change. Thus, paradoxically, violence would seem to be the consequence both of inadequate social controls and of the excessive use of force or repression on the part of groups seeking to impose such controls. This may contribute to another cause of violence — an apparent lack of nonviolent alternatives to conflict resolution. Conflicting parties may have no knowledge of nonviolent methods of change.

> Nonviolent alternatives to struggle require leadership, special organisations, tactics and similar resources. Thus, if there are no mediators, conflict adjudicating agencies, or established patterns of compromise, negotiation, and exchange, contending parties may see violence as their only resort. Ignorance of existing resources has the same practical effect as their non-existence. . . (and once these are known and utilised). . . it requires time and practice to distill and establish a body of nonviolent traditions. (Himes 1980, p 116)

As already indicated, violence may emerge as the central vehicle for change when struggle groups become disillusioned with the efficacy of negotiation and other nonviolent methods.

Various *structural conditions* and *psychological factors* may predispose groups towards violence. Himes (1980) mentions anomie (normlessness), alienation and prolonged and pervasive tension as contributory factors towards violence. On a psychological level, as already indicated, violence is likely in cases of frustrated expectations, especially where the obstacles to their achievement (people or systems) are seen as arbitrary or unfair. Following the work of Bandura (1983), violence is more likely to be used where people have learned to respond to aversive situations aggressively. This may occur at a personal or vicarious level of experience. Aggression may not be directed at the source of frustration owing to its superior power and the level of risk involved. Instead it may be displaced to other targets — strikers attack 'scabs', boycotters attack those breaching edicts not to pay rent or buy in certain stores. These are not the primary targets of aggression or sources of frustration, but their behaviour undermines group solidarity and evokes the full wrath of the group concerned (Cohen 1990; Vogelman 1989).

In crowd situations individuals may experience lessened feelings of personal responsibility (group authorisation); may be more easily aroused to violence through singing, dancing, overcrowding and the breakdown of meeting procedures; and may be subject to conformity pressures from the group which may act to promote violent behaviour. Anonymity in the crowd and the dehumanisation of victims assist in the commission of violent acts. Environments with high levels of frustration, aggression and violence contribute toward the evolution of values and attitudes which condone or promote violence — a culture of violence may emerge in such societies (Cohen 1990; McKendrick and Hoffmann 1990; Vogelman 1989).

A CASE STUDY OF CONFLICT ESCALATION AND VIOLENCE: THE SATS STRIKE OF 1987

The South African Railway strike of 1987 vividly illustrates the conflict escalation process outlined above. The efforts of the employer, workers and their trade union to settle the matter reflect how differently parties in conflict can perceive events and actions, how a history of relations affects efforts to resolve a current problem, and the importance of jointly acceptable procedures and forums for conflict resolution. The culmination of the crisis reveals how dramatically intra-group and intergroup relations can shift, locking the parties into conflict, reinforcing stereotypes and producing conformity pressures on individual players with, in this case, terrible consequences.

Structural factors

The emphasis of this case study is on the process analysis but several critical structural factors require brief discussion. SATS was established in 1910 and developed during the 1920s as part of the state's 'civilised labour policy' intended to alleviate the 'poor white problem' by providing jobs to this group. The trade-off, in a sense, was votes for jobs, and the victims were the disenfranchised black population. Right up to the time of the dispute described here, black SATS workers were seriously discriminated against in terms of job status and opportunity.

In terms of Conditions of Employment (SATS) Act of 1983, SATS would negotiate only with trade unions recognised by the Minister of Transport who accorded this status at his discretion. He accredited a union called BLATU as the recognised union. It is apparent that many workers were not satisfied with this union, that its structure, organisation and *modus operandi* were not clear to them, and that there were perceptions that it was a sweetheart union whose presence acted as an obstacle to more genuinely representative unions being established. The COSATU affiliate, SARHWU was attempting to establish itself at this time and certainly did not see BLATU's presence as helpful.

No recognition was accorded SARHWU, but SATS was aware that it was organising.

In terms of the Act, workers were prohibited from strike action. An extensive disciplinary procedure was evident allowing for appeals to the level of the general manager, with representation by a recognised union or employee of own choice. No access for progressing appeals to an independent arbitrator or industrial court or tribunal existed, and the procedures had not been negotiated with black workers, thus reducing their acceptability and perceived legitimacy.

The strike described below took place a few weeks before a general election being run on a security ticket, and in which there was a shift to the Conservative Party by the white electorate. White voters employed by SATS formed a substantial constituency and were by repute already conservative in leaning. It seems not unlikely that this factor was an important influence in the decisions management took in handling the strike, with a heavy government presence on the Board of SATS. Certainly, while government was vigorously running a 'total onslaught' political campaign, the chances of it recognising a trade union it perceived as having communist leanings, on the strategically important railways system of the country, were remote.

Process analysis

On Thursday 12 March a black driver was dismissed following a cash irregularity of R40,40 which had occurred five months previously. He had not handed in the sum on returning from a delivery on a Friday afternoon, but on his own initiative had handed it in on the following Monday morning. Serious questions of procedural and substantive fairness in the conduct of the disciplinary case are readily apparent (timeousness, fair representation, severity of sentence being some of these). It is possible that if an acceptable and trusted disciplinary process had been pursued that a rights dispute of this sort could have been relatively easily resolved at an early stage.

However, these regulatory mechanisms were not in place and, as already indicated, a deep rift in the relationship had developed over decades. Evidence in the extenuation trial indicated that this was the time at which annual bonuses were paid each year and that workers perceived that black labourers were annually dismissed in large numbers in an effort to contain costs. In the light of the perceived injustice over the dismissal and their suspicion that the event signalled the possible beginning of a larger process of contrived terminations, workers at the site embarked on a strike. Their demand was for the reinstatement of the dismissed individual.

An opportunity to settle the matter was provided the following day when the regional manager visited the site and discussed the matter with BLATU representatives. In an effort to settle he made three successive offers on the dismissal matter:

- reinstatement as a labourer;
- reinstatement as a lower grade driver;
- reinstatement to previous status with an R80 fine.

Each of these was rejected by the striking workers who stuck by their position of unconditional reinstatement. The parties clearly saw this exchange in quite different lights. The manager probably saw his efforts as genuine compromise offers to settle the matter and their rejection as intransigence on the part of labour. Workers perceived the moves as confirmation of their suspicions that management had not acted honestly in the first instance and was now trying to conceal its mistakes without admitting error and doing what was just, that is, apologising and reinstating the driver. Early on in the process then, there is some evidence of crossed perceptions even as the parties tried to resolve the matter. In the private sector a likely resolution of the matter would have been a return to the status quo while the matter was properly reinvestigated or submitted to independent arbitration. No such recourse was available to the parties in terms of existing procedural mechanisms.

At this point SARHWU, through its attorney, requested access to assist in resolving the matter. In the light of existing suspicions about the nature of the union, its unrecognised status in terms of existing law, and lack of knowledge about its actual representativeness, it is not unsurprising that SATS rejected this offer.

The strike continued over the weekend. On Monday 16th workers alleged that the regional manager failed to arrive for a pre-arranged meeting, this perception confirming their belief that management did not take their demands seriously. The employer then tried to use white drivers to drive the trucks in the depot, and black strikers responded by driving their vehicles into positions to block entrances to the site. This act by workers clearly escalates the process from one of a withdrawal of labour to one of preventing the work process.

On Tuesday 17th a personnel manager arrived claiming neutrality and offering to resolve the dispute. While this may appear naive in the context of modern thinking about the role of human resources personnel, it should be remembered that many traditional texts described the role as one of bridging the interests of management and employees. Although this message may have been sent in good faith, however, workers regarded it sceptically. While SATS policy restricted the personnel manager to talking to BLATU, he nevertheless showed considerable insight into its actual effectiveness and representativeness by requesting them to come forward *with* three other representatives chosen by the workers. This allowed a circumvention of policy restrictions without actually breaching them, and represented a creative attempt to engage with real leaders. In meeting with the elected team, however, he demanded a return to work before dealing with the matter of the dismissal. The status quo solution would have allowed a remedy to this impasse -workers could have accepted a return to work subject to reinvestigation or arbitration. But of course this solution was not one of those available to the manager in existing procedures, was not one customarily used, and quite possibly was not even known to him as an option.

Later in the day workers demanded:

- unconditional reinstatement of the dismissed driver;
- full payment for days on strike;
- all future disciplinary actions to be open to worker assessment;
- worker involvement in decision-making on their future;
- abolition of all racial practices in the management machinery; and
- freedom of expression in meetings sanctioned by SATS without fear of intimidation/victimisation.

Whatever the merits of these demands, clearly they were substantially expanded from the original demand for the reinstatement of an individual. It would not be unexpected if management began to suspect that the union was moving the goalposts, or using the original dispute to piggy-back a wide range of other grievances, or even that deliberate attempts were being made to sabotage a settlement on the trigger issue.

Negotiations proceeded late into the night when the personnel manager advised that he needed the general manager's mandate on proposals. While awaiting a reply, the worker representatives slept in the offices on site. At 04h00 on 18 March the personnel manager arrived with the police and a court interdict ordering workers to hand over the keys of vehicles. While this action was clearly to aimed at stopping workers fom inhibiting the work process, its timing, coming while they were waiting for a reply to demands, and while the personnel manager was assumed to be seeking a mandate for a response, did little to build trust between the parties, and certainly contributed to escalated use of pressure tactics in the process.

At this stage the strike started to expand with sympathy action, and workers from other depots sent representatives to assess the situation. SARHWU again offered to intervene, but SATS turned this down with the reply that workers should use recognised channels and organisations. SARHWU reiterated its offer the following day and suggested independent mediation or arbitration to resolve the matter. At the site SATS then excluded the three non-BLATU representatives from negotiations.

A week after the trigger event then, the dispute had shown the following features of conflict escalation:

- Demands had escalated from a concrete single issue to a larger number of grievances of a more grandiose and vague character, making negotiations far more complicated.
- The use of pressure tactics by each party had escalated: the union's from withdrawing labour to preventing the work process; and management's from demanding a return to work to using authority in the form of the interdict.
- There is evidence that the parties were misreading each others' actions in the light of misunderstanding and preconceptions.
- The parties had no commonly accepted set of procedures or dispute resolution mechanisms to contain the matter.
- Management's refusal to recognise the union that offered to assist, precluded possible engagement with genuine representatives and added to the dispute the further complication of a struggle for recognition.
- There were signs of the strike being likely to expand through the sympathy action of other workers.

On Saturday 21 March thousands of workers attended a meeting at COSATU house, but left peacefully on instructions from the police after discussing grievances. While SATS adhered to the position that policy prohibited it from talking to SARHWU, it was revealed how quickly policy could be changed when, in a special *Government Gazette*, powers of mass dismissal were conferred on the general manager, threatening thousands of jobs. At this stage about 10 000 workers were involved in the action.

Despite the the escalated stage of the dispute, a chance for settlement arose on 23 March when the elected representatives put forward, somewhat clumsily, a set of proposals:

- The general manager should deal with the issue of the dismissal before 31 March, provided an appeal was submitted before 24 March.
- Pending the outcome of this process, drivers would return to work from 24 March.
- Workers would accept the general manager's decision as final.
- Workers would use annual leave to cover absence from 13–23 March.
- Workers were to be paid if the dismissed driver were fully exonerated.
- Final decision in this regard would rest with the workers.

This represented some creative thought on the part of the bargaining team and allowed room for a considered management response for purposes of reaching settlement. The personnel manager's response to the proposals signed an undertaking:

- to convey the dismissal case to the general manager within 24 hours;
- to investigate other grievances immediately and to begin discussions on 25 March;
- to consider immediately the proposal of leave to cover the strike absence;

- to accept that if the dismissed worker was totally exon-erated management would pay for the period of the strike up to 24 March.

This positive exchange was negated, however, when workers rejected the proposals of their own team, and submitted new proposals that management:

- rectify the dismissal;
- provide a statement of intent on racism;
- not take disciplinary action on workstoppage when workers return to work;
- pay strikers should the dismissed worker be totally exonerated;
- let an independent arbitrator rather than the GM hear the case.

The management team could be forgiven for believing that the union was shifting the goalposts after an exchange of this sort, and must have had grave doubts about the serious intent of the union to settle the matter. Nevertheless, a close examination of the revised proposals reveals that the significant change was that an arbitrator rather than the general manager should deal with the case. Again the problem of the absence of acceptable forums and proce-dures for purposes of conflict regulation. Workers simply did not trust management to act impartially.

At this stage SARHWU estimates put the number of striking workers at 14 000. Lawyers from SATS and SARHWU engaged in a brief tussle over acountability, SATS denying the legitimacy of SARHWU but holding it accountable for the strike, SARHWU denying responsibility but acknow-ledging that strikers were its members and on this basis that they should be allowed access to attempt to resolve the matter. SARHWU lawyers cited existing grievance, disciplinary and dispute settlement procedures as being inadequate and again proposed mediation or arbitration as suitable mechanisms. A SARHWU member was detained at this stage by the security police.

On 26th March the workers sent a delegation of 98 repre-sentatives to meet the personnel manager, who was left with the impression that many were not even aware of the details of the dispute. Management clearly felt that workers were being obstructionist in sending forward a delegation this large for negotiation purposes. One can imagine how this series of events confirmed management's worst suspicions of workers' motives. Yet, when asked why such a large team was sent forward, a SARHWU representative stated that it was a democratic step. As the number of sympathy strikers across sites increased so the necessity for a larger bargaining team grew — sympathy strikers had a right to be involved in the process — another example of how easily parties misconstrue each others actions in conflict escalation scenarios. Newspaper articles at the time reflected growing levels of police/worker confrontation.

Finally on 31 March, when the worker committee arrived to negotiate, it found that management had already appointed people to 'negotiate' with from each site. These agreed to withdraw. Management rejected the use of independent third parties, and returned to a position of talking only to workers from the site of the original dispute. This was probably an effort to try to 'shrink' the dispute by focusing on original issues at the original site in an effort to render it more manageable. However, it failed to recognise the true dimensions of the problem and unilateral efforts by management to pick the other side's bargaining team further entrenched perceptions of bad faith. An estimated 19 000 workers were now on strike.

When no settlement was achieved SATS issued a notice on the same day indicating:
- a strict adherence to prescribed procedures as regards the dismissal case;
- that the disciplinary procedure for blacks is based on that for whites;
- a preparedness to negotiate the disciplinary procedure at some future date with the 'recognised union and employees';
- an unyielding no-work/no-pay stance with regard to strikers;

- an initiative to replace black workers with whites on a permanent basis.

This notice was in line with SATS written strike strategy which sought inter alia to 'neutralise SARHWU and CO-SATU', to restrict negotiations to BLATU, and to emphasise the 'absurdity' of the strike. The attempt to limit the size of the action artificially was accompanied by a commitment to the position that SARHWU would not be engaged with. This commitment to principle precluded the possibility that the union may have been able to assist in settling the matter. By refusing to discuss issues with the union, it was presented with no acid test of representivity or influence. Discussions could not have made matters worse — at worst the union would have been shown to be ineffectual and the strike would have continued, at best a settlement might have been achieved with a return to work before the costs of further escalation were incurred. SATS, however, seemed to have regarded the principle that it should not engage with SARHWU as more important than attempting to resolve the dispute through whatever means presented themselves. This produced the fundamental problem of the employer refusing to grant legitimacy to the union, whose members in turn refused to legitimise its conflict regulation procedures — a classic impasse and conflict spiral situation. In such a situation the very mechanisms designed to contain conflict become themselves major obstacles to a settlement.

On 3 April the Minister of Transport was reported as stating that ' it was the intention of these organisations (UDF and COSATU) to take the crisis from the schools and townships to the workplace'. COSATU's general secretary accused SATS of violating principles of freedom of association. SATS claimed mass intimidation to be the cause of the strike, SARHWU claimed mass support. SARHWU's appeals to the minister to adhere to sound industrial relations procedures failed to evoke a response. A smear campaign against the president of SARHWU was initiated. By 10 April 305 SARHWU members had been detained under emergency regulations. On 13 April trains and SATS property were burned. Lawyers on both sides threatened each other, and both sides while stating an abhorrence of violence, accused each other of violent acts.

On 21 April SATS delivered an ultimatum to workers threatening dismissal if they did not return to work, and initiated Operation Telbord with the SA Police and the SA Defence Force to crush the strike. In the face of this loss of control over the situation and the authoritarian stance, worker representatives met with management. After accusing SATS of intimidation and failing to deal with the impasse they withdrew 'leaving the matter in the hands of management to take its course'.

On national television Dr Grove claimed that SATS had adhered to an open approach in the negotiations and cited subversive intentions as the basis of the actions by nearly 20 000 striking workers over a small issue. He also held SARHWU responsible for the strike and stated that SARHWU 'originated way back in 1936 from the then SA Communist Party. SARHWU is now affiliated to COSATU and we all know what the further affiliations of COSATU with the UDF and other organisations are. So there is much more, especially in the political field, to this strike than meets the eye . . .' He went on to state that the majority of workers wanted to work but were intimidated not to. This interview evoked particular anger amongst workers. Basically the attempt was to demonise the organisation while holding the members out as innocent victims of the process and promising them no victimisation if they returned to work.

Confrontational action escalated — on 22 April police action in Germiston saw workers shot and killed. Workers left COSATU House to march to Germiston in protest but were violently confronted by police who laid seige to COSATU House. SATS fired all 22 000 strikers involved.

An AWB emblem was placed on the bonnet of a police vehicle outside COSATU House. Worker attitudes to non-strikers hardened and they became more unruly and violent. On the night of 27 April non-strikers were beaten in the basement of COSATU House. The coordinating committee which met in the upper floors of COSATU House twice requested workers to cease this action, but in the face of rising levels of violence were unsuccessful, and according to one became afraid that they themselves would be beaten. On 28 April five non-strikers were fetched from depots and beaten. After a 'trial' the decision was taken to kill them for 'betrayal of cause'. They were taken to Prolecon and killed — one escaped. COSATU tried to claim that allegations of these murders were part of a mass media attempt to discredit the organisation, but on 29th April police made arrests leading to the trial and conviction of 18 individuals involved in the killings. Of these eight were found guily of murder, and following an extenuation trial, four received the death sentence, the others receiving lesser sentences.

On 7 May 1987 a bomb demolished COSATU House. On 5 June SATS agreed to re-employ all the strikers with the retention of employment benefits. This victory was achieved on the basis of a legal technicality in the dismissals rather than a fundamental power base on the part of the workers. Their misinterpretation of this coupled with a somewhat slow reform process on the part of SATS management quite possibly contributed to the repeat mass strike experienced in 1989.

After the parties failed to reach agreement on 23 March relations reached a new low, with the parties suspicions about each others' intentions worsening. SATS ultimatum of 31 March was retrogressive and racially imflammatory. The intransigent stance adopted precluded options of a negotiated settlement. Relations devolved into exchanges of mutual demonisation, accusations of intimidation, and attacks on each others' credentials. The number of people involved and resources employed escalated, tactics became increasingly confrontational.

Finally important changes occurred within the worker grouping as the pressure grew. Many of the factors cited in the literature as contributing to violence were present. High levels of worker discontent were clearly evident, evoking high levels of threat and defensiveness from management. No acceptable forums were available or could be established through which to regulate the conflict, frustrating workers further. Their feelings of injustice having no outlet were compounded as the matter drew on leaving them progressively alienated from the social system. Having lost their jobs and been subjugated by the police there was little that they could turn to and arguably little reason to trust any of the institutions of the wider society. Having lost faith in the justice of the wider system they set up a system of their own. The only strength they had was to maintain solidarity for their cause. Casual labourers broke this and were subject to discipline by their own code of isolated morality. In short this alienated group established new norms of social control at the same time as its tolerance of deviants decreased. Notably a new leadership emerged effectively displacing the leadership elected for negotiating purposes. This more militant group acted to pressure conformity and discipline in the rank and file.

ANALYSIS

Symptoms of conflict escalation

- *Issues proliferated* from a single concrete demand to a larger number of more grandiose character, reflective of longer term grievances.

- *Worker tactics shifted* from a withdrawal of labour to attempts to stop the work process to attacks on property to eventual violence.

- *Management tactics shifted* from efforts to appease to interdicts to threats to dismissal and eventually to coordinated action with the military and police. When policy changes occurred, they moved in the direction of coercion rather than opening the way for negotiation.

- The exchange became progressively characterised by *mutual demonisation* and smear campaigns as each side began to conform to the worst stereotypes the other had drawn of it.

- *Communications* started off a low base but owing to policy and mistrust became progressively disorganised, deteriorating into a series of public attacks rather than concentrated effort to solve the problem.

- From a few *participants* the number grew steadily until there were 22 000 workers on strike, and there was large-scale involvement of railway, defence and police personnel.
- *Internal shifts occurred in the groups* with a progressively hardline approach being evidenced. On the union side this witnessed the sidelining of representatives elected for negotiation purposes and the emergence of strong conformity pressures enforced by hardliners.
- As the workers became progressively disenchanted with the available system of justice in the company, were refused independent third party intervention, engaged in confrontational exchange with the authorities and found themselves alienated and attacked by wider society, so they began to establish *systems of justice of their own*. Deviants who eroded solidarity, the only strength left to them, were tried and punished on grounds of betrayal, and as in the case of traitors and deserters in war they were executed.

The absence of stabilisers and regulators

- SATS did not accord SARHWU *legitimacy* in the interaction. While it could be argued that there was sufficient reason to refuse the union's early approaches on the grounds of unknown representivity, conditions changed as the strike grew. The refusal to negotiate formally with SARHWU never allowed it the acid test — successful negotiation based on genuine representivity might have produced a settlement, if the union was not representative and no settlement had been found what would have been lost?
- An *absence of internal organisation and coherence* is evident in the workers' approach. Poor organisation is evidenced in the way it sent forward negotiating teams and achieved mandates. Properly organised unions, with clear structures and mandating systems do not generally behave in this way. This is one of the reasons for promoting union organisation for purposes of effective conflict regulation.

- An *absence of agreed procedures, third-party institu-tions and bargaining forums* prohibited focused effort to settle the dispute — the union had to fight for recognition as a player rather than over the trigger issue itself. As the company refused the union legitimacy, so workers refused the company's conflict regulation mechanisms legitimacy, locking the parties into a war of principle with entrenched positions. No shared conflict limiting norms were evidenced in the exchange. In the event the parties relied eventually on coercive tactics to achieve their ends.
- The *imbalance of power* in the struggle gave rise to a situation where the stronger clearly believed that it could win the day through muscle, the weaker being obliged to fight not over an issue of difference, but for its very right to exist.

Conflict aggravators

- *Aspiration levels* of workers were heightened by percep-tions of legitimacy of cause, relating to the perceived injustice of the trigger event, wider grievances and recognition of their union. Their comrades in the private sector had had bargaining rights for nearly a decade, and access to a more developed system of industrial justice with independent courts, arbitration and media-tion. Thus invidious comparison probably played a part in aggravating matters.
- A long *history* of discrimination, lack of opportunity and oppression in the railways is clear, giving rise to large grievances and feelings of threat to those faced with change in the system.
- There was *no history of effective joint decision-making or meaningful conflict regulation* in relations between the parties, no tradition of negotiation.
- The *progressive use of coercive strategies* by each of the parties acted to confirm their negative stereotypes of each other and steadily released them from any moral constraints they might have had over the use of direct coercion.

STALEMATE AND CONFLICT DE-ESCALATION

Kriesberg (1973) writes that

> conflict behaviour does not increase in magnitude indefinitely. It must de-escalate, stagnate or stop (p 163).

Pruitt & Rubin (1986) propose four main reasons for the development of a stalemate:

- ❑ the failure of contentious tactics;
- ❑ exhaustion of necessary resources;
- ❑ loss of social support; and
- ❑ unacceptable costs.

In effect a situation emerges in which neither party can or wants to escalate the conflict further. Zartman (1985) suggests that conflicts are ripe for resolution in the face of two types of stalemate — *plateaus* or deadlocks, and *precipices* or deadlines. The former occurs when the parties realise that they are unable to achieve their aims, resolve the problem or win the

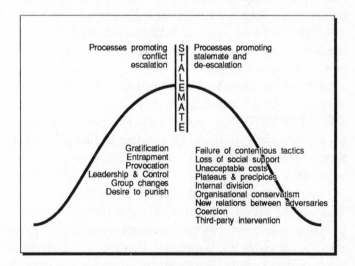

Figure 2.2
Stalemate and de-escalation

conflict. They begin to feel uncomfortable with the costly dead-end into which they have cornered themselves. Zartman states that the plateau is not a temporary resting ground, but a 'flat, unpleasant terrain stretching into the future, providing no later possibilities for decisive escalation or for graceful escape' (p 232). The precipice is the opposite, reflecting a realisation by both parties that matters will deteriorate rapidly if they do not negotiate a settlement. They are threatened by an impending catastrophe, or a narrow miss, which demands of them that they reassess strategies of confrontation.

Kriesberg (1973) postulates that when the costs for attaining a goal become too great, then it may be devalued. He suggests that a turning point of this nature is dependent on several other circumstances.

Competition for group leadership/internal division

Leadership competitions may witness the emergence of moderate constituencies as increasingly costly conflict behaviour produces no signs of achieving desired objectives. Leaders offering plausible alternatives for goal achievement, or acceptable reasons for decreasing commitment to it, may achieve dominance. This is more likely in non-cohesive struggle groups. The division in the Nationalist Party which saw FW de Klerk rise to power with a vigorous rejection of his predecessor's politics is an example of this process. De Klerk's strategy goes further than one of internal power play, however.

A party may seek to weaken an adversary through actions designed to promote internal division such as increased pressure on sections of its membership or conciliatory drives which are divisive in consequence. De Klerk's sudden opening of doors to negotiation took place as major international shifts were in evidence. Communist regimes were in collapse, weakening the resource base and models proposed by many internal and external struggle groups. Western countries' energies and resources seemed poised to be redirected to Eastern Europe putting further pressure on these groups to seek a solution sooner rather than later. The rapid repeal of 'second layer' apartheid laws, the unbanning of the ANC, the SACP, the PAC and the release of Mandela and significant others returned the government to the high ground as it sought to re-establish international credibility and ties, and to engage with struggle groups on a new political economy.

These struggle groups were clearly caught off balance. Splits are apparent in government opposition groups which may become larger as negotiation continues, probably alienating both the white right and the black left if and when a settlement becomes more achievable.

Organisational conservatism

Several authors have noted the tendency for organisations, once established, to make efforts to ensure their own survival. Thus struggle groups may become less willing to escalate conflicts in ways which threaten their own existence, for example, through an exhaustion of resources or through tactics which would evoke a high-risk confrontation with a stronger adversary.

This process was strongly evidenced in the military coups which took place in Greece in 1973, and in Portugal in 1974. In both these countries, governments of the day had been committed to high-risk costly conflicts: the Greek government stood at risk of a military engagement with Turkey over the Cyprus question, and the Portuguese government was committed to keeping its wartorn colonies in Africa. In both instances the 'military as institution' recognised these situations as being untenable in their own and national interests. The military coups were a means of preserving these interests and acted to de-escalate the conflicts in which their respective governments were engaged (Stepan 1986).

New relations between adversaries

As a consequence of conflict, competing groups may develop new respect and understanding for each other, and establish new methods of relating through procedural and institutional arrangements. Regular negotiation and pressure exchanges may contribute to the skills of leaders in reading each other's power capacities, needs and pressures, thus promoting the possibilities that one or both will take steps to de-escalate the conflict at critical points. As negotiuations between the South African government and the ANC/SACP continue, pragmatism is likely to set in. The fight for recognition and the right to be a player as issues of principle may give way to conflicts of interest, the hard realism required to build a nation's economy and preserve or build a measure of peace. A history of joint exchange may emerge to supplant the trackrecord of open confrontation.

Coercion

Coercion may see a de-escalation by the other side for two reasons. Firstly it may physically prevent the other side from continuing its conflict behaviour, obliging a de-escalation owing to a reduced *capacity* to continue by the other. The mass detention of leaders of struggle groups in South Africa during successive States of Emergency since 1984 had this exact effect. Secondly, and often as a consequence of loss of capacity, a side may lose its will to persist, doubting its capacity and questioning the desirability of pursuing competitive tactics. Empowerment to pursue conflict goals is the product of resources x mobilisation (Laue 1989). Thus relative control over resources is an important feature of the capacity to compete effectively. This may be of an economic or political nature. Arguably the South African government's containment efforts in the unrest of the eighties was directed at reducing the capacity of struggle groups to mobilise political power. Interestingly, however, the resources required for this purpose erode its own power base, leaving it weaker as well as its opponents. And, of course, coercion seldom removes, but may often enhance perceptions of the legitimacy of the cause, thus acting simply as a temporary lull in engagement between the parties while the weaker regroups for another strike at the system.

Third-party intervention

Third parties may de-escalate conflicts through intervention or non-involvement. Non-involvement can limit the expansion of the conflict confining it to the resource capabilities of the parties. By the same token direct intervention on a partisan basis may act to adjust power relations obligingly de-escalating efforts on the part of a party. Alternatively joint pressure may be exerted on parties to end the conflict. Mediatory assistance may also serve to reduce conflict intensity. These processes are discussed more fully in the chapter on mediation (chapter 7).

3
THE NATURE OF NEGOTIATION

Conflict provides the rationale for negotiation as a means of exchange between individuals and groups. However, it is not the only means of conflict resolution, or dispute settlement, and neither does its use exclude the employment of more contentious tactics. Moreover, effective negotiation would seem to be contingent on several factors, not all of which are present in every conflict situation. Therefore, prior to outlining the skills of negotiation, problem solving and peacemaking, it is necessary to make some broad observations on the nature of the negotiation process and outline some of its basic tenets. Further, effective negotiation is reliant upon certain attitudinal conditions, dependant on the nature of the negotiation environment and facilitated by the existence of agreed bargaining structures and forums. It is not a process which is solely reliant on the negotiating skills of the parties -these may be negated by ideological issues, the nature of their constituencies, external factors beyond their control and structural problems in their relationship.

NEGOTIATION DEFINED

Various definitions have been proposed for negotiation, most of which carry a similar emphasis:

> Negotiation is a form of decision making in which two or more parties talk with one another in an effort to resolve their opposing interests. . . a process by which a joint decision is made by two or more parties. (Pruitt 1981, pp xi–xii)

Negotiation is the process whereby two or more parties, who are faced with a problem or a conflict about some limited resources, attempt to agree on how best to solve the problem or resolve the conflict. (Falkenberg 1982, p 7)

. . . any form of verbal communication, direct or indirect, whereby parties to a conflict of interest discuss, without resort to arbitration or other judicial processes, the form of any joint action which they might take to manage a dispute between them. (Morley & Stephenson, 1977, p 26)

Negotiation is a basic means of getting what you want from others. It is a back-and-forth communication designed to reach an agreement when you and the other side have some interests that are shared and others that are opposed. (Fisher & Ury 1981, p xi)

Negotiation is a process for resolving conflict between two or more parties whereby both or all modify their demands to achieve a mutually acceptable compromise . . . a process of adjusting both parties' views of their ideal outcome to an attainable outcome. (Kennedy et al 1987, p 14)

Recurrent themes are evident in these definitions allowing the following elements to be identified as core to negotiation:

❑ It is a verbal interactive process
❑ involving two or more parties
❑ who are seeking to reach an agreement
❑ over a problem or conflict of interest between them
❑ in which they seek as far as possible to preserve their interests, but adjust their views and positions in the joint effort to achieve an agreement.

NEGOTIATION IN PERSPECTIVE

As will have become apparent in earlier chapters, negotiation is not the only means of dealing with conflict. It occurs when the parties involved in a conflict decide to use it either in place of, or in conjunction with other methods of conflict resolution to settle their differences. Specht (1973) offers a range of change tactics and categorises them in terms of appropriate conditions for their use.

Collaborative techniques include joint action, cooperation and education and are based on consensual relations between parties. Such relations emerge when parties are in agreement about a rearrangement of resources in their interaction, and tend to occur when none see the change as threatening in terms of money, prestige, power or status. Collaboration should not be confused with compliance. Collaboration is a mature exchange based in relations of power balance and the recognition of the need for cooperative endeavour. *Compliance* on the other hand, is based in relations of power imbalance and occurs where people obey the edicts of those in power despite their disagreement and resistance to these. Adam (1988) has noted that despite the oppressiveness of apartheid laws, the vast majority of black people actually complied with them, allowing the system to remain functional for a long period.

Campaign tactics are used in situations where differences exist between parties as to how resources should be distributed. Change will bring about realignments of power, wealth or prestige involving loss for some, but the consequent competition is seen as within the rules of the game of institutionalised competition. The parties therefore use negotiation, bargaining, compromise, mild coercion, arbitration, and normatively acceptable pressure tactics in the exchange as they seek agreement but attempt to preserve their interests as far as possible.

Disruptive tactics are used when there is a challenge to existing status relationships, and are rooted in a competition for power between parties. When a party sees its power, privilege or status as being diminished in a relationship, the response is dissensus. A struggle for reorientation of old values is undertaken by opposition groups, and the tactics used are essentially disruptive in character -a violation of legal or behavioural norms. Disruptive tactics are designed to prevent the target group from operating as usual. They are intended to disrupt but not to injure, harm or destroy in the sense of violence to people or property, and include acts of civil disobedience, protest marches, demonstrations, boycotts, renouncing honours, stayaways, fasts, factory occupations, and non-cooperation with laws.

South Africa is no stranger to the use of such tactics. Consumer, rent, and school boycotts have been prominent pressure tactics in recent years, as have strikes, stayaways and factory occupations. Detainees have undertaken hunger strikes to protest their circumstances and treatment (Hughes and Merret 1990). Van der Merwe (1989) acknowledges the power of civil disobedience in resisting oppressive laws, but voices concern that its methods may come to be negatively rather than positively motivated, and that mass emotion and charismatic leadership may prevail over individual judgement and commitment. He proposes in its place *conscientious affirmation* a more positive approach of promoting fellowship across racial lines, this being rooted in ongoing individual commitments rather than acts of organised mass defiance. While civil disobedience is directed at what is wrong in a society, he argues, conscientious affirmation is directed at promoting what is right.

Violent tactics are used where parties seek the overthrow of the existing order, and the reconstruction of the entire social system. They involve attacks on people and property, guerrilla warfare and efforts to take over government by force. Van der Merwe (1989) points out that non-violence became a discredited approach to resolving the South African situation for many opponents of the government, but argues that the use of violence is a major stumbling block to negotiations. He acknowledges that coercion and cooperation are not mutually exclusive means, but strongly advocates the use of conscientious affirmation as a powerful and constructive alternative to violence. He argues that violent tactics are not only hopeless tools to defeat the government in their own right, but serve also to provide a justification for government repression. Negatively, violence concentrates power in the hands of those who control the means of violence. The nature and risks of violence have already been introduced in chapter 2.

Specht (1973) of course only outlines the tactics available to those interested in changing a system. Apart from tactics of a collaborative and campaign character available to a party in power for purposes of accommodating or negotiating change, there are other tactics which are used for purposes of *maintaining the status quo and resisting change.* Coercive tactics include the use of authority to pass laws, declare states of emergency or unrest and mobilise armed suppression of opposition forces. Mass detentions, bannings, and restrictions have been used to control change agents in the system. Hit squads, assassinations and attacks on persons and property of opposition group members are features of resistance to change by groups in power. Over 65 rightwing attacks on individuals and property were listed by *SA Barometer* (1990).

Depending on how the parties involved perceive their relationship then, a range of tactics is available to them as they seek to preserve or change their relations. These are not mutually exclusive but may be used concurrently. Thus tactics of disruption and coercion may accompany the negotiation process, and indeed provide the essential energy for the parties to seek a settlement. The awareness of the capacity and willingness of the other party to injure one's interests focuses minds on utilising negotiation efficiently. However, it must also be recognised that where negotiation is accompanied by the use of contentious tactics it is also a more fragile process, susceptible to breakdown, brinkmanship, mutual suspicion and conflict escalation should the parties misjudge or lose control of the exchange.

Further, it must be acknowledged that committed ideologues may see the negotiation process on certain issues and its associated concept of compromise as undesirable, and as weakening fundamental stances of a moral nature. Strong ideological stances may thus render negotiation impossible, or unacceptable other than as a short-term tactic for longer term strategic purposes.

IDEOLOGY AND NEGOTIATION

The *World Book Encyclopaedia* states that an ideology is a

system of thought based on related assumptions, beliefs, and explanations of social movements or policies. Its content may be economic, political, philosophical or religious. (Vol 10, p 47).

Ideologies include the '-isms': communism, fascism, capitalism, feminism, Catholicism, Protestantism, totalitarianism as well as democracy. Competing ideologies are an important source of conflicts and they have important implications for negotiation as the alternative of choice for dealing with such conflicts.

Ideological conviction tends to supersede factual information — people who accept a thought system in its entirety tend to reject all alternative approaches. This produces problems in understanding, accepting and communicating with supporters of alternative ideologies.

Improved communication will only help if there is a willingness to listen and learn with an open mind. Unfortunately, this is seldom present in political conflict which usually has strong ideological content. Values, beliefs, and perceptions tend to exacerbate conflict, and ideologies such as race discrimination, apartheid, capitalism and communism may motivate people to act independently of their objective structural social positions or interests.. . . . Ideological commitment leads to excessive intolerance, oversimplifications, polarisation, and refusal to compromise or reconcile. (Van der Merwe 1989, p 77)

Ideologues tend to become convinced of the logic of their own beliefs and to utilise information selectively to reinforce these beliefs while closing out data which is contradictory or threatening. This obstructs rational analysis and objective needs-based discussion. In South Africa white fears of a 'total onslaught' have been matched by the mentality of 'total boycott' by opponents of the government resulting until recently, in an ideological standoff between interest groups (Van der Merwe 1989). While positive feelings of group belongingness, meaning, organisation and exclusivity may be experienced through ideological conviction and membership of a nation, a church, a club, a team or a social movement, these are also associated with processes of conflict creation and escalation — decreased communication, stereotyping, demonisation of the other groupings, and zero sum perceptions.

Solzhenitzyn (1974) writes:

To do evil a man must first of all believe that what he is doing is good, or else that it's a well-considered act in conformity with natural law. . . it is in the nature of the human being to seek a justification for his actions.. . . Ideology — that is what gives evildoing its long-sought for justification and gives the evildoer the necessary steadfastness and determination. That is the social theory which helps to make his acts seem good instead of bad in his own and others' eyes, so that he won't hear reproaches and curses but will receive praise and honors. That was how the agents of the Inquisition fortified their wills: by invoking Christianity; the conquerors of foreign lands, by extolling the grandeur of their Motherland; the colonisers, by civilisation; the Nazis by race; and the Jacobins (early and late) by equality, brotherhood and the happiness of future generations. Thanks to ideology, the twentieth century was fated

to experience evildoing on a scale calculated in millions.
(pp 173–4)

Pluralism, unitarism and radical change

The degree to which acceptance of difference and tolerance
of competing interests is embedded in an ideology therefore
has fundamentally important implications for the viability of
negotiation as a means of conflict resolution or regulation in
a society. Pluralist ideologies have the strongest track records
in this regard, and authoritarian or unitarist ideologies the
weakest.

Pluralism emerged from a criticism of the doctrine of sovereignty which held that every system should have a final
authority whose decisions are definitive. Contrary to this
notion pluralists propose that political systems are essentially
coalitions of individuals and groups with their own beliefs
and aspirations and that governments are dependent on their
consent and cooperation to be able to function. From this
perspective:

> There are no definitive decisions by final authorities: only
> continuous compromises with landowners, farmers, finan-
> ciers, industrialists, workers, the church, the army, and
> many other pressure groups, or with coalitions of two or
> more. (Clegg 1975, p 305).

Conflict is seen as entirely normal in society, the natural
consequence of interactive processes between groups which,
while having differences, also share a mutual dependence.
These differences are seen therefore to be best dealt with
through negotiation and compromise. Authoritarian control
is only possible at great expense and cruelty, and always with
the risk of oppressed groups overthrowing the existing political order. Clegg (1975) observes that stable societies are
most in evidence in developed countries where considerable
scope is allowed pressure group activities.

Where a broad balance of power between interest groupings prevails in a society, processes of joint social control
through negotiation and cooperation are allowed to emerge
as predominant. Tendencies to repression and insurrection
are blunted by the extent to which each of the competing
interest groups has a vested interest in stability rather than
disruption. Such social stability tends to become a self-reinforcing process characterised by strong social bonds, shared
conflict-limiting norms, mutual fear of conflict escalation, the
development of acceptable bargaining forums, and third-
party institutions and cross-cutting group memberships
(Pruitt and Rubin 1986).

Basic to pluralism is a philosophy of mutual survival
through which the parties recognise their differences and
their common ground, which in turn motivates the search for
mutually acceptable ways of regulating conflict inherent in
their relationship. As Fox (1974) points out, such an approach
hardly makes sense without the assumption that differences
are not so wide as to be unbridgeable through processes of
compromise or cooperation, and is only achievable where all
the parties limit their claims on each other to tolerable levels
thereby allowing the collaboration to continue.

The political vehicles established for exchanges between
differing interest groups are parliaments at national policy
levels, and provincial and local councils at lower levels. These
are empowered to enact laws that are in effect the expression
of compromise on issues between differing interests represented in the forum. The powers of these law-making bodies
are limited not only by electoral processes, but by independent judiciaries and constitutional boundaries in pluralist
systems (Hague and Harrop 1987; Boulle 1984). Pluralist
societies tend to be characterised by the rule of law which
underpins a wide range of rights, freedoms and protections
against discrimination and oppression. Typically freedom of

movement, association, assembly, expression, thought and religion, accompany rights to property ownership, political participation, social security, work, education and cultural expression. These are embodied in such documents as the Universal Declaration of Human Rights (Appendix A). Notably, these rights and freedoms are accompanied by certain duties — article 29 reads:

(1) Everyone has duties to the community in which alone the free and full development of his personality is possible.

(2) In the exercise of his rights and freedoms, everyone shall be subject only to such limitations as are determined by law solely for the purpose of securing due recognition and respect for the rights and freedoms of others and of meeting the just requirements of morality, public order and the general welfare in a democratic society.

Olivier (1990) argues that the individual-based approaches to human rights of the liberal democracies emphasise liberty, whereas socialists tend to place less emphasis on this and more on equality in the economy and welfare. The Freedom Charter (Appendix B) reflects this leaning. Olivier suggests that Third-World nations have emphasised social rights and the right to self determination following colonialisation. He distinguishes between individual or substantive human rights (general, civil, political and cultural); procedural human rights (due process of law); socio-economic rights and group rights (religious, language and cultural).

In industrial relations the pluralist philosophy is evidenced in the acknowledgement of rights to associate freely, bargain collectively, withdraw labour, safe and healthy working conditions, development and social security as well as the formation of acceptable bargaining forums at national, regional, sectoral and company levels. These forums and relations between the parties are usually underpinned by law, the parties' constitutions, and agreements negotiated between them. Constitutions usually govern how each party operates, its scope of operation, requirements for membership, electoral processes, systems of representation, control of funds and disciplinary powers. Agreements between the parties may be of a procedural or a substantive nature. This is an important distinction. In *procedural agreements* the parties establish the framework for their relationship, they negotiate 'rules of the game'. Typically they define the scope of their respective powers, the interests they represent (bargaining units), access to facilities and premises, negotiation and meeting procedures, and specific steps or procedures to be followed in cases of discipline, grievance, retrenchment, disputes, and changes to work practices. Essentially such agreements comprise agreed rules through which competing interests might be addressed, seeking to ensure procedural fairness so as to reach fair outcomes on *substantive issues*. They represent efforts by parties to regulate conflictual relations, and allow the search for settlement of disputes in a manner which does not oblige immediate use of force. Mutual destructiveness is avoided through procedural arrangements which are designed to render parties' behaviour consistent and predictable, allow the expression of pressure tactics within bounds, and achieve dispute settlement by means other than force, for example through the use of third-party assistance in the form of mediation or arbitration.

The procedural framework then, is the vehicle through which substantive issues are dealt with — wages, conditions of work, working hours, fringe benefits, leave and a wide variety of other matters are negotiated within the bounds of the procedural agreement.

Clearly then, negotiation, or more specifically collective bargaining is the central vehicle for conflict dealings within a pluralist frame of reference. In pluralist dispensations parties negotiate not only on issues of difference which arise between them, but on the procedures and institutions through which bargaining will take place. They institutionalise conflict handling processes in intergroup relations. Notably this includes agreement on appropriate steps to be followed should negotiation fail to achieve settlement on an issue — when coercive tactics might be used and in what form, the use of mediatory assistance and arbitration or adjudicatory intervention by an agreed external party.

From a *unitarist* perspective conflict is abnormal. There is a corresponding failure to understand the fact of differing interests and needs between groups and individuals, and, likewise the place of opposition groups in a society. As a result conflict is seen as dangerous rather than creative in character, the consequence of actions by subversive groups interested in undermining the social order. Negotiation as a process is then perceived as legitimating subversive interests, and even precipitating and crystallising unnecessary and destructive conflict in an order which would otherwise be naturally harmonious and ordered. Responses to opposition groups vary from paternalism (when they do not fundamentally threaten the existing order and there are means available to attempt to buy off those with grievances) to outright oppression and coercion (where the threat is seen as dangerous).

The *radical change* perspective denies the existence of a rough balance of power between various social groups. The capitalist system is seen as having quite different consequences, producing an increasingly inequitable distribution of wealth and power within society. Unlike pluralists, radical change theorists place little store by collective bargaining or negotiation to bring about fundamental change in the lives of working class people. The imbalance is seen as too great for this to occur, and negotiation is deemed to produce only very marginal changes for those at the bottom of the pile. Indeed, negotiation is seen by some as a means of veiling gross disparities of power creating an illusion of fair competition in society where none exists. This is seen as actually strengthening the power of those in control, rather than weakening it in any sense. No changes in the distribution of wealth, power or control are envisaged as likely through the negotiation process. Rather it is seen as having a limited tactical use, acting in a holding function, until sufficient power has been achieved for a major restructuring of society.

While pluralist societies reflect a predominance of the use of negotiation and cooperative approaches to dealing with differences between interest groupings, unitarist societies use authoritarian means to suppress opposition groups, often involving the destruction of civil liberties. The weight of activity in such societies is in repression and compliance — stability without legitimacy, as opposed to the stability achieved through ongoing legitimisation processes available in pluralist societies. Authoritarian regimes tend to evoke radical challenges to their legitimacy and their practices which may see a steady loss of control in the face of mass disruptive action or insurrectionist tactics. Where avenues for negotiation remain open, some prospect for ordered change is retained. Where these are absent an anarchic process of repression and insurrection may emerge wherein neither those in government nor the opposition can achieve full control. A total breakdown in society may then emerge.

Furthering the debate

Clegg (1975) has challenged the assumptions that a viable pluralism depends on power balance and processes of endless compromise between interacting interest groupings. He rejects the Marxist argument that pluralism must be discarded as unworkable owing to power imbalances, and the consequent argument that this produces agreements that are signed by one party under duress and need not therefore be honoured. He challenges the assumption that the duty to compromise dominates other moral values that parties may hold. If this was the case then bargaining would be an empty charade -negotiation occurs precisely because there are genuine differences in goals, values and action. In some cases parties may value their standards, positions and choices more than achieving an agreement through compromise. In such instances they may embark on trials of strength and direct pressure to achieve their ends, seek ways of continuing relations without an agreement or terminate the relationship. It would be unrealistic for pluralism to be premised on power balances — most relationships do not have this and seldom will a power holder relinquish power already achieved.

Following this line of argument pluralism is not based on an assumption that a power balance must exist or that every conflict of interest can be settled by compromise, but rather on the acknowledgement that all interest groups must have the right to mobilise and bargain to the extent of the power available to them. Likewise compromises may not always be available and there will therefore be tests of strength and winners and losers in conflict situations. Pluralism then would seem to be a relative concept, measureable by the extent to which groups have rights and freedoms to mobilise and bargain, and the extent to which compromise prevails over coercion as the central tendency in social relations, rather than balances of power. Where compromise, negotiation and problem solving do not predominate, or where one or more parties refuses to accept limits to its rights or to grant rights to others, pluralism is jeopardised.

Although pluralist societies are stable they are not static. Ongoing processes of mutual accommodation, compromise and concession making occur within accepted rules of exchange. These processes promote enmeshment and a sense of stakeholding in a society. The rules of the exchange are premised on rights accorded each other by the parties — to associate, to govern, to bargain, to lobby, to protest and pressurise — and are viable to the extent that they are used responsibly in a manner which does not seek to impinge on the rights of others. Acceptable rules of the pluralist game then provide room to operate but limit abuses of power.

Clearly pluralism then hinges to a large extent on freedoms accorded and duties and responsibilities assumed by all the players. This in turn is built upon the extent to which they accord each other legitimacy as players in the system. It relies on parties using their potential power with restraint in the sense that they have a vested interest in the overall stability of the relationship. Pluralism is threatened where there are perceptions that parties are abusing their power, or that legitimacy is being denied, or that the system is rigged to ensure unfair outcomes, or when a party perceives that it no longer has a vested interest in the continued existence of the system, because outcomes or returns from using the system have been unsatisfactory.

Pluralist societies are therefore finely balanced. They require a wealth base sufficient to allow the major interest groupings to have an interest in maintaining rather than disrupting them. They require a degree of ideological tolerance, the capacity not only to employ power, but to constrain its use, and the emergence of a track record of exchange that has negotiation and accommodation as the dominant form rather than repression and insurrection.

The conditions for negotiation are circumscribed not only by the attitudes of negotiators but by the circumstances in which they must negotiate and the availability of acceptable mechanisms (constitutions, parliaments etc.) through which to engage.

Where revolutionary change has been achieved, a crisis of government is faced. Choices must be made between democratic and authoritarian approaches. Commonly revolutionary change is followed by authoritarian rather than democratic rule. Where the necessary wealth base and social predispositions toward a pluralist based power balance are absent, societies are obliged to seek stability through other means. Scarce resources demand more competitive relations between interest groups as the inherent potential of meeting all parties' power and wealth interests is diminished. A paradox is evident in such scenarios. The need for wealth creation requires a disciplined, coordinated drive by diverse social groupings toward production. Power imbalances and wealth discrepancies between these groupings draws them into radical conflict which erodes their joint capacities for cooperation. In such situations stability is tenuous and tends to be maintained through authoritarian means.

Single party, authoritarian governments, centralised economies and controlled mass participation characterised the communist countries. In developing countries problems of national diversity and poverty are exacerbated and so, consequently, are those of social and political stability. Violent and non-violent coups are frequent vehicles for political change, and the most common forms of government are military rule, single party or single person rule or competitive oligarchies. Post-colonial Africa has experienced over 100 coups, and only two South American countries have not had military rule since 1945. (Hague & Harrop 1987; Hodder Williams 1984)

Very simply, any government in a poor country faces a crisis of delivery, regardless of its ideology. In wealthy countries, losing political campaigners survive to fight another election within a given time frame — they do not face direct state oppression, they may continue to operate their businesses, their means of earning a living will probably not be greatly affected, their children will still have access to education and jobs. In poor countries the struggle for political power is more fundamental, with strong survival overtones. As Hanf (1989) points out in his analysis of communal conflicts, the key to the game is to be a member of the group in power. This, rather than individual skills or merit, is the key to opportunities, jobs, education and privilege. Whether this is defined on a racial, tribal, religious, cultural or class basis, issues of control and survival are dependent on group membership. Scarce resources prohibit meaningful wealth distribution, and not unexpectedly groups in power choose to feed their own rather than opposition constituencies first. Failure to do so would erode the base off which power was achieved in the first place. Those radical change groups which achieve power then face radical demands of their own, often exacerbated by the expectations of those they mobilised to achieve change.

Stability tends therefore to be maintained through authoritarian measures: repressive laws, constraints on freedom of expression and organisation, and active use of various instruments of authority for 'law and order' purposes. In this sense radical change groups whether campaigning under banners of a classless society or national liberation, tend to be as unitarist and authoritarian as those whose power they have usurped. Social stability through coercion is inherently tenuous. The absence of shared norms, the presence of large unattended grievances and threat to the dominant group, and the failure to develop crosscutting group memberships and acceptable negotiating forums or third-party institutions are further hindered by repressive measures required for control purposes. Instead social process is dominated by structural imbalances, a constant feeling of threat, a desire to punish the oppressor, and eroded relationships. High aspirations fuelled by perceptions of legitimacy of goals and feasibility of change render reform steps less of a sop than a reinforcement of expectations. Communication between groups diminishes, an absence of alternatives produces zero sum perceptions, and residual changes are induced in competing groups as they compete for power and vest their energies in mobilisation efforts.

Radical change theory has foundered not so much in its analysis of sources and intensity of conflict in society, but in its failure to provide viable means for dealing with these. In general, revolutionary societies have failed to produce growth economies over the longer term, rendering wealth redistribution a meaningless concept, and have produced authoritarian regimes associated with the destruction of civil liberties and human rights across a broad international front. Radical change has a strong track record in bringing down oppressive regimes, a very poor one in establishing democracies.

The overall consequence of this is that negotiation is a very fragile process in such countries. It must operate in environments where it is simply not possible to meet every group's needs satisfactorily; where there are wide discrepancies in power distribution; where loser opposition groups face not a temporary loss of office but opportunity across a wide front of basic survival needs; where deep residual effects of previous conflicts prevail — in short where many of the factors allowing negotiation to become the alternative of choice in resolving tensions are simply not present. A glance at Freedom House's map of freedoms in the world confirms the scarcity of democracies across the globe, and the limited extent to which negotiation is the central vehicle for handling change in many societies.

However, Freedom House's 1991 report notes significant global shifts towards democracy. For the first time the num-

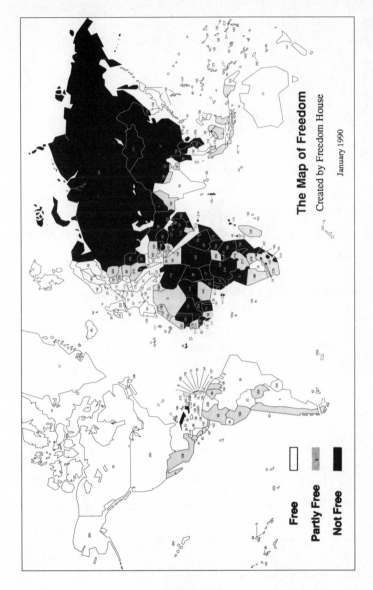

Figure 3.1
The Map of Freedom, January 1990

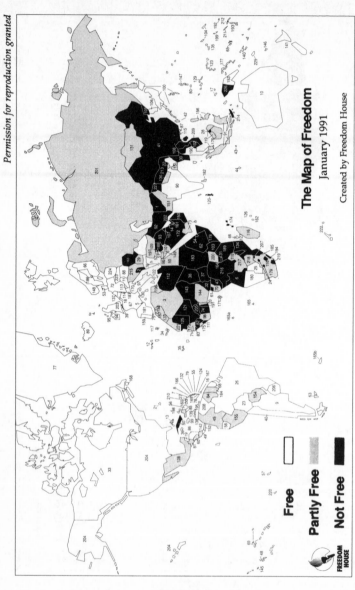

Figure 3.2
The Map of Freedom, January 1991

ber of free countries and their populations outnumbered those of not-free countries (39,2 % vs 32,9 % of world population). The Soviet Union for the first time moved out of the not-free into the partly-free category, and significant gains in freedom occured in Chile, Czechoslovakia, Hungary, Namibia and Poland. Nineteen African countries improved levels of freedom with moves toward multi-party systems. At the beginning of 1991, 76 democracies existed across the globe, with 36 countries in transition — 112 compared to 56 in 1980, and 44 in 1972. The shifts between 1990 and 1991 are reflected in figures 3.1 and 3.2.

However, the report also cautions that many of these transitions may not be successfully completed, and some countries claiming free status may not be able to sustain this. Obstacles identified include: violence, scarce resources, ethnic and ediological intolerance, the absence of a culture of democracy, and economic problems associated with social hardship across a broad front (McColm 1991).

APPROACHES TO NEGOTIATION

Discussion so far has attempted to illustrate that negotiation is not the only way to deal with conflict, and that its use may be sharply constrained by such factors as ideological conviction and scarce resources. In this section, attention will be given to various approaches to negotiation — where it is utilised, what are the choices available to parties? Several approaches to negotiation have been proposed in the literature. In their classic work on the subject, Walton and McKersie (1965) identify four sub-processes in labour–management negotiations:

❑ *distributive bargaining* through which pure conflicts of interests are resolved;

❑ *integrative bargaining* through which parties solve common problems and seek complementary interests;
❑ *attitudinal restructuring* whereby the parties seek to influence each other's attitudes and adjust the basic bonds
which relate them; and
❑ *intra-organisational bargaining* through which each side attempts to reach an internal consensus.

All these processes will be discussed in one form or another
in this work. The choice of approach depends on a variety of
factors including the nature of the issues at stake, the history
of relations between the parties, their respective bargaining
skills, ideological influences, constituencies and the intensity
of the conflict. Another influential factor affecting choice of
approach lies in the extent to which the parties have a concern
about their own and each other's outcomes — in a sense
whether they are concerned only about how much they can
achieve out of the exchange or whether they also have concerns about the relationship, and the extent to which the
other's needs can be met for purposes of nurturing positive
longer term ties. The range of negotiation options within
these parameters is illustrated in figure 3.3 based on the work
of Thomas (1976) and Moore (1986).

A few salient approaches or styles of negotiation may be
identified — contenders, yielders, compromisers and problem solvers (see also Johnston 1982).

Highly competitive bargainers or contenders may be concerned only about their own gains, and their use of tactics will
tend to reflect an aggressive win–lose style and intent. On the
other hand yielders are so concerned about the relationship
that they tend to assume subordinative styles, often losing on
substantive issues especially if they are in interaction with
tough contenders. Yielders have a lose–win style.

Generally, however, the major process is approached as
one in which some compromise is expected — an approach

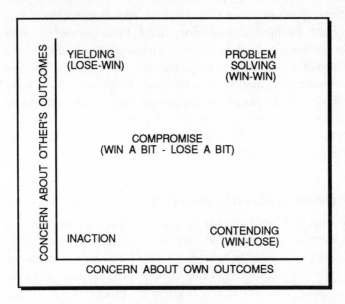

Figure 3.3
Negotiation options

which recognises that everyone will 'lose a bit to win a bit' in the exchange. This reflects the basis of distributive or positional bargaining. It is essentially a competitive process, but it requires some sensitivity to the needs and power of the other party, and a realisation that compromise based in pressure tactics and concessions is the route to settlement. This process is outlined in chapter 4.

In recent times considerable work has been done on alternative approaches to negotiation and problem solving. These are cooperative to the extent that despite differences the parties are willing to use techniques other than those associated with distributive bargaining. Joint problem solving, bargaining on the merits, no-fault bargaining, target specific bargaining are some of the approaches which have been developed as creative alternatives to traditional positional techniques. In essence they are all rooted in the idea that greater attention should be devoted to the needs and interests of parties which underpin their stated positions, than to the positions themselves. By addressing these needs, sharing relevant information and utilising problem solving techniques a wider range of solutions may be possible and a more positive relationship might be established between individuals and groups with differing interests. These techniques are discussed in chapter 5.

POWER AND NEGOTIATION

Power may be defined as the capacity to bring about desired outcomes, or to change the position or stance of another party. Perceptions relating to power have a fundamental influence on parties' choices regarding the use of tactics, and even as to whether they utilise the negotiation process at all. Thus, radical change ideologues may see few material gains as likely to emanate from use of the negotiation process but have insufficient power to achieve their real goals. As a consequence they may be obliged to settle for negotiation as the 'best of a bad set of options' — curiously then the power imbalance may act not only to discredit negotiation at an intellectual level, but also to oblige it in a more pragmatic sense. Lewicki and Litterer (1985) propose that power may oblige people to undertake actions that they would ordinarily not want to do. Unionists may negotiate wage decreases to save jobs or prevent a plant closure. Weak political parties may participate in structures they perceive to be flawed rather than be excluded from the political process altogether, arguing that it is better to remain in the game in this undesirable way than to risk never achieving a foothold. Lewicki and Litterer (1985) define power as 'the ability to get another party to do something they would not ordinarily do by controlling the options they perceive to be open to them' (p 241).

The settlement of the Rhodesian war involved pressure from Britain on both parties to take action they might not otherwise have. Lord Carrington basically used the pressure of the no-win situation to pressure a settlement with elements that neither party wanted — a new government to be formed on the basis of majority rule (resisted by the Rhodesian government) with a period of constitutional guarantees for the white minority (resisted by the African Nationalists). The first area of resistance was overcome by the promise of the second based on the awareness that it was a no-win war, the second by the reality of achieving power immediately. African Nationalist resistance to the plan was further eroded when the British government threatened to shift its support to the internal Smith/Muzorewa settlement, and the promise of economic assistance to facilitate the transition was offered (Zartman and Touval 1985).

Closer to home the ANC and the government have perhaps been obliged to talks they would otherwise preferred not to have by a range of pressures and incentives. The ANC would perhaps have preferred more time and a different entry to negotiations than that offered by the government. But the shortage of funds, the awareness that they could not win a military confrontation and that this might be best option available obliged participation. On the other side the government might have preferred not to embark on this route, but the realities of the economy, and the effects of prolonged international isolation obliged a shift in approach. Thus negotiation itself may be the consequence of power realities, not only the issues and outcomes arising out of the relationship.

Sources of power

Several theorists have attempted to classify sources of power in relationships. Expanding on Raven and French's (1958) categorisation, Raven and Kruglanski (1970) identified six types of power:

❑ reward
❑ coercive
❑ informational
❑ legitimate
❑ expert
❑ referent

(Anstey 1983)

Mayer (1987) enlarges this categorisation to ten sources of power:

❑ *Formal authority* derived from a formal position within a structure that confers decision-making prerogatives, such as a manager in a business enterprise might enjoy.

❑ *Expert/information power* based on information or skills in a given area.

❑ *Associational power* derived from association with others with power such as a lobbyist in political circles might have.

❑ *Resource power* based on control over valued resources, the ability to deny others needed resources or to force them to expend theirs — the extended control over world oil supplies achieved by Saddam Hussein's occupation of Kuwait as an example.

❑ *Procedural power* based on control over procedures by which decisions are made, such as the capacity to delay meetings on technical aspects of a constitution, or deny them a quorum.

❑ *Sanction power* based in the capacity to inflict harm or interfere with another's ability to realise interests — for instance the ANC's influence in the isolation of the South African economy

❑ *Nuisance power* rooted in the power to cause discomfort to another party, but falling short of a capacity to apply direct sanctions. A union may not have the power to call a strike at a given point in time, but still exert pressure on a company through go-slow tactics.

❑ *Habitual power* based in the awareness that it is often easier to maintain the status quo than to change it. In a sense the South African government enjoys this form of power after over 40 years in power which has seen it achieve an iron grip on the military, and administrative services of the country. Shifts in political power could result in chaotic infrastructures if this base of experience and control over the system is overly disturbed.

❑ *Moral power* is usually derived from the capacity to appeal to widely held values, such as the international support achieved by the ANC against apartheid — at this point in world history it is unlikely to achieve the same level of support for economic policies which are overly centralised, however.

❑ *Personal power* is rooted in a number of personal attributes which magnify other sources of power, such as self assurance, articulateness, determination, endurance, a capacity for problem solving.

These sources of power are commonly translated into specific forms of power in given situations. In labour–management relations management's traditional sources of power include: controls over contracts of employment, and financial resources, control over the production process and therefore employment, control over rewards and information, coalitions with other employers, and industrial action. Labour's sources of power usually reside in size of union membership, control over key skills, presence in strategic industries, financial resources such as strike funds, coalitions with other unions and industrial action. Both have access to such power sources as the media, use of the courts, negotiating skills and international pressures.

Another important concept is that of *power distance*. Mulder (1960) offers a set of propositions regarding power inequalities in relationships, their effects on the parties involved and their interaction. Discussion of this set of propositions is reserved for chapter 5, where some cautionary thoughts are expressed regarding interest-based negotiation processes.

MOTIVATION AND NEGOTIATION

If people are to negotiate they must not only know how to do it, they must want to do it. This basic assumption raises the issue of motivation to negotiate, a matter already touched on in the earlier discussion of ideology and its implications for negotiation. For what reasons do parties choose to negotiate or problem solve rather than attack each other? Some tentative answers and new thinking regarding negotiation lie in motivation theory. Two approaches will be discussed here — Maslow's needs theory, and valence–instrumentality–expectancy (VIE) theory which has its roots in social learning theory.

The needs approach

Maslow proposed the concept of a needs hierarchy, needs being the basic motivators of human activity. He suggested that there can be no substitute for a basic need owing to its intrinsic properties, that such needs exist across castes, cultures and classes, and that healthy individuals, families and societies are characterised by needs satisfaction. Five basic needs are postulated by Maslow, arranged in ascending hierarchical order (box 3.1).

Maslow proposed that individuals can move on to higher needs only when previous needs have been satisfied. In other words, until basic physiological needs of hunger, thirst, rest and shelter have been met, higher needs for safety and se-

---

- *Self actualisation* characterised by strivings for truth, justice, individuality, meaningfulness, perfection, independence and freedom.
- *Self esteem* needs are of two sorts — esteem from others(external) and true self esteem (internal). Self esteem is proposed to be self generated and centres in needs for achievement, recognition, dominance, prestige, and respect for others.
- *Love and belongingness* needs motivate individuals to search for group belongingness, that is, family, work, social groups. Such needs include affiliation, deference, conservance, nurturance, assimilation, and blame avoidance.
- *Safety and security* needs may be of a physical or interpersonal nature and include those of acquisition, retention, aggression and succour.
- *Physiological* needs include those of food, water, rest, shelter, sleep, etc.

Box 3.1
Maslow's needs hierarchy

curity will not act as motivators. Having said this, the theory acknowledges that behaviour may be driven by more than one motivator simultaneously — thus love and belongingness may be the primary motivator, but adjacent needs for self-esteem and safety may also be present as motivators.

Nierenberg (1986) proposes a matrix for a need theory of negotiation that recognises:

❏ needs,
❏ the levels at which negotiation is conducted, that is, international, interorganisational, and interpersonal, and
❏ varieties of application of needs theory.

He suggests six varieties of application exist and orders these in terms of control and risk. The applications are:

❑ Negotiator works for opposer's needs.

❑ Negotiator lets opposer work for his needs.

❑ Negotiator works for own and opposer's needs.

❑ Negotiator works against own needs.

❑ Negotiator works against opposer's needs.

❑ Negotiator works against own and opposer's needs.

He argues that negotiators working for opposer's needs have more control than those letting opposer's work for theirs. Kraybill (1990), in a discourse on negotiating deep-rooted conflicts, suggests that these are based not on transitory interests over land, money, or natural resources, but basic human needs for security, identity, recognition, and human development. Such needs supersede material interests, which are seen as mere avenues to need satisfaction, and are likely to be pursued regardless of consequences — desires for freedom, respect, and development may be stronger than those for survival. Kraybill argues that the recognition of the role of basic human needs in conflict situations is fundamental to their resolution and proposes that

> Due to the irrepressible nature of basic human needs, one's own long term interests are served best by recognising, honouring, and collaborating to meet the basic needs of an opponent with whom one is locked in conflict.. . . The practical implication is that if negotiations are undertaken within a framework which recognises and deals with the basic human needs of all parties, invariably there exists substantially more room for resolution of material issues than is commonly thought. (p 53–4)

Kraybill utilises this needs approach to underscore the difference between traditional positional bargaining and more creative joint problem-solving approaches which might well offer a wider range of alternatives for conflict resolution. This debate is furthered in chapters 4 and 5 where the techniques of various approaches to negotiation and problem solving are discussed.

The VIE approach

Valence–instrumentality–expectancy theory places emphasis on cognitive and drive theories, focusing on three cognitive beliefs which together predict effort.

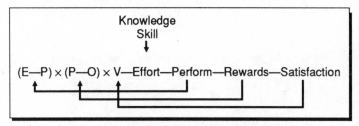

Figure 3.4
VIE Theory

The *expectancy* belief (E—P) holds that with sufficient effort, successful performance will follow: If I try, I can negotiate.

The *instrumentality* belief (P—O) holds that successful performance will result in a particular outcome. In other words negotiation will result in the achievement of a particular objective.

The *valence* component (V) refers to the positive or negative value people place on possible outcomes. Performance (negotiation) will have the consequence of rewards which are satisfying (raised wages, sale of an insurance policy) or averts a negative event (delays retrenchment, averts war).

If any of these beliefs is low then it is unlikely that an effort will be made to perform a certain behaviour. Thus if a group believes that no matter how hard it tries it will not be able to negotiate, or that negotiation will not achieve a particular outcome, or the likely outcome has only low value then the

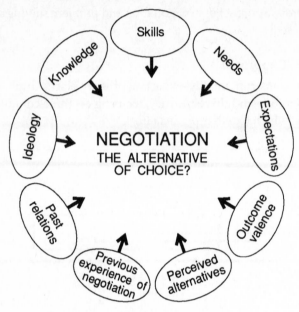

Figure 3.5
Some factors influencing the use of negotiation

motivation to negotiate will be low. Knowledge and skill are
insufficient in themselves, people must want to negotiate and
believe in the efficacy of the process.

The cognitive process implies that people make strategic
and tactical choices. Returning to the proposition that negotiation is not the only action available to parties in conflict, a
further proposal can be made about negotiation as the alternative of choice for settlement purposes. People make choices
about the utilisation of negotiation in relation to the perceived
effectiveness of other tactics to achieve an objective. If a party
believes that it can fight better than it can negotiate, or that
this approach will produce more rewarding outcomes then
coercive or disruptive tactics may prevail. It is not uncommon
to hear unionists state that negotiation gets them nowhere

compared to strike action. If managements move only under strike pressure, and usually do so, then in a sense they contribute to the belief that disruptive tactics are more rewarding than exchanges at the bargaining table. Likewise of course, weak parties may utilise negotiation as the best of a range of poor alternatives, that is, not because they believe in its inherent worth as a process, but because, in the light of the power imbalance and the consequences of a confrontational exchange, they have little option but to negotiate. Had they had more power, they might have chosen more confrontational tactics rather than negotiation in terms of the perceived effectiveness of approach.

SUCCESSFUL NEGOTIATION

Negotiation as a process of conflict resolution or dispute settlement is not a given. Its use depends on alternatives available to the parties in conflict, their perceptions of power relativities, ideological influences, their knowledge and skills levels, historical relations and the track record of negotiation effectiveness within this, and motivational factors such as needs, beliefs, and the valence of negotiated outcomes to the parties involved. The decision to negotiate is not simple. Where it *is* taken, how do the parties assess its success or failure?

Drawing on the work of Kressel (1972), Fisher & Ury (1981), and Whitney (1982), several criteria are proposed for assessing the successful outcome of a negotiation:

❑ achievement of an agreement/problem solved;

such an agreement should:

❑ meet the legitimate interests of all sides to the extent possible/ resolve conflicting interests fairly;
❑ be durable;
❑ not damage the relationship between the parties;

❏ be workable, that is, the parties must be able to live by it;
❏ be 'owned' by the parties, that is, not imposed or manipulated;
❏ be ratified by all the parties' constituencies and have no adverse political consequences for leaders;
❏ be unambiguous and complete;
❏ be achieved within an acceptable time frame; and
❏ promote the use of the negotiation process.

From the preceding discussion on conflict it is apparent that if successful outcomes are to be achieved, then a range of other factors are required to facilitate effective use of the process:

❏ an intention by all parties to achieve a settlement;
❏ a willingness to explore movement off a stated position;
❏ the possession of power — sufficient to persuade but insufficient to force total surrender;
❏ clear mandates from a coherent consistency;
❏ mutual accreditation as bargaining partners
❏ adherence to mutually acceptable 'rules of the game';
❏ acknowledgement of both the legitimacy of difference and the existence of common ground in the relationship.
❏ a belief that negotiation is the best option available for purposes of resolving differences; and
❏ sufficient resources to allow outcomes that do not discredit use of the bargaining process or those seeking to use it.

4
DISTRIBUTIVE AND POSITIONAL BARGAINING

Distributive bargaining is associated with situations where parties with competing interests are involved in a process of dividing a limited resource among themselves. Atkinson (1980) states:

> The distributive bargaining situation will be reached whenever the perception of the two sides in relation to an issue do not coincide and there is an unwillingness by either to abandon the issue or to modify their perception of it. (p 4)

Buyers and sellers of commodities, contractors, disputants in divorce cases, and insurance litigants all use tactics associated with this approach, but is perhaps most closely identified with the practices of labour negotiators.

Walton and McKersie (1965) observe that:

> Distributive bargaining is central to labour negotiations and is usually regarded as the dominant activity in the union–management relationship. . . . The term itself refers to the activity of dividing limited resources. It occurs in situations in which one party wins what the other party loses. (p 11)

This approach to bargaining tends to centre around substantive issues such as wages, overtime rates, leave or fringe benefits. Such issues have fixed sum, variable payoff characteristics with the consequence that parties find themselves involved in a conflict of interests with a win–lose orientation. Generally, parties move off divergent positions in a progressive manner towards a point of common settlement, employing power tactics to shift their opponents to a position that most closely approximates their own. Fisher and Ury therefore term this the positional approach to bargaining, noting that the process is characterised by parties successively adopting and then relinquishing a sequence of positions in an effort to achieve settlement without overcommitting or exposing their interests, while at the same time attempting to pressure the other party to do so.

This chapter seeks to describe the phases of the distributive process, to discuss the centrality of power in its use, and to elucidate some of the more common tactics associated with the approach as well as their consequences. Proponents of the distributive approach believe that it is more realistic than the problem-solving approaches. They point to the inherent adversarialism of many intergroup relations, fears of cooptation, ideological divides, and belief systems and influences of constituencies in arguing that the competitive approach is the norm. Some early research by Deutsch and Krauss (1960) indicates that even where higher opportunities for gain through cooperation are indicated, people tend to compete where they have a capacity to do so. Therefore, desirable as problem solving may be, this school proposes that competitive bargaining is a more realistic approach.

It must be stressed early in this discussion that with new developments in interest based bargaining and joint problem solving, there has been a tendency to discredit distributive negotiation somewhat carelessly. Where the approach is based in carefully reasoned positions, fully motivated and justified by the parties, and where the tactics are aimed at movement on issues rather than attacks on the other party, this is very different from a blunt confrontational approach. The latter is characterised by rigidly held positions, rejection of the other party's position as a legitimate expression of difference or need, refusals to motivate or justify positions, unreasonable delays, shifting 'goalposts', and the use of tactics intended to subvert the bargaining process or attack the other party. Despite the distributive nature of issues, a co-operative, cordial or respectful bargaining climate may be maintained in relationships. Criticisms of distributive bargaining tend, in my opinion, to have been a little too generalised and fail to distinguish between constructive and destructive approaches. Positional bargaining represents the worst face of competitive exchanges and here the critique has relevance, but to discard more constructive approaches with the same brushstroke, reflects a failure to recognise the complexities of the process and the fact that tactics may fall along a broad continuum with widely divergent consequences for relationships and settlement potentials. Once interests have been explored and understood, and once parties have considered ways to meet each other's needs, scarce resources or differing perspectives may still reduce the engagement to one of competition. Not all conditions lend themselves to cooperative problem solving, however desirable the process may be.

PHASES IN THE DISTRIBUTIVE BARGAINING APPROACH

The distributive bargaining process has been widely discussed in the literature, and several authors have proposed that it moves through a sequence of steps or phases (Douglas 1962; Karrass 1970; Atkinson 1980; Kennedy et al 1980; Scott 1981). These contributions are summarised in figure 4.1. I have been been most influenced by the approach of Kennedy et al and this chapter reflects their basic model, but seeks also to incorporate the contributions of a wide range of other theorists in the field.

Figure 4.2 shows the major phases in the distributive bargaining process, and some of the tactics for applying and handling pressure which provide its momentum.

DOUGLAS (1962)	KARRASS (1970)	KENNEDY ET AL (1980)	SCOTT (1981)	ATKINSON (1980)
1. *Verbal fireworks* Aggressive behaviour and demands, largely for constituents and as parties assess each other	1. *Preconference stage* Define requirements and objectives and formal pre-negotiation activities initiated.	1. Preparation	1. Preparation	1. Preparation
	2. *Verbal fireworks*	2. Argue	2. Opening – exploration – bidding	2. Clarify opponent's position
2. *Hard bargaining* Serious search of settlement range for compromise. Parties use tactics to gain concessions on issues	3. *Hard bargaining*	3. Signal 4. Propose 5. Package	3. Bargaining	3. Structure expectation of opponent 4. Get movement
3. *Crisis & settlement* Tense uncertain atmosphere and in-group bargaining. Closure and agreement.	4. *Crisis & settlement*	6. Bargain 7. Close 8. Agree	4. Settling	5. Closure
	5. *Post-conference stage* Agreement elaboration, agreement approval, contract administration and final contract closure		5. Ratifying	

Figure 4.1
Phases in the negotiation process (Source: Anstey 1986)

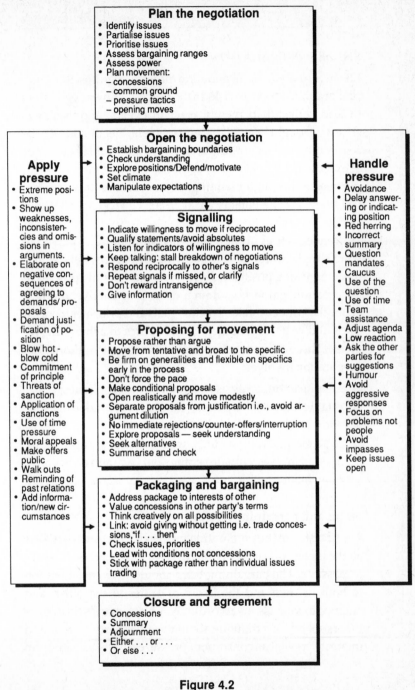

Plan the negotiation
- Identify issues
- Partialise issues
- Prioritise issues
- Assess bargaining ranges
- Assess power
- Plan movement:
  – concessions
  – common ground
  – pressure tactics
  – opening moves

Apply pressure
- Extreme positions
- Show up weaknesses, inconsistencies and omissions in arguments.
- Elaborate on negative consequences of agreeing to demands/ proposals
- Demand justification of position
- Blow hot - blow cold
- Commitment of principle
- Threats of sanction
- Application of sanctions
- Use of time pressure
- Moral appeals
- Make offers public
- Walk outs
- Reminding of past relations
- Add information/new circumstances

Handle pressure
- Avoidance
- Delay answering or indicating position
- Red herring
- Incorrect summary
- Question mandates
- Caucus
- Use of the question
- Use of time
- Team assistance
- Adjust agenda
- Low reaction
- Ask the other parties for suggestions
- Humour
- Avoid aggressive responses
- Focus on problems not people
- Avoid impasses
- Keep issues open

Open the negotiation
- Establish bargaining boundaries
- Check understanding
- Explore positions/Defend/motivate
- Set climate
- Manipulate expectations

Signalling
- Indicate willingness to move if reciprocated
- Qualify statements/avoid absolutes
- Listen for indicators of willingness to move
- Keep talking: stall breakdown of negotiations
- Respond reciprocally to other's signals
- Repeat signals if missed, or clarify
- Don't reward intransigence
- Give information

Proposing for movement
- Propose rather than argue
- Move from tentative and broad to the specific
- Be firm on generalities and flexible on specifics early in the process
- Don't force the pace
- Make conditional proposals
- Open realistically and move modestly
- Separate proposals from justification i.e., avoid argument dilution
- No immediate rejections/counter-offers/interruption
- Explore proposals — seek understanding
- Seek alternatives
- Summarise and check

Packaging and bargaining
- Address package to interests of other
- Value concessions in other party's terms
- Think creatively on all possibilities
- Link: avoid giving without getting i.e. trade concessions, "if . . . then"
- Check issues, priorities
- Lead with conditions not concessions
- Stick with package rather than individual issues trading

Closure and agreement
- Concessions
- Summary
- Adjournment
- Either . . . or . . .
- Or else . . .

Figure 4.2
The stages and tactics of distributive/positional bargaining

PHASE 1: PREPARATION

Effective use of the negotiation process requires thorough preparation. It reduces risks in the process, allows negotiators to lead rather than merely react to events, and demands creative thought *before* actual engagement. Negotiation can be a stressful process limiting creativity and flexible behaviour at exactly the moments they are most required for settlement purposes. Thorough planning helps overcome this problem (Whitney 1982; Kennedy et al 1980; Lewicki and Litterer 1985).

Kennedy et al propose that preparation must move beyond simple rehearsal of arguments for purposes of defending or attacking positions. It is a dynamic, ongoing process of information gathering, demanding constructive thought about the issues at stake, parties' goals and priorities, concessions and costs, and strategies and tactics to achieve movement. There is general consensus amongst authors that preparation involves:

❑ identification, analysis and partialisation of issues;
❑ establishment of bargaining ranges via definition of aspiration levels and fall back positions; and
❑ strategic planning as to power relativities, concessions, opening moves, climate setting, and pace and direction of movement .

Issues and bargaining ranges

The first step in the preparation process is to list and partialise all the issues, that is, break them down to as many sub-issues as possible. The bargaining team should give consideration to both its own and the likely priorities of the other, and attempt to rank issues accordingly. This demands that negotiators spend time thinking about the other party's needs and interests, as well as constituent pressures. Early sensitisation to the other party's priorities is useful in thinking through the approach it might use, possible movement and concessions.

Once all the issues have been identified it is helpful to construct a bargaining range around *each* issue, the outer boundaries being an ideal and a fall back position. The bargaining range planner is the basic tool of the negotiator. It demands a focus not on tactical manoeuvre but on the reality of the engagement — what do I want to achieve? what is my bottom line? what does the other side aspire to? what is their bottom line likely to be?

If there was no difference in the interests of the parties there would be no need to negotiate, so it must be expected that the aspirations of each as reflected in their ideal positions will diverge. Equally, if a settlement is to emerge through negotiation rather than coercion, it can be expected that both will consider moving from their opening positions. Compromise, concessions and trade-offs are the very essence of negotiated settlements. While it might be reasonably expected that the other party will endeavour to seek an agreement, and that this will involve movement away from a position at some point in the process, there is no certainty as to the direction, timing or extent of this — and if the conditions are not attractive, there is no certainty that any move will take place at all. If a company is facing liquidation a union would be naive to expect a wage increase or job security. Generally movement is the product of the pressures in the situation, the skills of the negotiators and their power relations.

Because the situation is uncertain, careful planning is required. The basic objective of each negotiating team will be to move the other party as close as possible to its own desired outcome. The first task then, is to assess accurately and honestly the ideal and fall-back of each side, and to understand the basis on which these determinations will be made. Nego-

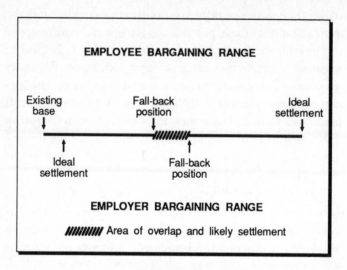

Figure 4.3
The bargaining range

tiators tend to plan only for their own side, and where they do think about the other side they often plan on the basis of what they'd *like* the other to demand rather than realistically projecting needs and interests from sound research.

Ideals and opening demands

Atkinson defines the ideal settlement as 'realism with a touch of optimism' — in other words if everything goes well, the other is unprepared, circumstances favour a party and it utilises its power better, this would be the best that could be expected in the situation. It is not meant to be reflect a 'fairy-land' scenario — it is meant, according to theory, to be achievable.

In South Africa, however, COSATU unions have regularly put in opening wage demands of up to 70 %. Extreme demands are often based on a fear on the part of a negotiator that he will misjudge the situation and not extract everything possible from the process. It has happened that unions have made wage demands of say 14 %, only to be embarrassed by the employer responding that he was prepared to pay 15 %! However, this is not the situation generally, and unions seem to have taken the line that demands should be based on the *needs* of their constituents rather than their affordability, that is, based on needs rather than resources. In this way employers are faced in an ongoing way with the reality of the needs of their workers.

Extremely high demands or low offers make for higher risk bargaining, as settlement will require one or both parties to make significant changes to their opening positions. Chances of loss of image, entrapment and miscalculation are obviously raised in these situations. Moderate demands or offers accompanied with reasonable movement achieve agreements more easily, and with less risk, but often not at the level of the more extreme positional approach (Bartos 1974; Pruitt 1981). COSATU has tended to adopt the higher risk approach, and its members have arguably achieved better agreements than other unions that assume a more moderate line generally. However, they are also involved in more frequent strike action which has risks, and carries the costs of a high level of dispute settlement which accompanies their strategy.

The determination of ideal/opening positions bears some serious thought in approaching negotiation.

Fall-backs

It is in the area of fall-back, however, that really serious planning must take place. Poorly prepared fall-backs have serious implications for the parties and for the bargaining process itself. Several aspects of this area of planning warrant discussion.

In labour negotiations employers and trade unions tend to plan fall-backs differently. It is important for an employer to plan fall-backs from the onset of the bargaining process. Usually projections have to be made for labour costs into the future to allow for accurate business planning and budgeting, and competitiveness. Where an employer must tender for business in a highly competitive industry this becomes particularly important. However, many employers do not think through their fall-backs, often carelessly identifying an inflationary increase as the point of no further offers. This is often naive, being based on what they desire rather than what is practicable.

In one negotiation, the union reduced its demand from 25 to 22 %, to which the company made a 'final offer' of 12 %. A mediator spent considerable time with the management team discussing the implications of this. If a final offer was made too early and too bluntly it would not allow the union side time and room to reconsider its position for purposes of further movement. It would be left with a 'take it or leave it' situation, in this instance, with a large gap to close. If the company stated that this was a final offer, but then moved at the first sign of a strike, it would be saying to the union that its 'finals' could not be trusted and inviting the union to strike every year to test the seriousness of a position. The factory manager stated that 12 % was the limit of the mandate, beyond that they had been directed from board level to 'dig the trenches and do whatever fighting was necessary'. The union rejected the offer and indicated to the company that it would be taking a strike ballot. When the factory manager returned to head office that afternoon he advised the directors that deadlock had been reached and that a strike was probable. Looking again at the order book and stock levels, the directors realised that a strike would be very damaging to the business — and immediately raised their offer to 21 %! This reflects some wise last minute shifts, but very bad planning and poor use of the bargaining process — in effect the union called a bluff which the company did not consciously consider making!

Companies might need to plan several fall-back scenarios, based on various business conditions, for example, stock levels, orders, competition, peak periods etc. A series of 'what-ifs?' need to be considered. A distinction between what would be desirable and what is possible under various conditions is necessary. An employer may actively resist movement from a given point, but whether it would accept a strike for two months at that point, or stand the risk of severing relations with workers is another issue. Points of resistance signal to the other party that a final position may be close, but it is incorrect to state that it is 'final' if it is not! It locks parties into battles of trust and entraps them in principles that might be expensive to live out.

Unions on the other hand do not seem to plan fall-backs early in the process. They often plan movement session by session. As they are largely in the demand role, an important task is to try to get a feel for what is possible in the negotiation, and then to plan around this in an effort to extract a bit more. Tactics would centre around trying to move an employer beyond what they think he intends trying to settle at, keeping bargaining open to allow this to happen and getting him to think again about his planned fall-back. It is my experience that unionists often have a very accurate suspicion about where the employer is trying to settle. Too early planning of fall-backs does not allow flexibility, and the chances of leakages to management through the grapevine, or careless shop-floor talk (not to mention the malpractices of some companies in 'bugging' union caucuses!) are too great to be too specific too early.

NEGOTIATION PLANNER

ISSUES		IDEAL	FALL-BACK
1	OURS: THEIRS:		
2	OURS: THEIRS:		
3	OURS: THEIRS:		
4	OURS: THEIRS:		
5	OURS: THEIRS:		
6	OURS: THEIRS:		
7	OURS: THEIRS:		
8	OURS: THEIRS:		
9	OURS: THEIRS:		
10	OURS: THEIRS:		

SOURCES OF POWER	
OURS	THEIRS

BARGAINING STRATEGY		
	Ours	Theirs
1. Opening moves		
2. Setting expectations		
3. Priorities (core interests & needs)		
4. Common Ground		
5. Possible concessions		
6. Trade-offs		
7. Time limits		
8. Pressure tactics		
9. Handling pressure tactics		
10. Plan in case of impasse		

Assessing power realities

The issue of power in negotiation has already been discussed in chapter 3. Suffice it here to state that having planned bargaining ranges in terms of ideals and fall-backs for both parties, attention must next be directed at the power relativities in the situation. Typically parties will give attention to their level of interdependence at given moments in time; strike and lockout capacities; stock levels; order book/market conditions; time factors; trade union strength in terms of numbers, location and strategic skills; company finances; control over benefits; legal factors; media/public sympathies; negotiating skills; international links; moral argument; constituency pressures; and the need to take a stand at a given moment in time. Several authors suggest formulae for assessing power realities. (Atkinson 1980; Whitney 1982)

Planning strategy

Having considered power factors attention may now be turned to strategy planning. After observing both managers and trade unionists over many years in role play situations it is striking how much time both sides spend on planning strategy rather than considering bargaining ranges. If there are no bargaining ranges then there is no place for the negotiation to go — strategies for movement are worked out in a vacuum. It may be that after considering power factors and considering strategic factors that parties return to their bargaining ranges and adjust them, but it is critical that attention is given first to these. Bargaining ranges focus minds on what the negotiation is actually about and what the parties are trying to achieve through it. Strategies are only constructive in this context — how might movement be achieved and in what direction?

Strategy planning gives consideration to such factors as the parties' needs and how these might be met or exploited;

appropriate concessions and trade-offs and their timing; identification of common ground; setting expectations for the process; appropriate use of pressure tactics; pacing movement; coping with pressure tactics; and identifying core themes around which to hinge the general thrust of one's arguments.

PHASE 2: OPENING THE NEGOTIATION

The opening moves of the parties in the negotiation usually set the tone for the remainder of the process (Atkinson 1980). Bargaining convention holds that, once parties have stated their position, they will endeavour to progressively close the gap identified in their opening declarations of demand and offer. The nature of these opening positions influences expectations of the process, the bargaining climate, trust levels and the tactics the parties choose to use to gain leverage in the exchange.

Typically this phase is characterised by the following elements:

❏ the establishment of bargaining boundaries,
❏ setting the bargaining climate,
❏ arguing, defending, motivating, justifying, clarifying positions, and
❏ manipulating expectations of the process.

Establishing bargaining boundaries

Normally parties open negotiations with their ideal demands and offers, thus setting the boundaries for the process. Not unusually one or both of the parties attempts to gain control over the process at this early stage, by assuming control over the order of items on the agenda, determining whether matters will be negotiated one by one or in the form of a package. Sometimes a tactical effort may be made by a party to delay indicating its position while it probes the aspirations, argu-

ments and motivations of the other. This may allow an adjustment of position before committing too early, and an unwary
adversary may start moving under pressure before establishing the other's position. This would allow a shift off the
original planned ideal to psychologically reset the bargaining
boundaries, and change the expectations of the process held
by the adversary. Movement before ascertaining the demands of the other side precludes the means of assessing
relative gains or losses in the process.

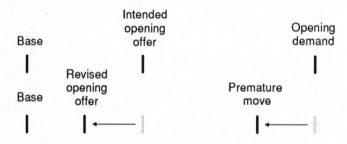

This process of influencing the bargaining boundaries is
shown in the figure above.

Setting the bargaining climate

During the opening phase parties to a negotiation try to
establish how the other intends to approach the exchange.
Scott (1981) states that one of the reasons why this phase is
important, is:

> . . . because attitudes are being formed. Each party is
> reading signals from what the other says and does, making
> continued judgements about the other's character, and
> framing its own behaviour in response . . . alert for anything
> which can be interpreted as aggressive and often ready to
> themselves to become defensive and counter-aggressive.
> (p 16)

Scott suggests working toward a climate that is businesslike and cordial. Messages of submissiveness or hostility by way of gesture or tone of voice may have consequences for the process in the longer term.

It is strongly suggested here that sincerity be conveyed where it is genuine. However, sending signals of conciliatory intent and empathy for the other party are counterproductive where it is known that these are insincere. One tactic that some negotiators like to use is *reminding of past relations* -efforts are made to bring to the other party's attention to how amicable relations have been over time, how effectively they have managed to overcome differences in the past and how it is hoped that future relations will not be jeopardised by 'today's problem'. Unfortunately some negotiators use this approach to soften the other side before delivering a really destructive blow to the process. In a protracted dispute in a bus company the managing director did just this. The company was facing serious financial problems, exacerbated by a months long passenger boycott which it was widely believed had been organised at least in part by the very union which was demanding a thirty per cent increase in wages. The parties had been in dispute over wages for over seven months. The manager spent a good half hour reminding the parties how wonderful the relationship had been in the past and how it must be nurtured into the future, before opening with a withdrawal of all previous offers from the table and announcing a return to a bargaining position held eight months previously! Apart from being insincere, the message preceded an offer which was retrogressive thus leading the union to believe that some progress was about to take place only to see this bluntly contradicted by the substance of the offer. Double messages of this sort create serious problems in trust relations!

Arguing, motivating, justifying, defending positions.

The beginning phase of bargaining is often characterised by prolonged discussion over the opening positions specified by the parties. Justification for demands and offers is demanded, positions are defended, research is referred to, ideas are motivated. This not uncommonly has the appearance of a prolonged argument, and many negotiators complain about constant repetition of motivations and the lack of movement in the process.

The prolonged period of repetitious argument has a purpose, however. It provides a vehicle for each to assess the underlying needs and interests of the other party, its strengths and weaknesses, possible concessions, priorities, and commitments, and power capacities. It is the means through which the parties attempt to gauge what might realistically be achieved through the engagement. It is rendered difficult quite often because it is also the means through which the parties attempt to manipulate each other's expectations, reducing each to having to try to separate bluff from reality before committing to a move in the negotiation.

Because the opening phase is often information based, parties tend to return to these arguments during later phases of the bargaining process when movement becomes difficult. My own hypothesis for this is that it allows 'breathing space' in negotiations. Parties feel safe with their arguments even if they have already been used and have been shown to have little persuasive effect. Repeating them at least gives nothing away, and at the same time allows time to think about alternatives and put out feelers as to alternatives from the other side. I suspect it also has some value in allowing parties to regroup around their core concerns — while it may not persuade the other side, it may reaffirm solidarity in one's own!

As mentioned earlier, the argument process is also a means for manipulating expectations of the process.

Manipulating expectations of the bargaining process

A central feature of distributive bargaining is that of manipulating an adversary's expectations of the process. Lewicki and Litterer (1985) suggest that negotiators must assess the following issues in this respect:

❏ How much value does each place on a particular outcome?
❏ What are the costs to each of a delayed or difficult negotiation?
❏ What are the costs to each of aborting the negotiation?

Each party needs to gain an accurate understanding of the costs and values of the negotiation process and outcome to the other, and not unusually each attempts to conceal the true nature of its own costs and values.

Thus if one party sees that the other urgently needs a settlement, is incapable of delaying one, or aborting the negotiation, then it is well placed to press for a more advantageous outcome. It is in this awareness that tactics such as *appearing unconcerned or unpressured* are rooted. Lewicki and Litterer suggest that the more the other can be convinced that the costs of a delay or cessation of bargaining are low for oneself, the more modest its resistance or fall-backs will be. Likewise, negotiators seldom throw away concessions even if they carry low costs — by *delaying,* or *appearing very resistant* on the matter or *demanding valuable concessions* in return, they attempt to make the other feel that an important victory has been achieved when it is finally conceded.

Typical tactics used for the purpose of assessing the values and needs of the other, and conveying impressions of one's own include those shown in box 4.1. (Atkinson 1980; Lewicki & Litterer 1985)

- Using *informal meetings* or organisational *grapevines* to obtain or disseminate information prior to negotiations.
- Dropping apparently *chance remarks* to evoke a response off which to assess commitment levels or feelings on issues likely to arise in formal meetings.
- *Researching the needs and bargaining activities* of the other party indirectly to assess its actual values and need for continued negotiation.
- *Probing questions* to assess values and needs.
- *Observation of responses* to matters or issues 'floated' to the other by way of test questions or proposals.
- *Delaying indicating own position* on the basis that a return to one's principles/constituency is required.
- *Selective presentation* of facts or arguments which support own case or highlight negative consequences of other's position.
- *Controlling own emotional responses* to the other's proposals to conceal or convey impressions of importance or relevance of issues.
- *Spending greater lengths of time on issues* to convey their significance.
- *Using presentations, or third parties* considered to be neutral and expert to provide input on a matter.
- *Using disruptive actions*, creating *alliances* with new partners, placing *time limits* on negotiations to bring home to the other party the costs of delaying or terminating negotiations.

Box 4.1
Typical tactics for structuring expectations

Clearly, the manipulation of expectations obliges negotiators into the area of *'bluff'*. It is often only a short step to dishonesty and bad faith bargaining from here. In addition, it is these tactics which lead to parties misunderstanding what is possible in negotiations, misjudging the other's commitment to a position or willingness to use direct power to achieve or defend one. While 'bluff' may be central to distributive bargaining, it is also central to its breakdown in many instances. It raises levels of tension, promotes defend–attack spirals, and may entrench already negative stereotypes and polarised positions. Furthermore, it raises serious ethical questions and may have destructive implications for trust relations.

PHASE 3: BARGAINING.

The exchange moves out of the opening phase with its characteristic argument process when the parties begin to signal to each other as to their willingness to move, and start making tentative proposals as to movement or concessions. Several elements demand attention:

❏ signalling;
❏ proposing; and
❏ packaging and bargaining.

Signalling

The fact that parties continue to talk to each other despite the frustration often incurred in the argument phase is essentially a signal of willingness to look for compromise and avoid breakdown in the exchange. However, arguments tend to lock people into their positions and thought sets — their egos become entwined with their positions, and efforts are directed more toward defending arguments than opening the way for creative problem solving. Parties become afraid to concede even small issues in case these moves are perceived as indications of weakness inducing the other party to apply even more pressure, and to adhere even more strongly to a position.

Kennedy et al (1980) suggest that:

> The way to handle concessions with confidence is to develop skills in signalling behaviour . . . a signal is a means by which parties indicate their willingness to negotiate on something. It is also more than that: it implies a willingness only if it is reciprocated by the other side. (p 53)

Signalling allows movement to be initiated in a safe manner. It is a means of informing the other party of a willingness to move provided this is reciprocated, in other words, a process of two-way movement is to be undertaken. It is a means of breaking out of unproductive circular arguments, for testing intransigence on the part of an adversary, and for opening the way to a course of bilateral concessions.

A signal may be made as clearly as:

> We have room to move on our wage offer, but can only consider an improvement if you indicate a willingness to revise your position substantially.

However, they are usually made in the form of qualified rather than absolute statements, such as:

> Generally, your demand could not be considered . . .
>
> At this point in time it is difficult for us to respond positively to your suggestion.
>
> As things stand, your offer does not allow us to revise our position with any confidence.
>
> Under current circumstances we might be able to exercise a little more latitude than usual.

Statements like these open the door to further exploration for movement — thus:

> We understand that this is the case generally, but surely there are special circumstances in this instance?
>
> Perhaps we could hold this matter over until our next meeting when the timing might be more appropriate.

What circumstances need to change to enable you to respond to our offer?

What 'latitude' do you have in mind?

Because signals are often sent during prolonged periods of argument or discussion, they are easily missed. Active listening is required, and negotiators require skills in noting nuances in language to respond to signals from others, and patience in repeating signals where they might have been missed to keep the exchange open.

Kennedy et al (1980) warn against movement without some understanding that it will be reciprocated. They propose that this will not convince the other of one's good intentions but will only reward intransigence, confirming to the other party that if he only holds fast capitulation will ensue. They note that goodwill moves are often defended on the basis that they 'soften up' the other party or 'get negotiation underway'. In a blunt rebuttal of this, they write:

Both of these defences, in a triumph of delusion over experience, indicate utter confusion as to the tactics that produce better deals.

Goodwill concessions, they suggest, harden rather soften the other party.

Proposing

A reciprocation of signals of willingness to move allows the parties greater confidence in moving from argument to making proposals. While argument locks them into defend–attack exchanges, proposals initiate an active search for remedies.

In the first instance they are often made tentatively, and in a manner which suggests firmness on generalities but flexibility on specifics. As such, while clarity may not exist on substantive detail, early proposals have a reassuring quality, signalling to the parties that movement and settlement are possible. They allow a process of cautious exploration without overcommitment. Thus a wage demand may be reshaped allowing a union to convey commitment to a broad principle but opening room for exploration:

> Our members demand an increase of R5 an hour, a 38 hour working week, annual leave of 20 days . . .

becomes:

> We cannot leave this table without a significant improvement in conditions of service of our members.

Sometimes it may help the process if a party can prevent the other committing too early to a specific position. An early commitment may oblige a party into defending a position for the sole purpose of preserving dignity, thus preventing reasonable exploration of problem. It might be useful to open with the following kind of statement:

> Before we make any exchanges of demands or offers, let's discuss the situation in broad terms . . .

As the process continues, parties become more specific as the parties acquire confidence in the other's willingness to move and become hopeful that a settlement is possible. Several tactics may be employed to ensure that proper exploration of proposals takes place. These are reflected in box 4.2.

Packaging and bargaining

As proposals begin to firm it is suggested that they be bargained as packages rather than as individual items. This initiates a process of concession exchanges and trade-offs, allowing each party to secure certain benefits or guarantees in exchange for movement on the same or other items. In this way some flexibility is allowed rather than tests of strength on each item on the agenda. Kennedy et al (1980) propose that packaging and bargaining is the most intense phase of the process, demanding creative reshaping of variables in a form that more closely approximates the fears and interests of each party. It is a creative process centred on moving parties from

- *Avoid interrupting proposals* — listen through before responding.
- *Avoid making immediate counterproposals* however unpalatable they may be — explore the thinking of the other party.
- *Use behaviour labelling* to ensure that proposals and recommendations are properly listened to and not lost in the interactive flow.
- *Check own understanding* of proposals.
- *Ask the other side how they understand your proposals* to ensure that they understand your suggestions as you intended.
- *Summarise* to ensure acceptable mutual understanding of proposals.
- *Caucus* to allow full consideration of proposals.

Box 4.2
Tactics to ensure proper exploration of proposals

where they are to where they might settle. Rackham and Carlisle (1978) concluded from their research that effective negotiators *link issues, do not dilute arguments and bargain in packages* based in preparation around individual items. Several important guidelines exist for effective packaging and bargaining.

The critical skill is that of *linking items*. This is not a careless lumping together of issues, but a carefully considered and creative exercise. Concessions, trade-offs and movement are most likely to be effective when they mean something to the other party, and show recognition for their concerns, and understanding of their pressures, values and inhibitions. *Concessions should therefore be valued in the other's terms* — not only in terms of what they cost to give, but in terms of their utility to the other side. A party may believe that it has made very important concessions at considerable cost to itself, and be angered to find that they are received with little excitement by the other side.

A report was received a few years ago of a milling company that closed wage negotiations with a trade union with an offer of a bag of mealie-meal as part of the remuneration. After an initial response of 'is this the 1980s or are we en route back to bartering with old boots and overalls?' I enquired how the exchange had come about. After a prolonged deadlock someone in the company team had the sense to start exploring what the major cost factor in the union's demand was — it was food. Further exploration indicated its demand was based on the cost of mealie meal bought in supermarkets. The company realised that it actually produced the meal at a fraction of that cost — a concession could be made then at low cost to the company, but with a high value to workers. This type of creativity has obvious limitations for a company manufacturing explosives of course, but the message is clear enough!

Effective linking demands that *conditions be stated before concessions*. Generally opening conditions are made large, and concessions kept relatively modest to allow room for trading, with the proviso, of course, that concessions must be sufficiently attractive to oblige the other party to seriously consider the proposed package.

A company and a union were in dispute over two separate cases of dismissal. The union had left matters too late to utilise the formal dispute machinery but wished to challenge the decisions. The company was anxious to clear the slate with the union. Management felt strongly about one case and was determined that no return to the workplace should take place, but had some flexibility about the other, and determined to try to trade the cases off against each other. This is clearly unacceptable — two separate rights cases should not be used for trading purposes — but the company was insistent that it proceed with its plan. The management team opened the negotiation with:

> We would be prepared to re-employ A under certain conditions, if you drop your demands on B.

The union responded angrily rejecting the linking of two rights cases each with its own individual circumstances, but suggested a caucus to consider the proposal. In this way they rejected the tactic but kept the proposal sufficiently open to respond with a counter:

> We accept your proposal regarding A, but reject entirely your demands regarding B and propose independent arbitration in this case.

Management tried to remind the union that the offer had been made in package form, but the union pointed out that they knew now that management was prepared to re-employ A under certain conditions, that an immoral linkage had been attempted — and why not cut a lot of bother and expense and simply re-employ A. B could be dealt with separately!

Apart from the problems of trying to trade rights issues, management made the fundamental error of proposing its concession before the conditions, thereby indicating to the other party how far it was prepared to go before ascertaining whether the idea of a package deal was acceptable. The union then simply separated the concession from the demand and applied pressure to secure what it knew it would probably get for A, and to deal with B as a separate matter. How different it might have been if the company had opened with:

> If you would be prepared to drop your demands on B, (large condition), you would give us room to review our position on A (signal of willingness to move but non-specific).

This would have obliged a response from the union, even a rejection of the idea, but the company would not have over-committed.

The key to packaging and bargaining is the 'if you – then we' linkage, the basic rule of thumb being never to give anything without getting something (Kennedy et al 1980).

My four-year-old daughter Jessica taught me the lesson of effective linking with a small bedtime exchange. With amaz-ingly accurate timing children seem to wind up just as bed-time approaches. Faced with an increasingly frenetic little girl I tried this approach: 'If you calm down, I'll read you a story.' This seemed to do the trick. She loved books and in utilising this route I'd valued the concession in her terms. As she'd never been on negotiating skills course, I was clearly in com-mand. After some time she was sitting quietly. I finished the story and with a sense of success, suggested she head for bed. Without hesitation she played her trump card: 'No, Dad, you said that if I calmed down you'd read me a story. I calmed down. If you want me to go to bed then you must read me another story.' She got her story!

PHASE 4: CLOSURE AND AGREEMENT

The central purpose of negotiation is obviously to endeavour to achieve a settlement in an area of disagreement between parties. However smoothly the preceding phases of opening, signalling, proposing and packaging and bargaining might have proceeded, closing negotiations is often a difficult task. Quite often proceedings 'bog down', with parties becoming cautious and suspicious of the process. New tensions may emerge as each tries to 'get the last inch', play a last power card, or 'wait out' the other in an act of brinkmanship. Parties may feel that they have given enough, and that the other should close the gap, or that matters have gone too smoothly and that they might have been 'conned' somewhere along the line.

Atkinson suggests five tactics which negotiators might use to make their offers credible to opponents in order to overcome suspicions that they are bluffing (box 4.3).

> • *Make offers public* through the media.
> • Put *offers down in writing.*
> • *Remind the other of consistency in past nego-tiations.*
> • *Walkouts.*
> • *Threaten or implement sanctions,* such as the strike or lockout to pressurise the other.

Box 4.3
Tactics to make offers credible

Some comment is required on these tactics. *Making the offer public* has become increasingly popular for employers who feel that they are facing unreasonable demands or action on the part of trade unions. Companies such as SA Breweries, VWSA and Mercedes Benz of SA have placed advertisements in the country's newspapers in the face of strikes by their employees in an effort to educate the public as to the 'true' story behind the action, and no doubt, to elicit public sympathy for their position and to isolate workers in terms of community support. While these tactics may be effective in achieving these objectives, they may also lock the other side into a position from which it becomes difficult to move without losing face.

Walkouts are dangerous tactics especially if the other side is clearly indicating that further movement is possible providing there is reciprocation. While it has the strong feel of commitment to a position, it also leaves the other party with an all or nothing, take it or leave it choice. If they call the bluff and leave it, it is a humbling experience to have to return to try to re-open negotiations. In one instance, a trade union organiser walked out of a negotiation while the company spokesman was conveying that further movement was possible but only if the union revised its demands. Months passed. The company did not implement a wage increase on the usual date. When workers queried the delay, managers stated that no increase could be given until negotiations were completed, that they had room to improve their offer but could not do so as the organiser had walked out of the meeting. Shortly workers frogmarched the said organiser back into the negotiation room and a settlement ensued — with the union operating from a base of weakness. Walkouts are only powerful if the costs to the other party of failing to conclude, or a delay in concluding an agreement are high.

The same applies to the use of *threats of sanctions* — a party can only make so many threats before it is obliged to exercise a sanction if it is to retain credibility. Once this threshold is passed, and the sanction is actually implemented the nature of the negotiation changes. While threatened or implemented pressure tactics may act quickly to focus minds on the consequences of failing to achieve an agreement, they may also act as obstacles to agreement. The attention of the parties is shifted off wages for instance, to how to defeat or progress a strike. Face saving becomes a factor in continuing or ceasing action promoting the chances of conflict escalation and entrapment. Many strikes have proceeded long beyond their economic rationale simply because there seemed to be no dignified way of de-escalating the crisis. It continues to amaze me how much companies will spend on defeating strikes that they would not have considered sharing with workers — and how much workers will sacrifice to back demands that are clearly unachievable. This is not the stuff of rational trials of economic strength — it is the stuff of conflict entrapment and brinkmanship.

Expressions of commitment then, are valuable sources of leverage in negotiations, but raise the risks of premature or unnecessary deadlocks. Kennedy (1984) observes:

> Playing 'chicken' with a dedicated ('irrational') opponent in fast cars on a highway is also a fast way to die. In negotiating, a mutual chicken game is known as deadlock (p 289).

He makes several suggestions for avoiding deadlocks (box 4.4).

- *Place moratoriums on public statements.*
- Replace attack language with *neutral statements* on feelings.
- *Use questions* to clarify and reclarify the needs and interests of parties.
- Move questions from *why* something should be done, to *how* it could be done.
- Use *open vs. closed questions.*
- Shift from us vs. you approaches to one of *acknowledging joint problems.*
- *Re-examine own levels of commitment* to assess the worth of continuing the process.

Box 4.4
Tactics for avoiding deadlocks

These actions constrain premature public commitments, and allow for the emergence of creative problem solving in place of costly trials of strength over issues of principle, or simply a desire to 'teach the other a lesson' or 'keep them in their place'. If the other party is sensitive to these issues, then some active searches for face-savers might be embarked on to allow both an honorable withdrawal from a deadlock.

In a dismissal situation a personnel manager admitted to the mediator that he knew they might lose a dismissal case if it went to court, and that he was not himself vigorously opposed to the idea of a reinstatement with some penalties. His concern centred around being seen by line managers as having 'given in yet again' to the union, and being perceived as actively undermining the authority of line managers. It would be better in a way, he thought, to lose the case in court and to have the decision obliged on them by an outside power. In this way he would not be seen to be the 'soft' one. Some exploration of concerns with the union finally brought worker representatives to an awareness of the fears of management, and they voiced willingness to publicly acknowledge management rights to discipline (without losing the right to challenge actions perceived as unfair) if re-employment occurred. Agreement soon followed.

Usually closure in negotiation is brought about by the following:
- ❏ 'either . . . or' offers (alternatives);
- ❏ 'or else . . .' offers (threats); or
- ❏ concession exchanges (reciprocal exchange).

Some exploration has already taken place on the risks of 'or else . . .' closures, and concession exchanges and the manner in which they are achieved are the essence of effective use of the distributive approach, but a short word is necessary on the 'either . . . or' method. Alternatives used to be reserved for executive appointments with senior managers being provided with menus of conditions from which they could compile a remuneration package according to tax benefits, personal preferences etc. With the advent of computer based systems it is possible for employers to accurately assess the implications of various alternative offers to a union -weight-ings at the lower end of grading systems offset with reduced offers for higher grades, alternative fringe benefits and so on. One consequence of presenting alternatives is that it might induce a mind set on choosing between proposed alternatives rather than thinking about others, or demanding improvements on any of them.

TACTICS IN NEGOTIATION

Tactics are to many the grist of competitive negotiations. It is my opinion that much of the tactical play advanced through negotiation skills courses is not only overblown but often counterproductive. Bargaining is a game of power exchange, it does involve bluff and the use of mutual pressure by the parties but there is more to it than this. As proposed in an earlier chapter, the negotiation process is only viable if the parties utilising it are sincere in their efforts to endeavour to achieve a settlement. *Tactics have one central purpose — to assist in achieving a settlement!* Too often negotiators utilise their preparation time planning how to split the team of the other, how to irritate or disrupt concentration, how to threaten or illustrate power. Often they do not plan bargaining ranges or think about possible areas of settlement. Tactics then are planned not to achieve movement within a framework of expectations but in an ad hoc careless manner, as if the process were solely one of tactics convened for a display of skills in pressure games. During the negotiation one witnesses long exchanges of mutual attack, of deliberate efforts to stall the bargaining process, or to make it difficult for the other party on quite minor points. Asked why they are doing these things parties respond — 'well it's a tough process' or 'it's important to keep one step ahead, and to keep the pressure on'. Seldom is there constructive discussion on the usefulness of a particular tactic in seeking settlement, or gaining movement in an exchange. In other words, much tactical play is not directly related to settlement searches but to efforts to obstruct the other party. The consequence is that negotiators become locked into defend attack modes of behavioural exchange rather than directing their energies toward solving problems.

It *is* a tough process — why complicate it with undirected tactical play?

In listing some common tactics then, the intention is not to turn negotiators into 'tactics technicians', but to assist people to recognise some of the means whereby pressure may be applied or handled, and to deal with rather than apply 'dirty tactics'.

Issues-arguments tactics

Tactics in this category are essentially focused in the issues on the table. They include:

❑ showing up weaknesses, inconsistencies, omissions and incorrect assumptions in arguments;
❑ demanding justification of demands or positions;
❑ providing additional information;
❑ using comparisons;
❑ avoiding argument dilution; and
❑ pointing out the positive consequences of own proposals/ negative consequences of other's proposals.

Pressure tactics

Pressure tactics are directed at achieving movement on the part of the other bargaining party. They might include:

❑ blow hot — blow cold;
❑ splitting the other's team;
❑ imposing ultimatums/deadlines;
❑ threatening to terminate negotiation;
❑ indicating that constituencies are impatient; and
❑ demands of principle.

Process tactics

Process tactics are directed at changing the order, direction or pace of the negotiations in an attempt to achieve leverage over the other party. These include:

- ❑ adjusting the agenda;
- ❑ delaying indicating a position;
- ❑ avoidance of issues;
- ❑ red herrings;
- ❑ asking for time to achieve a new mandate/report back to constituencies; and
- ❑ keeping issues open.

Obstructive tactics

Obstructive tactics are those which are used to deliberately stall the process by rendering it unworkable, attacking individuals on the other side, or eroding unity in the other's team. They might include:

- ❑ extreme demands or offers;
- ❑ single or overloaded agendas;
- ❑ not bargaining honestly on the issues on the table (hidden agendas);
- ❑ non-negotiable demands;
- ❑ refusals to justify or explain demands or positions;
- ❑ early use of threats or actual sanctions;
- ❑ emotional outbursts;
- ❑ incorrect summaries;
- ❑ focus on emotionally upsetting areas making the other feel inferior or dependent, inexperienced, incompetent etc.;
- ❑ active use of irritators;
- ❑ refusal to acknowledge finality of agreements; and
- ❑ walkouts.

Tactics to handle pressure

Whether under pressure from argument or confrontationally based tactics, it is necessary to have skills in dealing with tight situations. These include:

- ❏ the caucus;
- ❏ low reactions to emotive threats;
- ❏ request the other party for proposals;
- ❏ use of humour;
- ❏ problem vs. person focus;
- ❏ the threat-free apology;
- ❏ stick to bargaining procedures;
- ❏ expose the dirty tactic;
- ❏ keep issues focused;
- ❏ respond to needs and emotions;
- ❏ listen for real vs. overt concerns;
- ❏ adjourn for a 'cool off';
- ❏ avoid aggressive responses — keep issues focused.

OBSTACLES TO EFFECTIVE NEGOTIATION

Many factors may derail or sour negotiations. Some of these may not be in the direct control of the parties — violent acts by groups not involved in ANC talks with government threaten the process; government acts in the past have produced tensions at labour–management negotiation tables. Constituent demands may not allow for a meaningful search for settlement. Scarcity of resources may render any negotiation an inherently stressed process.

However, many factors *are* within the control of the parties -how they frame their demands, the use of tactics, their preparation for negotiations, their skills in giving and responding to signals, making proposals and closing a deal.

Many of these factors have already been discussed. A checklist for diagnosing obstacles to the process is provided on page 162.

PROCESS EVALUATION

Pro forma evaluation forms for negotiation process are provided on pages 163 and 164. It is important that designated members of bargaining teams acquire skills in observing and analysing negotiation process, noting signals, tactics, proposals, behavioural shifts, flows of power, and obstacles to progress. Recorder/analysts may suggest caucuses to their own teams at critical moments, and lead discussion on progress and options based on their analyses during caucus on the basis of their observations. Their role may be critical in assisting negotiators hear each other more fully, and keeping negotiation on track in the search for settlements.

CHECKLIST: OBSTACLES TO PROGRESS			
OBSTACLE	US	THEM	PLAN
1. AGENDA • too few items • too many items • hidden agendas			
2. POSITIONS • extreme • rigid • confused/unclear			
3. MANDATES • unrealistic • absence of			
4. RELATIONSHIP • no respect/trust • no legitmacy • history • stereotypes • no sensitivity to needs			
5. STRUCTURAL • inadequate procedures • no trusted third parties/forums			
6. CONTEXTUAL • social/political economic			
7. NEGOTIATION PROCESS • poor planning • poor justification • hostile tactics • missed signals • poorly expressed/no proposals • poor linking • inability to close • absence of genuine desire to settle • public commitment to position • misjudgement of capacity to move			

PROCESS EVALUATION				
PARTY A	Tactic	Power flow	Tactic	**PARTY B**

SUMMARY EVALUATION FORM		
	US	THEM
1. Movement		
2. Signals		
3. Proposals		
4. Tactics		
5. Needs		
6. Obstacles		
7. Plans		

5
CREATIVE ALTERNATIVES TO COMPETITIVE BARGAINING

Chapter 3 discussed approaches to negotiation and the issues determining which might be used in specific circumstances. It will be recalled that integrative bargaining, or the dual concerns approach is really one of joint problem solving rather than competition based on positional power plays.

The process is one of collaboration with a win–win orientation on the part of the parties as they look for solutions of mutual benefit, that is, the best solution for both is aimed for by both.

INTEGRATIVE BARGAINING: JOINT PROBLEM SOLVING

Many negotiators — usually management negotiators, in my experience — bewail the tendency for negotiations to become distributive and wish that they might be conducted on a more 'cooperative' level. In many instances it appears that they want the climate of the joint problem-solving approach without any desire to get to grips with the elements which make it work. Joint problem solving takes place between parties who respect each others' legitimacy, needs and interests, who are willing to be open and honest and will share relevant information with each other. If these elements are not present, what is being sought is subordinative rather than integrative bargaining!

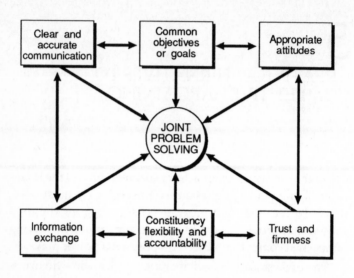

Figure 5.1
Prerequisites for joint problem solving

Several prerequisites exist for effective joint problem solving (figure 5.1) — if these are absent then successful use of the process is unlikely.

PREREQUISITES FOR INTEGRATIVE DECISION MAKING

Several authors have identified conditions necessary for joint problem solving to take place (Filley 1975; Pruitt 1981; Lewicki & Litterer 1985). These may be summarised as follows:

A common objective or goal

If joint problem solving is to occur, then it is important that the parties believe that greater benefits are likely to ensue from collaboration than from competition. Lewicki and Litterer (1985) propose three types of goal offering the potential for this approach:

❑ *Common goals.* The parties are offered equal shares in benefits that can be created only by collaborative effort, such as a business partnership where individuals bring different talents (manufacturing, finance, marketing and sales) and agree to an equal distribution of profits created by the joint efforts required to make the business a success.

❑ *Shared goals.* The parties work toward a common objective but benefit differently, such as a sub-contracting arrangement where a contracted builder and a subcontracted plumber work towards completion of the construction of a house but the latter receives a far smaller reward, being dependent on the other for the work opportunity.

❑ *Joint goals.* The parties may have quite different end goals but combine in a collective effort to attain a common objective, as in the case of the broad alliance against apartheid in which a wide diversity of groups have united their efforts in pressurising for the repeal of racial legislation, but who themselves have very differing goals regarding the final shape of post-apartheid society in terms of economic and political restructuring.

Appropriate Attitudes

Filley (1975) suggests several key beliefs that must be shared by the parties if integrative decision making is to occur:

❑ a belief that mutually acceptable solutions are available;
❑ a belief that such solutions are desirable;
❑ a belief in cooperative endeavour vs competition;
❑ a belief that everyone is of equal value;
❑ a belief that the others' views are legitimate statements of their positions;
❑ a belief that differences of opinion are helpful;

❑ a belief that the other party could compete but has chosen
    to cooperate.

Lewicki & Litterer add:

❑ a belief in one's own problem-solving ability.

Trust and firmness

Mistrust inhibits collaboration, inhibiting open exchanges of
information and communication. Trust is a prerequisite for
open sharing of needs, positions, underlying interests, fears
and information. Where it is absent therefore positional bargaining is almost obliged.

Trust should not be confused with yielding — it actually
implies a commitment to an end objective. Yielding may
prompt a hardening of position by the other party even in a
trusting relationship, undermining cooperative endeavour.
(Lewicki & Litterer, 1985) Joint problem solving emerges
from high trust — high limit situations. Low trust — high
limit situations produce competition (Pruitt 1981).

Similarly rigid goals coupled with inflexible means or
positions promotes competition. Rigid goals coupled with
flexible means promotes joint problem solving (Pruitt 1981).
Rubin and Brown (1975) suggest that where parties indicate
a commitment to their own needs but a willingness to engage
in a search for a joint solution this promotes trust in a relationship.

Lewicki & Littterer (1985) outline several factors emerging
from research which contribute to the development of trust,
including:

❑ perceptions of similarity;
❑ perceptions that a positive attitude is held toward one;
❑ perceptions of the other's dependency;
❑ perceptions of the other's desire to cooperate and make
    concessions;

❏ opening moves in a negotiation which are open and co-operative; and

❏ histories or patterns of cooperative engagement.

Constituency accountability

An important aspect often neglected by writers on negotiation is that of the constituency. In collective or representational situations negotiators are not participant on their own behalf but are mandated by and report back to constituencies. These are often somewhat vague as to the process of negotiation, or may have unrealistic or inflexible expectations of outcome and place serious constraints on their bargaining team. In a sense this ensures that negotiators do not 'sell out' under pressure, but it also limits the potentials for problem solving.

Pruitt (1981) points out that low accountability to a constituency may allow collaboration but not necessarily problem solving. On the other hand high accountability tends to promote competition as negotiators try to meet their constituents' demands, and show strength in the bargaining process. Constituencies must then also provide their bargaining teams room for manoeuvre if problem solving is to occur — *high limits with flexibility about means.*

Information exchange

Parties cannot participate in joint problem solving meaningfully unless they have all the information relevant to the matter in hand. Important here is that information exchange promotes feelings of psychological closeness, allows a proper focus on problems and reduces power differentials associated with monopolies over data. In short it is a means of promoting trust in a relationship, or a working relationship.

On a cautionary note, negotiators should not be so naive as to believe that simple information disclosure will reduce conflict. On the contrary, conflict may actually be exacerbated in cases where genuine values or interests differences exist. Clearer understanding may only confirm suspicions of exploitation, injustice or corruption, enhancing feelings of moral outrage and entrenching the use of pressure tactics.

Clear and accurate communication

Clear, accurate communication is not the same as information exchange — the former refers to the process whereby understanding is achieved. Lewicki & Litterer (1985) state that negotiators should be able to state their needs in specific, concrete terms; to understand those of the other party; grasp the full meanings of statements to all parties involved, and avoid ambiguities. Skills to improve communication skills are outlined in chapter 6.

These prerequisites for effective joint problem solving provide a useful checklist for parties considering this route in their relationship. Where the conditions for such an approach are absent, and where it appears unlikely that they can be created, hopes for a more cooperative style of engagement should be realistically tempered.

STEPS IN THE PROBLEM-SOLVING PROCESS

The major steps in joint problem solving or integrative decision making have been outlined in a variety of stage models (Filley 1975; Pruitt 1981; Lewicki & Litterer 1985). A summary of steps is presented in figure 5.2.

Acknowledge that a problem exists

Before parties can embark on a common solution search they must jointly acknowledge that a problem exists and that it is the interests of both parties to resolve that problem. Thus, if one party is intent on deliberately escalating a conflict in the belief that greater gain can be achieved through this course of action, then a joint definition of a problem may be hard to

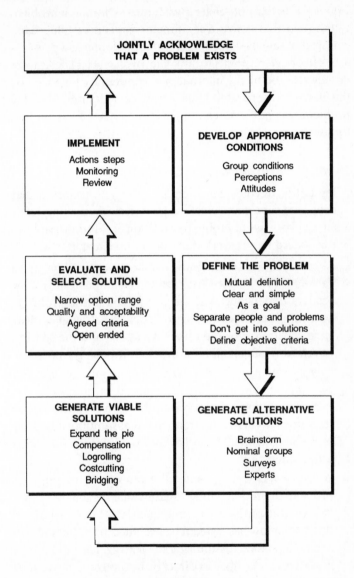

Figure 5.2
Steps in joint problem solving

achieve. Iraq did not see its invasion of Kuwait as a problem but argued that it was a legitimate acquisition. Like many countries it saw the Israeli–Palestinian situation as a problem and efforts were made to link the two issues. These were largely rejected by the international community who viewed the issues as separate. Thus a common definition of the problem was not achieved in the diplomatic efforts leading up to the war.

Development of appropriate conditions

Filley (1975) devotes considerable energy to ensuring that appropriate conditions exist for joint decision making *before* entering processes of problem definition or solution searches. In this regard he suggests attention to three major areas:

❑ *Group conditions:* seating arrangements; optimal group to facilitate face to face interaction; insurance that group leaders understand and are committed to the problem-solving process rather than competitive strategies; clear time constraints or the removal thereof; and the sharing of relevant information for problem-solving purposes.

❑ *Problem perception* by the parties may require review and adjustment. They should be assisted to check out the accuracy of their perceptions of the problem and those of the others involved; inferences and assumptions need to be replaced with facts, and evaluative attitudes with open mindedness.

❑ *Attitudes* and feelings enter the process at the point of problem definition. Filley suggests that personality types that inhibit problem solving, such as authoritarians or those with low self-esteem be excluded from the process as far as possible. Authoritarian persons tend to be con-servative, seek either to direct or be directed, need order and rules, are intolerant of minorities and tend to be less trusting, trustworthy or flexible, while those with low self-esteem are vulnerable in power exchanges, need structure, inhibit aggression, and because they are easily threatened and persuaded, yield too quickly to group pressure. Appropriate problem-solving attitudes and behaviours include perceptions of others' needs as valid, a willingness to check out motives, attitudes and feelings of others rather than infer them and seeing others as helpful resources in the search for a solution of joint benefit. Authoritarian persons may hold senior positions in organisations, and may have prevailed in many competitive situations being seen as the reason for success in such circumstances. As a consequence it may in reality prove a very difficult decision and task to exclude them from a team.

Various methods exist to develop appropriate attitudes including:

- ❏ 'levelling' conferences;
- ❏ pre-problem-solving meetings to discuss possible obstacles to the process;
- ❏ simulation exercises;
- ❏ sensitivity training to improve insights;
- ❏ skills training in problem solving.

Efforts to depersonalise situations, clarify values and fight antagonism rather than antagonists are useful pre-conditioning devices.

Define the problem

Filley (1975) advises that as far as possible processes of problem definition be separated from those of solution searches and their evaluation. It is important that problem definition precede discussion of solutions to achieve a joint clarification of issues at stake and to prevent parties entrenching themselves in positions.

Only parties to a dispute can accurately identify their goals and thus define the problem — a facilitator may however be useful in assisting them to do this in a mutually acceptable manner. The process involves a clear statement of goals and perceived obstacles in achieving these.

Lewicki and Litterer (1985) observe that problem identification is often the most difficult of the steps in the process. They suggest several key elements:

❏ *Define the problem in a way that is acceptable to both parties.* Feelings that the other party may be withholding information or manipulating the process to identify problems in his terms may inhibit the required openness and 'neutrality' required for problem definition. Parties may have to negotiate the problem statement a few times before jointly acceptable wording is achieved.

❏ *Keep the problem statement clear and simple.* Separate secondary from primary problems to work fully on the latter (unlike distributive bargaining where additional items may be introduced to confuse, or facilitate the trading process). Separate problems to prevent confusing the work on any one of them.

❏ *State the problem as a goal and identify obstacles to its achievement.* State the problem as a clear end objective to be achieved rather than a solution.

❏ *Depersonalise the problem.* Separating people from the problem is important. Evaluative or hostile attitudes directed at people inhibit openness and evoke emotional responses which get in the way of problem solving.

❏ *Separate problem definition from solution searches* to obviate premature commitments to positions which constrain creative thinking.

In addition it is proposed here that:

❏ *appropriately defined problems (in form of objectives) be used as criteria against which to assess later alternative solutions.* This ensures that the process remains as neutral as possible, preventing ideas -competition or either-or evaluation of solutions.

Generate alternative solutions

Once the problem has been clearly defined in a way that is mutually acceptable to the parties, and in a form that reflects objectives rather than positions *then* the search for solutions can begin.

Generally this is a participative process wherein all persons may contribute, unlike the distributive or positional approach in which each bargaining team operates under the control of a chief negotiator. In the integrative or joint problem-solving method the idea is to generate as many alternatives as possible, to open up exploration and raise debate in an open exchange. This is of course not the process described in the previous chapter where parties act to conceal their interests and use bluff and pressure tactics to oblige movement through a series of positions. Several methods have been suggested in the solution search process (Filley 1975; Palomares & Logan 1975; Lewicki & Litterer 1985; Van Gundy 1988). Van Gundy's work provides an expansive inventory of useful techniques.

Brainstorming or *brainwriting* are perhaps the techniques that most readily spring to mind in any discussion of solution searches. Brainstorming is a technique whereby people are asked in small groups to generate as many possible solutions as they can, someone recording these as they are suggested. Participants are urged to be spontaneous and to avoid censorship of any ideas as unworkable, too expensive or impractical. Brainwriting emphasises the silent generation of ideas in a group context for later collation and evaluation by the group. Osborn (1963) outlines a number of basic rules for the process (box 5.1).

- *Defer judgement on any proposal*: evaluation restricts idea generation and acts to constrain proposals.
- *Quantity breeds quality*: list as many ideas as possible.
- *The wilder the idea, the better*: breakthroughs are seldom the product of cautious, conservative approaches.
- *Combine and improve ideas*: build on each others proposals.
- *Be exhaustive in the process*: stay with the problem.
- *Take a break from the problem*: it is difficult to generate fresh ideas when people are tired.

Box 5.1
Osborn's rules for brainstorming

These rules underpin the effectiveness of many other solution search techniques.

The nominal group technique involves asking each negotiator or the negotiating teams, or subgroups of these, to prepare written lists of solutions for the problem at hand. In common caucus these are then shared with the wider group and recorded on flip charts. This prompts the generation of a wide variety of solution searches in a short space of time.

Surveys may be used to solicit ideas from persons not directly participant in the negotiation, usually by means of a questionnaire sent to a wide range of people defining the problem and asking them to list as many solutions as they can think of. This has the advantage of obtaining a wider range of ideas, but of course has limitations in that the parties surveyed cannot see or hear other's ideas of views for stimulation.

Expanding the pie

Many conflicts occur because there appears to be a scarce resource which does not allow each party to satisfy its needs under the current allocation. Efforts are then directed at exploring ways to 'expand the pie' so that each might meet its needs — generate more money, take more time etc.

Compensation

In cases where it is not possible to expand the pie, it may be agreed that one party will obtain his goal with the other being compensated with an accepted or valued alternative.

Logrolling

In cases where there is more than a single issue at stake concession exchanges may be possible on the basis that if one party achieves its objectives on the first item, then the other party's objectives should be realised on the second, and so on. Ideally parties might be able to exchange items of differing priorities, that is, high priority items on one's list may be low on the others. The success of this approach depends on perceptions of equivalence of exchange and involves movement by both rather than one of the parties. It may be helpful to develop secondary or additional items to allow logrolling to develop.

Cost-cutting

Here the parties seek to reduce each other's costs or fears in developing a solution. For instance in a dismissal situation, the management negotiation team was not in itself intransigent about reinstating a worker, but was very concerned about line manager's remarks that '. . . all that was required was the union demand — and then management gives in' and '. . . all that industrial relations is about is giving the authority of managers away . . .'.

To the union the reinstatement was a very important issue. When they became aware of the management team's fears they offered to make a public statement acknowledging management's rights to discipline in the workplace should the reinstatement take place. This was seen as sufficiently significant (in reducing fears) to warrant a deal.

Bridging

Bridging takes place when the parties are able to invent new options to meet their mutual needs. This requires in-depth discussion of real wants underlying parties' opening positions.

Box 5.2
Methods for achieving integrative agreements.

External assistance or expertise may be sought in cases where problems are too complex or expert information is required for their resolution.

Generate viable solutions

Another approach utilised in the wider process of solution searches and which moves beyond simple brainstorming is one in which parties try to define their underlying needs and develop alternatives that will successfully meet those needs.

Pruitt (1981) and Lewicki & Litterer (1985) identify five methods for achieving integrative agreements which refocus issues under dispute and require increased information on the other side's true needs (box 5.2).

Lewicki & Litterer (1985) note that while the generation of alternative solutions may 'luck' the parties into a solution to solve a problem, generally this is not the case. Solutions emerge as a consequence of focused thinking on mutual needs and interests, information exchange — and hard work by the parties, that is, a commitment to the joint problem-solving process!

Evaluation and Selection of Alternatives

At this stage, solutions generated by the parties can be evaluated and a mutually acceptable route ahead agreed on. If parties have defined problems clearly in terms of needs, then these may be used as criteria against which to weight solutions. Some negotiation on option ranges may be required but the dictum of objective criteria, and separating people from problems, if applied rigorously, may act to prevent the development of either-or, or positional bargaining. Filley (1975) and Lewicki & Litterer (1985) suggest the steps outlined in box 5.3.

- *Narrow the range of solution options*, focusing on options strongly supported by either party.
- *Evaluate solutions on the basis of quality and acceptability* both to the negotiators and to those who must implement them.
- *Criteria should be agreed in advance* especially on controversial items to ensure objectivity in the evaluative process.
- *Use subgroups* in complex situations thus breaking down the size of the task.
- *Keep decisions tentative and conditional* until the whole 'package' of a solution is together to keep thinking open, allow retraction or sidestepping and maximise flexibility.
- *Minimise formality and record keeping* until the end to prevent people becoming bogged down in formal minutes, records of positions, etc.

Box 5.3
Steps for evaluating and selecting alternatives

Implement solutions

Having reached a solution, the parties need to contract on steps to be taken, responsibilities, deadlines, monitoring structures and processes and means of evaluating progress. A solution is not a solution until it has been effectively enacted! Further problems may arise out of trying to action a plan, requiring a return to the problem-solving process either for problems arising or on the original issue.

BURTON'S APPROACH TO RESOLVING DEEP-ROOTED CONFLICT

John Burton (1987) expands on this problem solving approach in a practical exposition of the skills involved in resolving deep-rooted conflict. He addresses the issue of conflicts involving not merely differences of interest which can be negotiated, but deep motivations, values, and needs which cannot be compromised, ie. *deep-rooted conflict*. This form of conflict, he asserts, occurs at all levels of relations, and because it involves deeply felt human needs, cannot be compromised or settled by the order of an arbitrator or more powerful body. Such conflicts, he asserts

> . . . may seem endless, erupting into emotional displays and even violence from time to time, contained only by imprisonment or social, political and sometimes military pressures. Containing serious conflicts, however, does not resolve them. On the contrary, it tends to protract them. (p 3)

This kind of conflict is different to the normal types of conflict based in competition of interests or ideas, or even personality differences — it requires skills that move beyond 'managing' or regulating conflicts to reaching fundamental values and needs of the parties involved. These skills are not those associated with achieving compromise but are centred in an 'analytical problem-solving process which seeks self-sustaining outcomes.'(p 5)

The process requires facilitators, comprising a panel of four or five persons who work with the parties seeking to assist them to resolve rather merely to settle the conflict in their relationship. In international disputes, Burton refers to *second track diplomacy*, a process of informal, analytical and exploratory discussions between the parties which takes place outside the formal structures of political engagement which tend to constrain creative endeavour.

Burton suggests that there has been a shift in approach from traditional power bargaining to approaches that avoid positional play, and are exploratory and analytical in nature. Like De Bono's design approach, this approach requires third parties — their task being to infuse discussion with knowledge and information about human behaviour and conflicts generally, and to keep the process within the analytical framework. These people sit in the form of a panel, and avoid making recommendations or assuming evaluative stances.

Burton's key concept is that people pursue basic needs regardless of 'objective' power realities or consequences. Universal needs of security, identity and development cannot be compromised, negotiated or adjudicated. This demands a recognition that traditional approaches to conflict handling are limited in their capacity to resolve conflicts, serving at best to produce settlements and at worst failing altogether.

> . . . traditional concepts of law and order, the common good, majority decision making, 'democracy' and the right to rule and to expect obedience, were often at the root of conflict situations. Furthermore, the empirical evidence seemed to show that authorities who deny people identity and development, and attempt to impose the norms of the powerful are, in themselves, a source of conflict. . . . It seems likely that the traditional processes of power bargaining and mediation are themselves an additional reason for some conflicts to be protracted. Such processes often lead to temporary settlements without tackling the underlying issues. (1987 p 18)

Burton points out that incorrect definitions or understanding of the causes of conflict lead to inappropriate approaches to their resolution. He proposes that the facilitated resolution approach is based on analysis of the goals, values and motivations of the parties acknowledging a difference between interests which can be negotiated, and values which cannot be traded. It also suggests that the unit of analysis is not the power holder in the form of the state, for instance, but various identity groups defined by culture, ethnicity, class, religion or language. Because basic needs and values cannot be traded, attention is devoted not to win–lose, but win–win outcomes in relations. The basic elements of Burton's approach to facilitated conflict resolution are reflected in Box 5.4.

In the first instance Burton suggests *rules for sponsorship* dealing with the manner in which the body offering assistance should behave. Sponsors should offer services only if

---

BURTON'S FACILITATED CONFLICT RESOLUTION APPROACH

- Differentiates between negotiable interests and basic needs and values which cannot be bargained away.
- It is analytical of motives and values, perceptions of these, and confusions between interests, tactics and goals.
- It allows the opportunity to explore the costs of failing to respond to needs revealed in the analytic process.
- It attempts to assist parties to recognise the changes in existing structures and policies to facilitate need fulfillment of all involved.
- It assists parties to monitor events and communications carefully, to anticipate responses and to to be aware of policy details in improving relationships.

Box 5.4
Burton's Facilitated Conflict Resolution Approach

Burton proposes fifty six rules for effective conflict resolution. These are summarised here but readers should consult the original text, *Resolving Deep-rooted Conflict: A Handbook*, for a full grasp of the approach.

they have facilitators who are trained, and if they can stay with the situation until services are no longer needed. The sponsor should identify the parties and relevant issues before initiating action steps. *Analysis* starts with the point of breakdown in the closest relationships, extending outward to include all parties, and an ordered approach devised to tackle issues is communicated to all involved with assurances that no action will be undertaken until it has been discussed with everyone affected. *Communication* should be directly to leaders of those involved, invitations should be simultaneously conducted and identical in content and parties invited to send participants who are not decisionmakers but are close to them. Factional elements should be sought out and invited.

The parties should communicate directly in *analytical rather than bargaining dialogue,* and in the presence of a third party whose task is to facilitate analysis of goals, tactics, interests, values and needs. A balanced panel of facilitators is required across a range of disciplines to assist accurate analysis, but should not include exclusive specialists in the issue in dispute (in case of bias and influence). Efforts should be made to bridge parties into the problem-solving mode, and facilitators must be prepared and coordinated in their actions.

After meetings sponsors must report back to leaders, and should consider *transition periods* between informal and formal negotiation processes. Facilitators should work out responses/tactics regarding publicity and the media with the parties. Funding should be adequate for the first meeting, and parties encouraged to contribute thereafter with a reserve funding capacity for rapid responses. Locational factors must be addressed, and parties housed separately. Seating arrangements need to be thought through. No observers should be present and no recording carried out, but interpreters may be required. Caucus rooms should be available. Lists of those involved should be circulated, each person in the process should be clearly identifiable, and the parties should be fully aware of the role of the facilitators and the process before the first sitting.

Matters of substance should be confined to conference, and facilitators should be aware of re-entry problems of participants when they return to decisionmakers — shifts in relations may occur during meetings that do not have a direct bearing on issues at stake as a consequence of relationships established during the working process. The panel of facilitators acts as a unit in the process with one assuming chairmanship of the process. *The analytic framework* moving from perceptions, to situational analysis, to evaluation of perceptions, to finding an agreed definition, and to exploration of options capable of meeting the needs of all should be adhered to without rigidity on timing or ordering of issues. The task of the facilitators is to organise and control this process, essentially holding the parties within the framework for purposes of the exploratory endeavour. In line with the problem-solving approach no solutions should be proposed until a complete analysis of the situation and definition of the problem has been carried out. Initial statements should be heard without interruption, followed only by clarificatory questions. The focus should be on values and goals, and the panel should respond to these with questions and then move top preparing a statement on what appear to be shared goals and values (common ground). Free dialogue on values should be allowed along analytical lines, with facilitators sharing relevant expert knowledge and information. The panel is responsible for pushing discussion forward and preparing a final statement of propositions for detailed debate.

The search for options takes the form of facilitators assisting parties to deduce the necessary shifts in structures and policies to respond to identified needs and values and discussing these. Transition steps should be sought for longer term solutions, with the panel abstaining from firm proposals but making suggestions as regards possible options for debate. Time should be allowed at the end for discussion of next steps and continued communications, and each meeting should build on the last for progress to occur in use of the process at a pace that does lose the enthusiasm of participants.

PRINCIPLED NEGOTIATION: BARGAINING ON THE MERITS

Two books have emerged from the Harvard Negotiation Project which have made a substantial contribution to thinking on the subject of bargaining: Fisher & Ury's (1981) *Getting to Yes*, and Fisher & Brown's (1988) *Getting Together: Building a Relationship that gets to Yes*. Readers are strongly advised to consult these texts directly as they are full of practical guidelines and case examples, and are written in an easy-to-read manner. While much of the content of these books is not new in social science literature, its presentation is innovatively and refreshingly constructed. For this reason, rather than simply absorb their work into the theory of other sections it is presented here as a model on its own. I have taken the liberty of welding the two books into a single construct for introductory purposes here.

Fisher & Ury (1981) propose that distributive bargaining is characterised by the parties successively adopting and then relinquishing a sequence of positions. In the course of this process, they argue, negotiators tend to lock themselves into positions, their commitment to these increasing as they try to defend them and to convince the other party that movement on their part is impossible. Ego identification with a position is the consequence, introducing a 'face-saving' component into the negotiation which assumes a greater influence than

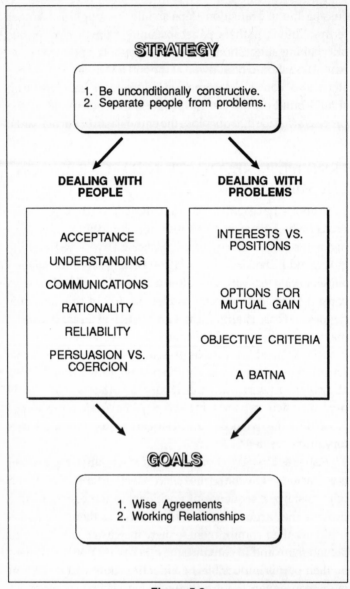

Figure 5.3
Principled negotiation: bargaining on the merits

achievement of a workable agreement. Attention to positions supplants attention to underlying concerns of the parties rendering agreement unlikely. Fisher & Ury argue that position based bargaining is inefficient, endangers ongoing relations and becomes increasingly ineffective as the number of parties involved grows. They propose an approach of bargaining on the merits to avoid the win–lose tone that distributive bargaining inevitably assumes. Four basic elements characterise their approach:

❑ Separate people from the problem.

❑ Focus on interests, not positions.

❑ Generate multiple options before deciding on action.

❑ Insist that the result be based on some objective standard.

Fisher & Brown's (1988) sequel to *Getting to Yes*, focuses on building the kind of relationship that promotes principled negotiation — what they term, a 'working relationship'. They propose that such a relationship is based not on approval or shared values but such elements as:

❑ communication,

❑ understanding,

❑ rationality,

❑ reliability,

❑ persuasion vs. coercion, and

❑ acceptance.

The appropriate elements, they suggest, lie in an overarching strategy: *be unconditionally constructive*, and is rooted in the basic precept: *separate people from the problem*.

Figure 5.3 reflects these elements of the principled negotiation approach which proposes two major objectives -the achievement of 'wise agreements', and the establishment of a 'working relationship'.

The Strategy: Be unconditionally constructive

Fisher & Brown (1988) suggest that to achieve a working relationship, a clear strategy is required to replace the often ad hoc, reactive approaches people commonly pursue.

They suggest that two common mistakes are to:

❑ ignore partisan perceptions or forget how differently people see things; and to

❑ rely on reciprocity in relations.

People arrive in negotiations with widely divergent interests, needs, values, backgrounds, constituencies and resources — they tend not to see issues in the same light.

If they did the chances of conflict would be considerably diminished!

Likewise, while expectations of reciprocity underly many exchanges it is a dangerous foundation for a relationship. Positive reciprocity may be difficult to establish, resources may be difficult to equate and negative reciprocity (an eye for an eye) leads quickly to conflict spirals.

Fisher & Brown (1988) propose that being *unconditionally constructive* is a strategy that is:

❑ independent of disagreement on substantive matters;

❑ independent of concessions or requirements to give in to demands;

❑ independent of partisan perceptions;

❑ independent of reciprocity; and

❑ independent of permanent 'sides'.

They suggest that this strategy is one which allows the pursuit of guidelines which are good for both in the relationship, and for 'me' regardless of whether 'you' follow them as well.

This should provide the basis of a working relationship which if combined with an approach of bargaining on the merits has the potential for achieving *wise agreements*, that is, agreements that meet the legitimate interests of both sides as far as possible, fairly resolve conflict, are efficient and durable, take into account community interests, and improve or at least do not damage relations between the parties. (Fisher & Ury 1981)

An example of an attempt to follow these guidelines is reflected in the overt steps taken by the South African government to shift relations with the black population and its representatives after years of oppressive action, an insurrectionist response and rapidly escalating conflict. The precondition for the cessation of the armed struggle before the release of Nelson Mandela was dropped. A large number of discriminatory laws were repealed; the ANC, SACP and ANC were unbanned and invited to discuss the removal of obstacles for talks about a new dispensation; prohibitions on mass gatherings and peaceful protest were eased; commissions were established to investigate allegations of state atrocities; the state of emergency was lifted; and forces were removed from the townships until their presence was requested. In the second phase of the process President De Klerk announced that all remaining apartheid legislation would be repealed. In this way the government rapidly moved from the role of 'international pariah' to the moral highground. By appearing to be trying to get its own house in order, without demands on other parties (no reciprocity), the pressure to respond accordingly was placed on the other parties. It has become harder to rationalise the armed struggle and sanctions other than as bargaining chips, and as safeguards in the face of a sudden reversal in the process. A new dispensation is far from being in place, and is unlikely to be achieved without some major obstacles being encountered, but the manner of getting the process in motion has been almost textbookishly pursued.

Separate people from the problem

Negotiations take place between people with differing values, emotions, perceptions and backgrounds. Fisher & Ury (1981) suggest that problems arise in positional bargaining as substantive and relationship issues become entangled. A working relationship does not require that the parties approve of each other's positions, goals, or conduct, nor that they share values — indeed, the more serious their differences and the consequences of confrontation, the greater the requirement for an effective working relationship. Fisher & Brown (1988) propose that a necessary first step requires a disentangling of relationship from substantive issues, and a capacity to think about the relationship as a process which should not be subordinated to short-term substantive concerns. Although the relationship is important, it does not imply that all demands by the other be acceded to — appeasement does not provide the basis for effective working relations. Fisher & Brown (1988) propose that what is essential is a viable process for dealing with differences, one 'involving reason, understanding, communication, reliability, noncoercive means of influence and reliability' (p 21–2).

Using these strategic guidelines it is possible to separate two broad activity areas: those for dealing with people, and those for dealing with problems.

Dealing with people

Understanding

Misunderstandings of the nature of a problem or the other party's perception of it are a common obstacle to achieving accords. They arise out of poor communications, incorrect information, incorrect assumptions, ignorance, fears of loss

of face or position in a dispute. Fisher & Brown (1989) suggest
several steps to improve understanding between parties:

❏ Explore their thinking to ensure sensitisation to real perceptions rather than your assumptions.
❏ Always assume a need to know more.
❏ Start by asking 'what do they care about?' — what are
   their interests, perceptions and values in relation to issues
   and our relationship?
❏ Overcome fears of new learning that entrench positions
   and lock people in outdated or incorrect preconceptions
   or date.
❏ Be open and confident in receiving and/or looking for
   new information and understanding.
❏ Learn their story.

Fisher & Ury (1981) in similar vein suggest that people open
up their thinking to better grasp the perceptions and emotions of the other party. In this regard they suggest:

❏ Empathy: put yourself in their shoes.
❏ Don't deduce their intentions from your fears.
❏ Don't blame them for your problems.
❏ Discuss each other's perceptions and look for oppor-
   tunities to behave inconsistently with their incorrect pre-
   conceptions.

A small company and a trade union negotiating a procedural
agreement became locked into a dispute over the number of
shop stewards that could be elected. The union demanded
that at least six shop stewards should be elected. The company strongly resisted this on the grounds that as there were
only 30 workers this would result in each steward having a
constituency of five. Matters became embittered. The union
vigorously opposed the idea that management should have
any say in how many shop stewards they might elect, and the
company proposed that the demand was irrational and sus-

pected that it was designed to stall the process. Behind this was suspicion that it was an attempt to get extra leave for as many workers as possible for purposes of union training, a motivation the union strongly denied. With the assistance of a mediator the company was able to think through some of the reasons the union might want so many elected representatives. If normal criteria were used only one shop steward would have been elected. This would have resulted in a very lonely exchange for this individual in meetings with management. The union was clearly concerned less about the size of constituencies than that it should have a decent sized negotiating team that would not undermine feelings of strength in meetings. With this new understanding of worker motives, the management team was able to put forward proposals that allowed for a larger union team for purposes of negotiation and to secure assurances as regards its own fears.

With regard to emotions Fisher and Ury propose:

❑ Understand emotions — theirs and yours.
❑ Make emotions explicit and acknowledge them as legitimate.
❑ Allow the other side to let off steam.
❑ Don't react to emotional outbursts.
❑ Use symbolic gestures.

Fisher & Brown (1988) conclude:

> . . . we can overcome the common barriers to better understanding in our working relationships by pursuing three unconditionally constructive steps: explore their thinking, be open to learning, and use tools to break into their world. Each of these steps can be taken unconditionally without concern that the other side will gain or benefit from our unilateral action. Every effort we make to understand those with whom we deal is good for us, and good for the relationship, whether or not they follow suit.' (p 83).

Communication

Efficient communication is basic to a working relationship.

> Good communication need not indicate friendship. Communicating effectively with those with whom we have fundamental disagreements is more difficult but more important than communicating with those we like.' (Fisher & Brown 1988, p 85).

Communicating is a complex process involving verbal, tonal and nonverbal signals, and conveying meaning of both an informational and emotional nature. This subject is explored in greater depth in chapter 6, but Fisher and his colleagues identify some important barriers to effective interaction and some remedies in their work.

They propose three major barriers to effective communication:

❑ an assumption that there is no need to talk;
❑ a tendency to communicate in one direction — to 'tell';
❑ sending of mixed messages conveying ambiguous and inconsistent values; emotions and beliefs, sometimes owing to the mixed audiences or constituencies people report to.

Fisher & Ury (1981) and Fisher and Brown (1988) suggest several steps to improve communications including:

❑ *speaking in a manner which ensures understanding* by the other;
❑ *speaking about yourself* rather than the other;
❑ *speaking purposefully.*
❑ *Always consult before deciding* (ACBD)to promote understanding, help balance emotion with reason, to avoid perceptions of coercion, and to promote two-way communication, acceptance and reliability.
❑ *Listen actively* to engage the other person meaningfully and promote understanding and direct constructive responses.

❑ *Plan the communication process to minimise mixed messages.*
Various steps proposed here include clarifying purpose
and being honest about ambivalence; using privacy to
minimise the problem of multiple audiences; planning
ahead how to deal with difficult questions or creating
forums to promote efficient exchange.

Communication is the lifeblood of a working relationship
. . . we can always find ways to improve it . . . but the
simplest and most power- ful rule of thumb is to consult the
relationship partner. Really consult. Ask advice before
making a decision — and listen carefully.' (Fisher & Brown
1988, p 106).

Rationality

Emotions are an integral part of all relationships, affecting our
thinking and behaviour. They have the potential both to
facilitate and to damage people's capacity to deal with difference. Affection and empathy can motivate a settlement of
differences, but so can anxiety and frustration. By the same
token logical thinking may be impaired by strong anger, grief
or fear. A balance of emotional arousal is required — too little
and there is no motivation to get to grips with a problem; too
much and one's capacity to do so effectively is impaired.

Fisher & Brown (1988) propose four ways of achieving a
balance in emotion and reason for purposes of establishing a
working relationship:

❑ *Develop an awareness of emotions — ours and theirs*: by sensitising to verbal and nonverbal signals of emotional arousal. This requires conscious practice and training in
observation. Check out ambiguity through questioning of
the other to ascertain your
interpretation is correct.

❑ *Don't react emotionally — take charge of behaviour*: simple
awareness of emotions may not be enough to control
behaviour. Sudden threat may evoke emotional reactions

which transcend rationality, as may deeply entrenched learned behaviours such as aggression which may have been socially reinforced over a lifetime. Taking an adjournment or delaying a response to reevaluate circumstances may be useful in resisting impulsive expression.

❏ *Acknowledge emotions*: it is hard to conceal emotions although social training may caution their expression. Hiding emotions does not allow them to be dealt with and may result in build-ups of resentment and anger. Again the inhibition of supportive emotions constrains the development of positive relations. Fisher & Brown suggest that feelings be acknowledged, expressed, talked about and used purposefully in relationships. Where outbursts have occurred people should take responsibility for them and apologise in a threat-free manner.

❏ *Prepare for emotions before they arise*: anticipating and rehearsing events may prevent surprise emotional reactions to events. Anticipation of this sort may include preparing for one's own reactions as well as likely reactions from the other party.

Finally, Fisher & Brown propose efforts be made to 'recruit' constructive emotions such as security, optimism and confidence in oneself and acceptance, respect and concern in the other. Emotions such as insecurity, hopelessness, rejection and hostility tend to damage or blunt the relationship.

> the injunction to be rational is not a prescription to reject emotions, or to ignore or suppress them, but rather to think about them, exercise control over how we express them, and enlist them. In any relationship, being honest about emotions, discussing them candidly, and dealing with them jointly will enhance an ability to deal with conflicts and problems — rational and emotional — that are bound to occur. Preserving a balance between emotion and reason is unconditionally constructive.' (Fisher & Brown 1988, p 63).

Reliability

Trust is commonly recognised as an important but elusive component of good working relations. Attention must be centred in creating a trust that is well founded and balanced. Inappropriate trust is as dangerous as inappropriate suspicion. Fisher & Brown (1988) propose that the key element in creating a trust-based relationship is reliability on the part of both parties.

Starting on the premise that a party has reasonable control only over himself really, these authors propose that parties should look first to their *own levels of reliability*. In this regard Fisher & Brown suggest some self analysis:

❏ Is our conduct erratic?
❏ Do we communicate carelessly?
❏ Do we treat promises lightly?
❏ Are we deceptive or dishonest?

They propose some important remedies:

❏ Be predictable.
❏ Be clear.
❏ Take promises seriously.
❏ Be honest while having the integrity to retain appropriate confidentiality.

In brief Fisher & Brown (1988) advocate that each party should devote energy to becoming wholly trustworthy in a relationship.

Parfitt's (1989; 1990) research into strikes in the Eastern Cape indicates that over 85 % of industrial action by workers in the area is unlawful and non-procedural. This has seriously eroded trust levels, so that employers accuse trade unions of failing to live out agreements and honour contracts, of being unreliable or even deliberately subversive of relations. Unionists on the other hand have countered that employers show gross inconsistency in applying procedures, favouring workers with skills, especially white personnel. They argue that spontaneous strikes are often a response to employer inconsistency or unreliability, and that employer breaches of contracts tend to be merely less visible than the strike response evoked. Clearly, reliability is an issue of major concern in labour–management relations in the area, and a reminder that contracts and procedures are insufficient for industrial conflict regulation. The relationship is the grease which allows the consitutional machine to operate.

A major obstacle to settling a factional dispute was rooted in one group's perception that the other could not be trusted to live out an agreement — that in due course it would be subject to an 'interpretational twist' against their interests, or some reason would be found to declare the agreement invalid. This was eventually brought into the open when the mediator suggested writing the agreement down and signing it. When the other party resisted, on the basis of lacking a mandate, it confirmed the fears of this group and their perception that the other party could not be trusted. With some assistence parties were able to recognise that a written agreement should not be used to trap another into a position, but likewise the exercise showed they had not in fact reached an agreement, and it was dangerously misleading for them to pretend that they had. A party anxious for settlement may 'read' into discussions the agreements it wishes for — and then accuse the other of reneging on positions it had in reality only indicated a willingness to consider. A cycle of distrust and disappointed expectations is set in motion.

Dealing with the reliability of the other party is a more difficult task. Here Fisher & Brown (1988) again suggest that parties look first to their own behaviour — are they encouraging unreliable behaviour by overloading trust, trusting too

little, and overharsh judgements. They suggest several steps
to promote reliability on the part of another:

❑ Do not overload trust; act to reduce risks.

❑ Trust when the other party deserves it.

❑ Give praise and blame precisely (not generally).

❑ Treat problem behaviour as a joint problem, not a crime;
— look forward not back.

❑ Focus on behaviour rather than people.

The basic cautions are to be careful in assessments of other's
conduct as unreliable, as there may be quite valid reasons for
apparent inconsistencies, and to avoid generalising isolated
incidents to all levels of the other's behaviour.

Fisher & Brown (1988) suggest that *trust be based on risk
analysis rather than on moral judgement.* People may be unreliable in different ways, for different reasons. Deceit rooted in
hostile intentions is not the same as unreliability in an honest
yet conflictual relationship.

In essence these authors suggest that negotiators endeavour to be wholly trustworthy but not wholly trusting, and
propose that they endeavour to establish systems that will
promote reliability, that is, jointly acceptable systems of operation with legitimated sanctions.

Persuasion, not coercion

Just as my ability to negotiate with someone is affected by
the quality of our relationship, so the quality of the relationship is affected by the way I negotiate. How we try to
influence each other has a significant impact on the ability
to deal with future differences' (Fisher & Brown 1988,
p 132)

Coercion damages working relationships, inhibiting mutual
understanding and trust as emotions of anger and frustration
are evoked. Agreements emerging from coercive relations are
likely to lack a commitment from the subjugated partner as

they will probably have ignored his interests and his capacity to contribute creatively to its content.

Coercive tactics are characterised by:

❑ a tendency to attack people rather than problems;
❑ a perception that the negotiation is a contest rather than a problem-solving exercise;
❑ premature commitments to position;
❑ a focus on positions rather than interests;
❑ simple either/or rather than multiple option approaches;
❑ efforts to break the will of the other party rather than persuade on the basis of fairness; and
❑ threats of sanctions for failure to comply rather than improving options by looking for alternatives.

Acceptance

Effective conflict regulation and dispute settlement demand that parties accord each other legitimacy, and that they legitimate the procedures, institutions and forums they will use to resolve their differences (Deutsch 1973).

> No amount of rational thinking, clear understanding, accurate communication, trustworthy behaviour, or persuasive influence will build a working relationship if each side rejects the other as unworthy of dialogue. (Fisher & Brown, 1988, p 149)

Refusing to legitimate or accept the other party obliges the use of coercive tactics at the same time as it produces a situation of increased emotionalism and closes doors on the exchange of information between the parties which might contribute to a settlement. A refusal to accept the legitimacy of another contributes to all the negative aspects of conflict escalation discussed in chapter 2: negative stereotyping, attribution of moral blameworthiness, selective information induction, decreased communication, deindividuation. South Africa's interest groupings have a long history of mutual intolerance which has proven a major contributor to the country's levels of conflict and violence. Examples are numerous — SATS' refusal to accept SARHWU; government's refusal to accept the legitimacy of the ANC; the ANC's reluctance to acknowledge Buthelezi and Inkatha, to name a few.

Fisher & Brown (1988) suggest:

❏ Unconditionally accept the other party as a legitimate partner — not to be confused with acceptance of objectionable behaviour.

❏ Show concern, and a willingness to listen and work together in a problem-solving relationship.

❏ For purposes of a working relationship others' values or perceptions do not have to be accepted as correct, nor does their behaviour have to be approved of.

❏ Deal with respect: look behind stereotypes to deal with the real people.

❏ Give others' interests the weight they deserve.

Importantly, Fisher & Brown (1988) attend to the dilemmas of acceptance. They note that, while it positively opens channels for joint problem solving, improved understanding and communication, it may also be seen to reward unacceptable behaviours (such as violence), and encourage more. They propose that if a constructive working relationship is to be achieved, this implies also limitations on peoples' expectations. Acceptance in itself should therefore not be seen as a concession, but should be general policy in dealing with others. It does not imply a contamination of values or interests to engage with those we do not like, nor a weakening of bargaining power. Fisher & Brown see withholding of acceptance as a negative tactic:

> . . . bargaining over acceptance is like bargaining over an apology. The longer it is held back, the less valuable it becomes. Like an apology acceptance is constructive when given, not when withheld. (p 165)

Withholding acceptance promotes distrust and coercive exchanges and precludes creative problem-solving initiatives.

Dealing with problems

Focus on interests, not positions

Fisher & Ury (1981) suggest that conflict really lies not in positions, but in conflicting needs, fears, desires and concerns. There are often more solutions than reflected in a single position — behind opposed positions lie shared and compatible interests, not only conflicting ones. They propose:

❑ Identifying the interests of the parties.
❑ Realise that each has multiple interests — basic human needs being the most powerful.
❑ List interests.
❑ Talk specifically and clearly about interests.
❑ Acknowledge others' interests as part of the problem.
❑ Put problems before answers.
❑ Look forward not back.
❑ Be concrete but flexible.
❑ Be hard on problems, soft on people.
❑ Be firm and open.

In a wage mediation the parties had taken firm positions, resulting in a deadlock, with the union demanding a R40 per week increase across the board, and the company offering R30. Each felt that it had moved more significantly and that the other should therefore concede. This resulted in increased intransigence and soured relations. In private caucus the company indicated that it was under serious trading pressure and that it was terribly important that no industrial action be experienced as it was peak season for consumption of its product. While sales volumes were good, falling prices had seriously reduced profit margins, and it was now vitally important to contain costs and maintain volumes and market share. The company indicated that it could increase its offer by R2 across the board, but was reluctant to put this on the table unless there was an indication that it would be accepted — there was a fear that the union would simply hold out and continue to demand more. If the union reduced its demand to R34 they would feel more confident in re-initiating the trading process.

The union indicated that there was no way that it could come down to R34 — the previous year an increase of R35 had been achieved and union members expected no less this year, particularly in light of harder work to achieve increased volumes. In addition union members had become aware that non-unionised workers in the lower grades were receiving much higher wages in a depot of the company in a neighbouring town. This was perceived as clear evidence of union bashing. Lower grade workers were aware of this discrepancy and this was where the major consituency pressure was being experienced.

Through this discussion the mediator helped the parties identify the key interests underlying their stated positions. By talking about their pressures, fears and needs, the parties were able to move away from the thinking which had entrapped them to this point, to make proposals which would be responsive to each other's priorities.

Invent options for mutual gain
Fisher & Ury observe that agreement is often blocked by limited diagnosis of problems and conflict situations.

Obstacles to effective diagnosis include:
- premature judgement;
- searching for *the* single answer in the form of splitting the difference between positions;
- assumptions of a 'fixed pie' which limits resolution to competitive tactics; and
- thinking that says 'it's *their* problem'.

They suggest that creative options must be invented and propose several guidelines in this regard:

❑ Do not confuse option invention with option evaluation.
❑ Broaden options by using experts, inventing agreements of different strengths, changing the scope of proposed agreements.
❑ Look for mutual gain by identifying shared interests, dovetailing differing interests, or asking the other party about its preferences
❑ Make the other party's decisions easy by understanding problems in the other's terms.

Insist on objective criteria

Realistically, the authors of negotiating on the merits point out that win–win solutions are unlikely — conflicts of interest will remain. However deciding issues on the basis of contest of wills is costly. They suggest that solutions should be sought on the basis of principles rather than pressure, and that the parties be open to reason but closed to threats. Techniques to establish objective principles include:

❑ developing fair standards and procedures for solution searches;
❑ framing each issue as a joint search for objective criteria; and
❑ openness to reason.

Returning to the example used above, the mediator was able to use the signals of core interests to help the parties explore alternative options. The union acknowledged the business pressures faced by the company, the management team acknowledged that there were inconsistencies in approach to remuneration and that workers in the lower grades faced particular hardship. Within this frame an active solution search was initiated. The union signalled that it would be amenable to dropping its demand for an increase across the board, and the company indicated that it would have room to improve its offer for lower grade workers if those in higher grades would restrain their demands. Various options were costed and eventually settlement achieved on a wage package which saw lowest paid workers receive a R35 increase, and all others a R31 improvement. By assisting the parties to signal their key interests to each other, the mediator was able to help them leave the positional bargaining approach to establish a broad framework for a settlement search which acknowledged the needs of each. The parties left negotiation with not only a settlement but a greater understanding of each other's pressures and a relationship which had not had to endure the stress of a direct power confrontation.

BATNA

Fisher and Ury (1981) note that if all the leverage lies with the other side a party should seek to protect itself against entering an agreement which should be rejected, and to make the most of assets which it does have to meet its interests to the best extent possible. The fall-back position is one means of protecting interests, but these authors warn that it limits imagination and may prohibit acceptance of terms that should be accepted in the light of new information — that is, they produce rigidity. In place of the fall-back position they suggest the BATNA (Best Alternative to a Negotiated Agreement), that is, the standard against which any proposal should be measured. It is a protection against accepting unfavourable terms and not accepting favourable ones. A BATNA is developed by exploring what you will do if you fail to reach agreement. Planning is further assisted by thinking through the other side's BATNA. Depending on the process it may sometimes be wise for parties to advise each other of their BATNAs to assist in reality appraisal. Thus an alternative given to an intransigent liberation front in the Rhodesian conflict by the British was the recognition of the Smith/Muzorewa government — this prompted a shift in position by Mugabe and Nkomo and facilitated a settlement.

Fisher & Ury's contribution to negotiation theory is unique — it bridges distributive and integrative approaches to conflict resolution. 'Negotiating on the merits' recognises that conflicts of interest do occur, and that win–win outcomes may be unlikely. Attention is given to power realities (although somewhat weakly), and the use of dirty tactics by the other party. In this sense, the approach differs from the purely problem-solving techniques associated with integrative bargaining. However, tactics suggested by Fisher & Ury borrow heavily from this body of theory. In a sense their approach is an attempt to provide an alternative to distributive or competitive approaches — it represents an effort to create interest based cooperative joint efforts towards conflict resolution in competitive situations.

DE BONO'S DESIGN APPROACH

Like other critics of the positional approach, De Bono (1985) proposes that argument-based forms of negotiation are inadequate for purposes of conflict solving. Clash of ideas seldom produces synergistic solutions, rather it produces 'grudging compromise or retreat from a position' (p 19). It produces rigidity in thinking, directs the creativity and ingenuity of parties toward defeating opposing ideas rather than improving them, and ends in the adoption of answers that are not necessarily better, but merely more strongly expressed. Argument, he suggests, tends to be used to prove that the other party is wrong, stupid, ignorant or untrustworthy; to impress others; or to set the emotional climate for negotiation. More positively it may be used to oblige exploration of a matter, to cast doubt on certainty and to bring about new insights. However, De Bono feels that these positive results are seldom the consequence of argument, and he proposes the exploration idiom as a more effective approach whereby existing ideas are not attacked (allowing a return later without discredit, should better solutions not be located); a joint and early commitment to creative search and design; no time wastage occurs owing to stand-offs; and an avoidance of your idea vs. my idea competitiveness.

De Bono suggests that traditional approaches to problem solving are also inadequate in the face of complex interactive situations. Logical ordered approaches to cause identification and treatment or removal might suit our needs for rationality and orderliness but they constrain thinking on outcomes and possible ways of getting there.

> Problem solving certainly does have a place in conflict thinking. The main limitation is that we may put too definite a view on what we believe the solution should be before we have really done our thinking about the matter. As soon as we say 'this is the problem' we have defined the sort of solution we expect' (p 41).

Having examined the limitations of both argument based negotiation and problem solving, De Bono advances a *design idiom* for approaching conflict situations.

> With design we set out to design something. There is an output. There is something to be achieved. It is not just a matter of removing a problem or effecting a compromise. There is a designed something which was not there before. With design there is a sense of purpose and a sense of fit. Things are brought together or shaped in order to fulfil some purpose. . . . Argument, negotiation and problem analysis are always looking back at what is already there. Design is always looking forward to what might be created. (p 41)

De Bono initiates his analysis of the design idiom by trying to locate *reasons for disagreement* between people. He ascribes these to mood, the context of a conflict, limited views and differing logics, perceptions, circumstances and exposures, universes and information. Beyond this generalised behavioural styles, rigid adherence to principles, competing values and beliefs, and the adoption of slogans act to constrain paths of creative thought and lock people into conflict as opposed to design outcomes. De Bono proposes that people's need for consistency, truth and logic and the accompanying emotionalisation of thinking blocks creative approaches to conflict resolution. Instead of looking for new and novel 'fit' in situations of contradiction, people find security in the simplistic 'either ... or' choices that such contradictions seem to demand. 'If we are obsessed by the principle of contradiction, then we are condemned to the negative exclusion type of thinking. We need to escape from this obsession in order to develop the positive constructive type of thinking: the design idiom' (p 73).

The design idiom

Design thinking involves constructive exploration of a situation with the aim of designing an outcome. De Bono likens it to a process of mapmaking, creating a variety of routes and choosing one. In this regard he suggests a variety of simple thinking tools to free people from becoming locked into traditional logic based conflict modes. These include:

- ❏ PMI (Plus–Minus–Interest)
- ❏ C & S (Consequence and Sequel)
- ❏ APC (Alternatives — Possibles — Choices)
- ❏ ADI (Agreement–Disagreement–Irrelevance)
- ❏ OPV (Other People's Views)

De Bono proposes that in the face of the complex multivariate designs of conflicts a process of *un-design* is required, 'unravelling the strands that have come together in this way and seeking to put them together in another way' (p 82). This involves recognising that minor disagreements may lie at the root of major conflicts, perceptions of difference having become exaggerated over time and obscuring alignments of interest on other issues or during different periods of time. Ideologies may start far apart but evolve closer over time, reducing actual polarisation on issues except in the minds of the parties involved. Design tools may be used to explore possibilities of achieving outcomes that accommodate seemingly incompatible views, or that are built on common elements of perceptions, that is, by focusing on areas of agreement rather than disagreement.

Other design efforts:

❑ Attempt to *shift perceptions* so that things are seen differently, and offer conflicting parties new outcomes. In this way conflict situations are broken down into *sub-elements* and then an effort is made to reconstruct them into a new design.

❑ *Leave central conflict points* and focus on working towards resolution of other issues.

❑ Identify desirable end points or outcomes and then *work backwards* to see how these might be arrived at.

❑ Brainstorm *'dream solutions'* as possible outcomes.

❑ Unfreeze thinking by making small *speculative* changes (if *x* were the case then . . .).

❑ Overcome and *remove preconditions* and blocks, design requiring working back into boundaries rather than within them.

❑ *Work down* from broad pictures towards values and objectives rather than vice versa.

❑ Establish a *core principle* and then build outcomes around this.

These are all mapping approaches and can be used with parties who must, while they employ them, agree to forego argument approaches to conflict resolution.

Realistically, De Bono recognises that in situations of intense conflict the parties are often involved in a 'tension of hostility' which they dare not relax for fear of being defeated by the other party. This state prohibits design type thinking and for this reason he suggests that conflict situations require *third-party involvement*. Parties in dispute are, he proposes, in the worst position to resolve the outcome, except through force. De Bono states that 'for the design approach to work there has to be "triangular thinking" and the involvement of a third party' (p 100) who is not so close to the situation as to preclude the evolution of other perceptions or outcomes.

As conflict situations develop, sequences of stances, events, and arguments evolve which progressively lock disputants into constrained methods of viewing their situation structures, concepts and positions produce a continuity trap for each party which impels them onward into inevitable and escalating conflict. The creativity demanded for new outcomes is simply not available to them. De Bono's perception of creativity is that it is a logical rather than a mystical process — it 'is specifically concerned with the ability to escape from existing perceptual (and conceptual) patterns in order to open up new ways of looking at things and doing things' (p 114). Currently held concepts and ideas may actually block the emergence of better concepts demands for logic obscure possibilities of creative new outcomes. 'Concept evolution is not good enough. We need ways of backtracking out of dead-end concepts. We need ways of freeing up elements imprisoned obsolete concepts in order to use them in better designs ... lateral thinking is a more specific term than creativity and is concerned with pattern changing. There is movement instead of judgement' (p 123). Lateral thinking techniques revolve around provocation and movement to elicit new openings and outcomes in deadlocked situations. For De Bono, the third party is not an aid or an addition but integral to the process of design thinking in conflict resolution. The third party is required because parties in conflict are usually 'bogged down by tradition, training and com-

placency in the argument mode of thinking' (p 125) and because their positions in the conflict prohibit certain thinking
operations. The participation of this party allows the development of a triangular thinking mode.

The third party is there to detect and defuse conflict
initiatives; to set the stage for exploration and design exercises; to set and control the agenda; to orchestrate the process;
to define focus. Further, to harvest ideas; provide detached
overviews; indicate connections; review concepts and provide additional alternatives, De Bono proposes the map or
design thinking tool to facilitate the task.

SOME CAUTIONARY THOUGHTS

Alternatives to distributive bargaining have received considerable attention and excited an enthusiastic following in recent years — and deservedly so. However, there are
dynamics at play which these approaches either pay little
heed to or ignore altogether. Of central concern is the somewhat superficial manner in which they deal with the issue of
power. The argument is that efforts are made in these approaches to avoid confrontational exchanges of power between parties, and that the techniques employed are centred
on assisting parties to resolve problems on the basis of fairness or meeting each other's needs, rather than the superior
leverage of one. This has a ring of sincerity about it, but in my
opinion neglects many aspects of the reality of aggravated
conflicts.

What happens, for instance, when the parties have explored each other's interests and the values and needs under-
pinning these, but are unable to find an integrative solution
to their differences? What is the situation when scarce resources limit the range of solutions — is not competition inevitable? From a theoretical perspective scarce resources may be
transitory and not a reflection of deep underlying needs, but

in practice may bear costs or promise rewards that prohibit meaningful application of integrative methods. Arguably meeting the fundamental needs of the oppressed and disenfranchised black population will demand very real substantive sacrifices on the part of white owners of wealth. Further, are no the fears of whites regarding loss of identity, security and opportunity in South Africa likely to be aggravated through the process of meeting black needs for these? Surely meeting such needs demands not only some kind of constitutional guarantees, but access to and control over resources as well? In these terms competition may be the inevitable outcome.

Advocates of integrative approaches will of course criticise these observations as leaping to conclusions before allowing the process a chance to develop options of its own. They will argue that it is precisely such thinking that constrains affective implementation of the approach. This must be acknowledged, but it would be naive to expect negotiators or problem solvers to embark on a process without thinking about what they will do if integrative solutions do not emerge from use of the method. In such instances, one or more of the parties involved may see little option but to return to the competitive approach and the use of power based tactics. One approach that has been developed recently is that of *target-specific bargaining* (Power 1991) which advocates an information-based, problem-solving orientation phase to collective bargaining, but acknowledges that final process may remain competitive in character. In effect it attempts to remove the 'dishonesty' of bluff, and crude confrontational tactics from the interaction so that by the time interests competition is embarked on, the battle field has been considerably reduced in size, and relations between the parties are sufficiently trusting to avoid serious intent to damage or destroy each other. It represents an attempt to recognise the values of an

integrative approach at the same time as it recognises the
realities of distributive relations. As Coser (1957) noted so
early in the development of the field, relations are characterised by a tension between cooperative and conflictual
tendencies — the future may lie in developing approaches
which more clearly acknowledge both these tendencies.

The question of competing interests and scarce resources
may not then have been adequately thought through in mainstream integrative approaches at present. Similarly they may
not have given sufficient consideration to issues of power,
role and group structure in conflictual relations. Use of alternative negotiation methods may evoke considerable changes
in traditional power relations, leadership requirements and
group resources, cohesiveness and structure. The incapacity
of the parties to meet these demands may have the consequence of resistance to the approach, collapsing well-inten-
tioned initiatives. Fundamental needs of identity, security
and development, in other words, may be seen to have
greater opportunity of being met through continued adversarialism than through conflict resolution for one or more of
the parties involved.

In a labour–management dispute on wages, the employer
(offering a 17 % increase) and the union (demanding a 35 %
increase) agreed to refer the matter to mediation. A long
history of blunt confrontation was evident, including lockouts and dismissals and poor shopfloor relations. The company opened by removing its 17 % offer from the table and
stating that losses over the period had been so severe that
closure of the factory might be required, a situation aggravated by a very high level of 'shrinkage' of stock. Rather than
talk about specific wage proposals, they would be prepared
to discuss new creative means of repairing relations and
saving the business in the interests of all. In this respect they
would be prepared to provide full disclosure of information

to the union through an agreed auditor, and on the basis of this enter a more participative way of managing the business involving the union. Workers aggressively rejected this when their representatives mooted the idea. When asked about the possible closure of the firm they said 'it serves them right'. The union, when it was pointed out to them that there seemed to be a choice between unemployment and one of the most enlightened agreements in the country, confessed that it was taken by surprise by the offer, that despite demanding such practices for years, now that a concrete offer was on the table it did not know how to deal with it, and in fact had no policy position on the question.

Assuming that the problem was one of surprise and that workers were understandably resistant to the offer of something rather more vague than a wage offer somewhere between 17 % and 35 % which they had been expecting, the mediator adjourned the meeting for ten days. In the interim the union had time to discuss issues with members, and on meeting again an agreement was signed providing for a 10 % increase with a further increase of 7 % in 6 months' time and should the company achieve profitability over the last three months of this period, a further increase of 7 %. Full disclosure to an auditor acceptable to the union with a report back to workers immediately and in 6 months time was agreed, and so was a commitment to utilise this information to set up new joint structures to tackle obstacles to profitability in the company, and organisational and industrial relations problems. The first disclosure exercise was arranged, and the agreed auditor conducted the exercise over two days performing a thorough examination of the company's business situation. When the exercise had been completed, the union simply failed to turn up for the arranged report back — active resistance being replaced by passive resistance.

What would have sparked such resistance in the face of clearly sincere efforts by the company to respond to worker demands, and to establish more acceptable/participative management systems?

Once one has finished with considerations of the history of relations, a lack of trust in relations, and the surprise element, another factor must be attended to — the shift in power relations. Some understanding may be provided by Mulder's (1977) theory of *power distance*. Mulder makes the following propositions (adapted and shortened):

❑ The mere exercise of power gives satisfaction.
❑ More powerful parties strive to increase power distance from less powerful ones, this striving growing as the distance grows greater.
❑ Less powerful parties strive to reduce power distance, the tendency growing stronger as the inequality is reduced.
❑ The tendency to power distance reduction on the part of less powerful parties increases regardless of recent improvements of position.
❑ In reality, as the power gap closes, costs increase more sharply than benefits.
❑ More participation in decision making increases rather than reduces power distance.
❑ Crises in social systems demand leaders capable of exerting strong exercise of power and showing self confidence.
❑ When leaders exercise power forcefully, people ascribe self-confidence to them.
❑ When less powerful persons find they have greater self-confidence than more powerful ones, the tendency to reduce the power distance increases.
❑ Parties perceiving themselves midway between the powerful and the powerless show strong tendencies to reduce power distance.

❑ Efforts by the powerful to increase power distance and by the less powerful to reduce it reinforce each other.

❑ Where less powerful parties perceive the gap to be too large to be reduced and desist from reduction efforts, they tend to show other tendencies such as solidarity with other powerless parties.

❑ Those who no longer strive to reduce the power distance may refuse to follow the powerful any further and resist (non-cooperation).

❑ A unified, and well organised group of the powerless achieves power and behaves accordingly in terms of tendencies toward power distance reduction.

Several of these propositions may have relevance to the case described, allowing the following hypothesis. Workers in their relatively powerless situation joined a collectivity (the union), and from this base mobilised for improvements in conditions. Management in turn resisted this seeking to maintain the power distance. The actions reinforced each other resulting in confrontational behaviour to the extent that the survival of the social system (the company) was threatened. At this point motivation to experiment with alternatives to existing relations increased and the offer for disclosure and participation was made, in effect reducing the power distance. At this juncture the paradox becomes apparent — as the distance appears to be reduced, it in fact increases. Suddenly the union, and workers, are faced with demands for a range of knowledge, skills and responsibilities for which they are ill-prepared. Participation requires a move beyond adversarialism to shared responsibilities, and concrete proposals for making things work rather than stopping them. Challengers must suddenly adapt to roles of contribution. Workers and their representatives are faced with understanding and responding to balance sheets, income and expenditure statements, market projections, cash flows, budgets, and decisions regarding distribution of profits.

Workers and their representatives (save in a few instances) are ill-equipped for this terrain where the skills of mobilisation and disruption must give way to discussions about business complexities. In other words, the offer of participation and disclosure moves the exchange onto the terrain of management where the MBAs, the CAs and the engineers and production graduates hold force by virtue of their education and training. The inadequacies of workers in this area may be cruelly exposed — thus just as the power gap appears to be reduced, so it increases.

If this was the process which occurred in the case described, then the behaviour of workers may be more easily understood. The sudden shift of strategy by management shifted the power balance in an unexpected way, in defiance of the tradition of adversarialism demanding new behaviours and skills of the (to now) adversary. A sense of the underlying reality of disempowerment may have resulted in worker resistance in its various forms. The apparently irrational behaviour in the face of the sudden willingness of the old adversary to be open and reasonable does then reflect some rationale. It is the ultimate trump — the powerless must now explain why reasonableness, joint decision-making and openness are not sufficient to end resistance. They must either appear irrational or confess their powerlessness.

The old resistance to 'cooptation' is not sufficient in this new game of 'getting to yes', because it is played in many instances far more genuinely by the power holder. On a more cynical level it could be argued that the approach may have attraction for some in that, rather than attempting to trip the other party with rigged forums, or weighted boards of control, there is a sense of certainty that it will fall down by itself through its own incompetence or naivete, and that leaders unable to meet constituency expectations in the context of the realities they must now work, will discredit themselves or find their constituencies divided.

A complex shift in power relativities may then be concealed by the apparent objectivity, reasonableness and openness of the alternative bargaining approach. As Zartman (1985) has noted, some groups are structured solely for purposes of fight. Adjustment of goals is not possible without collapsing the group. Canny negotiators may then utilise the approach to disempower an opposition whose only skill is one of adversarialism, appearing reasonable and fair in doing so. Because the power distance element is not discussed openly in the theory and because the approach is so overtly reasonable, the fundamental power imbalances in the engagement are often concealed in the process and the powerless group not only has its state confirmed but appears unreasonable if it resists.

Some thought must clearly be given to applying this critique to the engagement between the South African government and the ANC at the time of writing. President De Klerk, through his moves in dismantling apartheid and in the face of risks of white resistance to the release of opposition leaders and the unbanning of and engaging with their parties, has achieved very rapidly an unprecedented level of international acceptance and opened the door to a peaceful solution to the nation's longstanding crisis. However, this very shift to reasonableness from crude confrontation has arguably acted to weaken rather than strengthen opposition groups. They must suddenly transform themselves into a political party from a liberation movement, rhetoric must give way to concrete proposals on matters economic and political, consistency must be shown by leaders across public platforms, a unity of vision and values is expected — these transformations have to the time of writing not been successfully completed. Thus as De Klerk has improved his power, so has the opposition lost some. It would not be inconceivable if, with a sense of this opposition groups attempted to regain some of the old solidarity and apparent strength of mass resistance campaigns, but the game will have changed in terms of external support. The old adversary has transformed into a being against whom it might be perceived to be grossly unreasonable to resist.

To this point it might be thought that this critique has been something of an indictment of the alternative approaches and to the extent that they do not properly explore the possibilities and consequences of power shifts and the implications for negotiations, it is. The criticism lies in failing to explain the process fully so that well intentioned (rather then strategic) negotiators may find themselves faced with apparently irrational responses to their efforts which their 'motherhood and apple pie' manuals do not explain in any way.

There can be no escape from the fact that power inequalities are part of social living. These cannot be concealed by cooperative rather than competitive approaches to negotiation which may actually aggravate power differentials.

This critique is however, insufficient to discredit these approaches. They still represent in many ways a less devious, more open and more objective approach than competitive approaches which lend themselves to blunt power exchanges and misrepresentation. As such they may reflect more honest efforts to respond to problems in terms of parties' needs and interests than leverage based approaches at any given moment in time. Brinkmanship, bluff, concealment, dishonesty, direct pressure tactics may be diminished in relations which can move to addressing core needs and interests on the basis of shared information and concerns, and jointly identified problems.

With regard to the question of power, further discussion is warranted. If a party is assuming a more open, reasonable approach than in the past, is this not more desireable? If this reveals a lack of preparation, skills or knowledge on the part of the other, is it not that party's duty to acknowledge this reality in the context of the relationship at a given time and respond accordingly? Are power inequalities alone sufficient to excuse confrontational responses to reasonable gestures from the other? If the ANC seeks to govern, is it not reasonable to expect greater coherence, vision and organisation before it achieves power? If trade unions wish to control or share control over industry, is it not reasonable to expect a higher level of competence in understanding the business process? Equally, however, it must be acknowledged that a current power holder may also not have a coherent vision to offer, but the fact of power possession may allow this to be disguised and a degree of control over the interaction exerted which the weaker party cannot match.

This critique then, does not seek to discredit the alternative approaches to negotiation, but rather to progress the debate as to their application. It is proposed here that the issue of power and competitiveness in relations requires greater attention and a more overt place in the theory of integrative endeavour than it seems to have been accorded thus far. Only in this way can the associated dilemmas and obstacles to effective practice be properly addressed.

6

PERSUASIVE COMMUNICATION — THE BASIC SKILL

Persuasion is the central purpose of the negotiation process, communication the medium through which this is achieved. Parties are usually concerned with using the interaction to move others to viewpoints and positions more closely approximating their own, or to improve mutual understanding for purposes of problem solving.

THE COMMUNICATION PROCESS

Communication generates understanding, spreads information, provides negotiators with a means for assessing the social reality of each other's expectations, is the vehicle for shaping attitudes and behaviour between and within the party's teams, and is the means for achieving the core objective of the negotiation or problem solving process - agreement (Douglas 1979; Heap 1977). Four major functions of the communication process have been identified for negotiators by Tedeschi and Lindskold (1976):

❑ *discovery* to ascertain information regarding the values and preferences of others;
❑ *disguise* of one's own values and preferences;
❑ *manipulation* of others' behaviour; and
❑ *relationshipshaping,* such as the degree of trust or attraction the parties invest in each other.

People use a variety of means to transmit their thoughts, and feelings to one another — language or verbal communications, non-verbal signals such as facial or bodily expressions, semi-verbal signals such as expressive sounds, laughter or sighs, and written or symbolic media such as letters, posters and placards.

Bales (1950) noted that communications might be of a *task-oriented* nature as people ask for or give suggestions, opinions, directions or information, or of a *social-emotional* nature in which case they might be positive (giving help, raising other's status, relieving tension, agreeing, accepting or complying) or negative (disagreeing, passively rejecting, withholding help, showing tension, withdrawing, antagonism, defending or asserting oneself often through efforts to deflate the status of others) in character.

Basically the communication process comprises the transmitter of a message, the message itself and the receiver thereof, and is characterised by a complex combination of verbal signals, facial expressions, tones of voice, and bodily stances. Effective communication demands organised thought, clear expression and focused listening.

Several assumptions can be made about communication as a transactive process (Gaw and Sayer 1979):

❑ It occurs within and is influenced by a situation.
❑ Each communicator continually creates and interprets words and actions.
❑ Each has an effect on and is affected by the other.
❑ Any communication factor can be seen as a cause or effect depending on the perspective taken.

In effect, then communication between people is a complex, changing and continuous process to which each of the participants brings his own unique background of life experiences and consequent ideas, beliefs, intentions, feelings and behavioural predilictions. Thus individuals find themselves in interactive exchanges with sets of expectations of each other and the interaction itself, and sets of behavioural skills which will facilitate or inhibit their intended communication.

Previously established ways of thinking (cognitions) and feeling (affects) act as a screen through which messages are transmitted and interpreted, and act to influence the manner in which each sends signals to the other.

It is always a revelation to me in negotiation skills training how many newcomers to the process arrive with strong preconceived notions of what negotiation involves. Quite often they believe that that they will be facing hostile or radical opponents whose trustworthiness will be low, and whose primary intent is to trick, subvert or coerce them into submission. Early simulations are quite often conducted with a level of aggression and suspicion which exceeds the norm of real-life exchanges. Preconceived notions as to the nature of negotiation and the character of bargaining partners may then translate into quite inappropriate behaviour, based not on experience in the first instance, but a series of stereotypes. If the other party then responds in like vein the exchange may quickly establish itself as one of hostility and aggression. It is terribly important therefore, that negotiators be aware of the stereotypes and biases which they carry with them, and of the implications these have for the issues to be bargained and the relationships to be established and utilised for this purpose.

Figure 6.1 illustrates the complex interplay of cognitions (thoughts), affects (feelings) and behaviours in the communication process. The moment two parties face each other in a process of message exchange, each becomes a receiver as well as a sender of interpersonal signals. Party 1 may wish to impart a message to Party 2, but this is not blandly or mechanically carried out. He brings with him the baggage of attitudes and behavioural skills learned from past experiences. He may lack verbal skills or abilities to control non-verbal behaviour. His personal feelings may be unclear to him, or he may be anxious about the message to be transmitted. He has

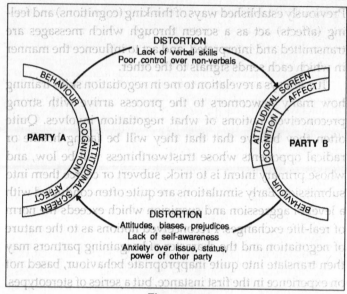

Figure 6.1
The basic communication process

to translate or encode the information he carries into a mutually understandable series of verbal and non-verbal signals to convey it to the other effectively. In facing Party 2 he looks at her in an effort to interpret her level of interest, mood, attitude to himself, her status and receptivity to the intended message. This interpretation is carried out, correctly or incorrectly, on the basis of the other party's appearance, and such behaviours as eye contact, facial or bodily expressions, and verbal or semi-verbal signals. These are interpreted through the screen of thoughts, feelings and expectations with which he arrived. A similar process of interpretation is being conducted by the other party.

Clearly, a great deal can go wrong in such exchanges -messages may be poorly transmitted or interpreted, the ur-

gency, mood and receptivity of the other party may be misunderstood, there may be disortions of communication
owing to pre-existing stereotypes or biases.

IMPROVING COMMUNICATIONS

A wide variety of techniques have been proposed for improving communications. These can be summarised into several
main categories:

❑ Establish a listening environment.
❑ Improve the communication climate.
❑ Improve listening skills.
❑ Improve skills in message transmission.
❑ Increasing levels of self awareness
❑ Understand communication networks.
❑ General techniques.

Establish a listening environment

Consideration must be given to creating or locating an environment that will be conducive to effective listening and
communication in all negotiations. Such factors as seating,
distracting noises and activity should be attended to if participants are to retain a level of alertness and attentiveness.

In a negotiation in a rural dairy where the buildings were
next to the railway line to facilitate transportation of produce,
trying to maintain a focused and businesslike climate for
wage negotiations was a nightmare. At critical moments, with
both parties attempting to convey the seriousness of the
situation through their eye contact, earnest expressions, and
pointed comments, the milk train would rumble past — so
close that the building shook and nothing could be heard in
the room until the train had passed. Try 'holding the moment'
for several minutes while you stare at each other across a
shaking table, the pictures trembling on the wall, and no
audible communication possible! The climax of this particu-

lar negotiation occurred when management determined that it would make a 'final offer', and that this should be conveyed in such a way that the union could not possibly misread the seriousness of intent. As the director of the company (flown specially from Johannesburg for the task) completed his wrap up speech and prepared to make the final offer, a large herd of lowing and mooing cows clattered across the courtyard outside the office for milking. Needless to say, the climate was never quite achieved.

Interruptions from anxious secretaries, telephone calls to union officials relating to disputes in other factories, and urgent calls from the production line do not create an efficient communication environment, and steps should be taken to ensure that such disruptions are reduced to an absolute minimum.

Improve the negotiation climate

It is not only the physical environment that requires attention in negotiations, but the bargaining climate, which may be seen as the general psychological or emotional state of the relationship. The climate might range from defensive to accepting in character. Typically *defensive/punitive* climates inhibit free flows of communication, and produce hostile or apathetic exchanges. They are induced by communications which are evaluative, controlling, or strategic in nature and which reflect attitudes of carelessness, superiority or certainty. These tend to carry messages of blame or judgement, often disguised in the form of unasked for advice or analysis. *Supportive/accepting* climates on the other hand induce listening, understanding and trust, and promote a willingness to cooperate and provide mutual assistance. Such communication styles are descriptive rather than evaluative, are problem oriented, spontaneous and empathic, and reflect attitudes of equality and provisionalism rather than superiority and certainty. (Douglas 1976; Anstey 1983)

The negotiation climate may be generated by the parties' interaction, their capacities to be honest and sincere, to trust, and their past experiences of each other and other negotiations. Negotiators should analyse the nature of their communications and the effect that these may have on the bargaining climate, and think carefully about the nature of the relationship they desire with the other party. It is suggested here that regardless of the distributive nature of issues on the table for negotiation, some latitude exists as to the climate of the bargaining process, in other words, it is possible to have a trust-based relationship and a positive bargaining climate despite substantive differences of interest.

A service organisation facing a trade union for the first time panicked at the thought of entering a recognition/procedural agreement with the union. A mediator spent considerable time helping the management think through its options — it could use a host of legal technicalities to block the union, or it could play open cards as to the nature of its function, its scarce resources, and its fears as regards strike action in respect of aged patients, acknowledge the place of the union as the freely chosen representative of its employees and try to establish a more open, trust-based relationship from the start. Management was ambivalent. Conservative members of its board of trustees advocated that unions were inherently problematic and sought to avoid it all costs. Others realising that the union might have to be recognised eventually, whatever early legal obstacles were thrown in the way, wanted to start the relationship off in a positive manner. The latter group prevailed and with the realisation that placing obstacles in the path of the union might embitter long-term relations, embarked on recognition discussions. A remarkable process ensued. The parties did not caucus separately once. They openly discussed their needs and interests in relation to contentious clauses together, management confessed its naivete in the field of labour relations and its central concern with the aged patients in the organisation, the union acknowledged that it was dealing with 'patients rather than profits' in this instance, volunteered to forego its right to strike and suggested mediation and arbitration in all cases of dispute whether of interest or right. The parties began to relax in each other's presence. Shortly before signing the agreement, a change of leadership in the board occurred. In the belief that the union could be negated, the new chairman briefed a lawyer to initiate a process of keeping the union out by whatever means possible. A sharp turn in the relationship occurred — the union was reduced to having to fight over the question of its legitimacy and a more hostile climate in relations emerged. Fortunately, with some assistance management revised its thinking again to return to its more open approach, and the parties eventually achieved an agreement acceptable to both of them to regulate relations into the future.

Improve skills in receiving messages (effective listening)

Barker et al (1979) define listening as 'the selective process of attending to, hearing, understanding and remembering aural symbols' (p 211). While hearing only implies that sound waves have been recorded, listening requires understanding. These authors also identify several pitfalls to effective listening:

❑ getting overstimulated or emotionally involved;
❑ preparing to answer questions before fully understanding them;
❑ tolerating or failing to adjust to distractions;
❑ allowing emotionally laden words to interfere with listening; and

❑ permitting personal prejudices or deep-seated convictions to impair comprehension and understanding.

There are several ways to improve listening. These include demonstrating good listening behaviour, increasing self-awareness, understanding defence mechanisms, and focusing on the purpose of the communication.

Demonstrate good listening behaviour

Good faith listening can be demonstrated through such behaviour as 'attending' to the other, showing interest and alertness, establishing and maintaining eye contact, and 'squaring' with a speaker. Effective listeners avoid interruptions, and search for meanings in messages (Carkhuff et al 1975). Drawing on the work of Carkhuff et al (1975), Shulman (1968), Johnson and Johnson (1975), Rackham (1979) and Rackham and Carlisle (1978), the following good listening behaviours can be identified:

❑ *Show attention and interest* through eye contact, and body squaring.

❑ *Avoid interruptions.*

❑ *Avoid immediate counterproposals* — these reflect a lack of respect for the other's proposals and a tendency to operate off preconceived ideas rather than a willingness to openly explore the needs and interests of the other.

❑ *Reach for facts* by asking for elaboration of a message, or for more information.

❑ *Reach for feelings* by asking the other to describe his feelings in order to gain fuller understanding of what a proposal or a problem means to him.

❑ *Respond empathically* by showing a desire to understand the feelings of the other — 'you probably feel angry/frustrated/hopeless in this situation ...'

❑ *Wait out feelings* when people appear to be struggling to get to grips with an emotion or its expression -there is often a tendency to try to fill a silence with some remark of one's own or to push ahead with another issue.

❏ *Paraphrase messages* to ensure that understanding is complete and accurate — 'so what you are saying is . . .' or 'correct me if I am wrong . . .' or 'as I understand you . . .'. Carkhuff et al (1975) suggest the most complete method of paraphrasing is stated in the form 'you feel . . . because . . .' thus responding to both the nature of the problem communicated and its emotional content.

❏ *Withhold evaluation* of communications until the message is complete — pre-emptive judgements may preclude accurate listening to the total message. It is not uncommon to hear an emotive response to a proposal mid-way through a communication, or to hear a message receiver wait until the transmission is complete but focus a response on some element mid-way through its content showing a fixation on some point, and possibly an end to listening at that point. In such a case the remainder of the message which may have been positive, or in the respondent's favour is simply not listened to and may get lost in the exchange as the parties squabble about a specific issue rather than the entire proposal or message.

Improving message transmission

Numerous skills for improving message transmission have been proposed:

❏ *Make messages complete and specific,* including frames of reference, assumptions and intentions.

❏ *Ensure congruency of verbal and non-verbal messages* — if a verbal signal of calm and reassurance is being conveyed, what message is being sent by the white knuckles tightly holding notes, anxious glances at others in the room and a sudden increase in smoking?

❑ *Adjust messages to the frame of reference of the listener* in order to maximise understanding.

❑ *Repeat messages* using more than one type of medium such as demonstrations, presentations, and written documents to back up verbal messages — for instance, management teams quite often use technical experts (production, finance, business planners) to make presentations to unions in order to convey a picture of the business climate, changing markets or production requirements.

❑ *Ask listeners to repeat their understanding* of a message, or to give feedback on it to ensure that it has been received and understood as intended — thus 'how do you understand our proposal?' or 'could you give us an indication as to how you think our proposal might affect you?' Ensuring understanding is not the same as asking for agreement or compliance, it attempts to ensure that everyone is operating from within a common frame of understanding rather than assuming an accord between parties.

❑ *Label behaviour.* Often in the heat of an exchange positive efforts to direct communications, improve understanding or make proposals are missed. A simple way to ensure that this does not happen is to label one's intentions — 'may I make a suggestion', or 'I would like to make a proposal', or 'can I summarise'. This informs others that someone is attempting to do something with the communication, focuses listening and ensures that such efforts do not fall on barren ground.

❑ *Avoid double bind messages.* These are ambiguous and uncertain in content, in their most serious form containing mutually exclusive signals calling for a response from the receiver. This places the receiver in an invidious position wherein acceptance of one part of the message is interpreted as rejection of the other. For instance when management suggests to a trade union that a more

participative cooperative approach is desired, but refuses
to share the information that would allow this to become
a reality, two messages are sent — we would like to
embark on a joint endeavour but also we don't trust you.
If the union accepts the cooperative mode without information, it could be coopted and easily duped in the relationship, if it refuses the offer it could be accused of failing
to respond to the realities of business pressures, radical-
ism and a stance of unrealistic adversarialism. It is a
no-win situation based in a double bind message.

Increase levels of self-awareness

As already indicated, people listen to each other through a
screen of their own biases, prejudices, experiences and expectations. Needs for power or for acceptance, a lack of empathy,
over-identification with another, suppressed anger, stereotyping, defensiveness, feelings of inadequacy, and strong
emotional responses get in the way of effective communication. The more one is in touch with one's own feelings,
attitudes and behaviour, the greater the chance that these will
not be allowed to distort understanding or clear message
transmision. The self-aware negotiator is freed to be more
objective and empathic in response to others in the process.

Improve understanding of non-verbal and semi-verbal communications

People do not only communicate through verbal signals.
Effective negotiators require sensitivity to physical posture,
facial expression, tones of voice, silences, and non-verbal
exchanges in the other negotiation team such as touching or
glances (where do all the eyes go when the tough question is
asked?). Signals of power distribution may be transmitted by
the manner in which negotiation teams arrange their seating.
Changes in patterns of behaviour may reflect a change in
stress levels. One negotiating team noticed that whenever the

chief negotiator on the other side was under stress he stopped
smoking cigarettes and reached for his pipe!

Eye contact indicate support and interest but if prolonged,
scepticism or a critical attitude. It may seek or invite responses, convey needs for support or interest or attempt to provoke a challenge. People tend to look away when they wish
to break the other's speech or respond to something. They
look back at the other when when they wish to start speaking,
but as soon as they have done so to look away. While talking
they tend to look at the other about thirty per cent of the time,
while listening for about sixty per cent. Prolonged looking
increases feelings of credibility and influence in a speaker,
conveying signals of listener interest in what he has to say.
Avoidance of eye contact may indicate fears of rejection,
manipulation or authority, guilt or a wish to conceal emotions
(Argyle 1967; Heap 1977; Carkhuff 1975). Gaze aversion may
also be a response when people are faced with questions or
situations which make them feel uncomfortable. If, however,
the situation evokes hostility then the pupils become enlarged (Nierenberg & Calero 1973).

Cultural factors may influence interpretation of eye contact patterns. In training black counsellors with a Western
based model, one trainee pointed out that the eye contact
required to convey interest in the model might be construed
as rudeness or a lack of respect for more senior persons in her
culture.

Facial expressions may carry significant messages to
others. Raised eyebrows indicate *envy or disbelief*; frowns,
displeasure, confusion or anxiety; a dropped jaw, *shock*; a tight-
ened jaw and lips, *anger or irritation*. Different forms of smiling
and greeting, handshakes and hugs indicate the degree of
warmth and openness or *tension* in the relationship. Walking
style and bodily posture indicate *mood*, levels of *anxiety* or
urgency. *Openness* may be indicated by open hands, unbut-

toned or removed coats; *defensiveness* by crossed arms or a hand to the back of the neck; *anxiety* or *hostility* by clenched fists; *evaluation* by hand-cheek gestures; *interest* by head tilting; *thought* and concern by pinching the bridge of the nose and closing the eyes; *readiness to proceed* by hands on hips or sitting on the edge of a chair; *frustration* by short breaths, 'tsk' sounds, and tightly clenched hands; *dominance and control* by the raised or pointing finger; *confidence* by finger or hand steepling, more eye contact, upright posture, or clasped hands behind the back; *superiority* through leaning back with hands clasped behind the head. Generally behavioural signals occur in clusters -changed breathing, pupil dilation, posture, walk, hand gestures, sitting style, flushing — and negotiators should be sensitive to behavioural patterns in their opponents to assist in evaluating the consequences of their messages, pressure experienced by the other, emotional changes, and receptivity. In outlining typical behavioural signals and clusters in their work *How to Read a Person Like a Book*, Nierenberg and Calero (1973) raise awareness to a wide range of non-verbal behavioural signals all negotiators should be appraised of.

However, such signals should be interpreted with care. People may cross their arms because there are no arm-supports on the chairs rather than through defensiveness, or sit in certain ways out of habit or comfort rather than a prevalent emotion. In one training course, a delegate kept squirming in his chair. During the feedback, the other team advised that he should learn to control this behaviour as it clearly conveyed his anxiety in the situation. With an embarrassed smile he announced that his squirming had little to do with anxiety — he had had a haemorroid operation a little while previously and could not remain comfortable for very long in a single position! Don't misread it and continue your negotiation on the basis of some fantasy of what the other side is experiencing.

Mediate others' communications

Quite often people do not transmit their messages effectively. They may lack the verbal skills, or strong emotions may obscure the central message in a smokescreen of abusive language, or reticence and shyness may make them hestitant to share a valuable proposal in the face of more assertive participants. Shulman (1968) proposes several techniques which sensitive others might use to facilitate a contribution, clarify a message or focus listening.

❑ *Step up weak signals.* Amplify a weak message to make it more fully understood, by enlarging on it, or asking someone to provide input that might have been missed. Here, non-verbal signals indicating a possible contribution, such as clearing the throat, sitting forward, or partly raising a hand on the part of a quieter participant, may be the cues to invite an input.

❑ *Step down strong signals.* Strong communications such as shouting, angry facial expressions, or aggressive tones of voice may obscure a message, or evoke an unwanted response. Thus, a negotiator may respond not the proposal or suggestion made by an opponent, but to the emotion which accompanied it, dragging everyone into a conflict spiral. Thus someone who can say 'Obviously Mr X is upset by the situation, but I think what he is trying to suggest is . . .', facilitates a focus on the proposal rather than the accompanying emotion, if it is getting in the way of progress. As already indicated however, it might be useful for some discussion to take place around the emotions involved — they are part of the process.

❑ *Redirecting signals* is a technique often used by mediators when negotiators start complaining to them about the opposition. Here the mediator may suggest that the message be delivered directly to a party on the other side, and remind people that it is important that they deal with problems directly between themselves and that solutions must lie in what they have to offer each other rather than in anything he can produce. This also serves to oblige parties to take responsibility for their relationship themselves.

Understand communication networks

Communication networks or patterns affect leadership roles, levels of satisfaction with a group experience, accuracy in information dissemination and peoples' behaviour in group situations (Leavitt 1951). In essence the more centrally placed an individual in a team, the more independently he behaves, and the greater the likelihood that he will assume and be assigned a leadership function. Thus when two bargaining teams face each other in an across-the-table format, the chief negotiator usually occupies a central seat on each side, and those at the ends of the teams tend to participate less in the process. Likewise, the across-the-table format is associated with adversarial, 'your team vs. our team' approaches. Circular arrangements produce a more evenly distributed communication system and leadership patterns, as they allow everyone a greater degree of eye contact and participation because no-one is left out on the shoulders of a team, and everyone has an equal opportunity to participate. This style of seating is associated with problem-solving approaches, which promote participation and openness.

In a multi-team scenario, various community groups were meeting under the chairmanship of two mediators. The two teams with the greatest interest and real power in the situation seated themselves close to the mediators, while the other groups distributed themselves around the bottom ends of the formation of tables (figure 6.2).

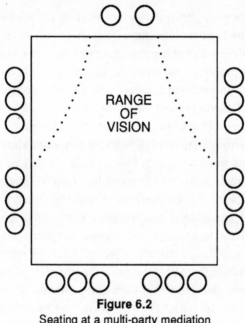

Figure 6.2
Seating at a multi-party mediation

What transpired was that the groups occupying the bottom end of the table actually dominated the proceedings, and the attention and focus of the mediators. Apart from the personalities involved, this was partly due to the fact that those occupying the shoulders of the table around the mediators had least opportunity to gain their attention through eye contact or gestures, thus diminishing their chances of participation. Those teams at the end of the table owned the territory within the range of vision of the mediators and were able to exploit this situation.

Other communication techniques

Apart from those techniques already mentioned several others are mentioned in the literature o the subject.

❑ *The threat-free apology* may be used in situations where someone is extremely angry: 'I'm sorry you are so angry, it certainly was not my intention to upset you, but we do have a problem that must be looked at.' This keeps the interaction problem focused while acknowledging emotions, clarifying intent and indicating concern but an unwillingness to get into an emotional exchange.

❑ *Humour* may be used to defuse tense situations but several cautions must be noted. Firstly, humour can be used to evade real issues which must be faced in conflict situations. Secondly, humour can be used aggressively in the form of sarcasm to humiliate another person in a way that is difficult to respond to. Finally, a spontaneous joke which suddenly comes to mind may carry elements that pertain directly to the tension in the situation and actually aggravate matters rather than defuse them.

❑ *Purposeful expression of feelings* acknowledges that feelings are part of the process, but effective negotiators express theirs carefully. Generally, a rule of thumb would be: give negatives to the process, positives to people. Thus, rather than accuse the other party of being intransigent, stupid and inducing serious proctalgia and suggesting a departure of a sexual nature (this more than likely would create further obstacles to progress) it might be more appropriate to state 'I find the lack of movement here immensely frustrating' or 'it is intensely irritating that we can make so little progress'. Positives, however, can be given to people as they nurture relations and the desire for ongoing progress. Thus: 'Your move is encouraging and allows me greater hope that this matter can be resolved.'

The use of the question

Perhaps the most useful tool for a negotiator is the question — it allows the application of pressure, buys time, obtains information, suggests alternatives without commitment, and provides a means for deflecting attack.

Nierenberg (1973) provides a qualitative analysis of the value of the question for negotiation purposes. He suggests five basic functions for questions:

❑ They draw attention.

❑ They obtain information.

❑ They give information.

❑ They start thinking.

❑ They bring matters to conclusion.

Quite often questions carry more than one function, thus providing pressured or confusing messages to others. For example: 'Would you mind checking this (start thinking/start thinking) and then sign here (bring to conclusion).'

Salespeople are often trained to invoke a mental set in a potential buyer through achieving a series of 'yes' answers to pre-ordered questions. These start with the children's encyclopaedia salesperson asking apparently innocuous questions like 'Would you agree that your child's education is the most important factor in her future opportunities?' to which it is dificult to say 'no'. Then, after a series of such questions interspersed with short comments of approval from credible and expert sources: 'Professor X, a world authority on developmental psychology has stated . . .' the central questions are reached — 'How much do you spend on an evening out in a restaurant? A R100?' before 'I'm sure you'd agree that your daughter's education is worth every bit of a small investment of only R100 a month.' And into the sale, with the buyer finding it increasingly difficult to say 'no' after so many commitments to 'yes' in the build up. It would appear quite unreasonable for the buyer to agree with all the points made by the salesperson only to turn down the offer at the end!

Nierenberg distinguishes between two large groups of questions: those that are *manageable* (generally those that prepare thinking, get information and start thinking), and those that *cause difficulty* (those that give information and bring discussions to false conclusions).

Nierenberg also deals with the skill of answering or not answering a question. He suggests four skills here:

❑ Leave the other person with the assumption that the question has been answered. Ensure that answers respond to the assumptions of the questioner rather than your own — there may be a difference which allows a different emphasis in response.

❑ Answer incompletely, by responding to parts of the the question.

❑ Answer inaccurately by restating the question in a way that allows more room for a response that you would prefer — 'as I understand your question . . .'

❑ Leave the other party without a desire to pursue the question: 'Yes we could discuss a productivity-linked increase Mr Manager, but this would require a full disclosure on your part, and a far more participative information-based style of management than exists at present. Perhaps we could discuss these first.'

In essence effective communicators listen to and behind messages, ensure clear transmission of their own signals, maintain focus on the problems or issues to be addressed in a negotiation, reduce conflict spirals and attacks on persons and positions, keep matters open, strive to understand the needs, interests and feelings of others, promote flexibility, and are assertive without having to appease. They use questions creatively to obtain information, focus attention, give information, start thinking, buy time, apply pressure and bring matters to conclusion.

PERSUASION AND ATTITUDE CHANGE

Zimbardo and Ebbesen (1970) define attitudes as follows:

> Attitudes have generally been regarded as either mental readinesses or implicit predispositions which exert some general and consistent influence on a fairly large class of evaluative responses. These responses are usuallly directed toward some object, person, or group. In addition attitudes are seen as enduring predispositions, but ones which are learned rather than innate. Thus, even though attitudes are not momentarily transient, they are susceptible to change. (p 6)

Attitudes have generally been understood in terms of three components:

❑ the *affective component* comprising the evaluation, liking or emotional response to some object or person;

❑ the *cognitive component* comprising beliefs or factual knowledge about the object or person; and

❑ the *behavioural component* comprising overt behaviour directed toward the object or person.

Zimbardo and Ebbesen (1970) suggest that all three components should be taken into account in any attitude change strategy, and note that all such strategies find their roots in the assumption that change comes out of conflict, discrepancy or discontent with the status quo. Thus attitudes may be changed when a person realises that his beliefs are not in agreement with group norms, or when there is a communication of what must be done to avoid punishment, be rewarded or be rational. By subtle pressure people may be induced to engage publicly in behaviour that is against their

own attitudes, thus inducing self-generated attitude change
as they endeavour to make their actions, feelings and thinking
congruent. Attitudes may also be changed through behaviour
modification techniques (modelling and conditioning
through reinforcement).

Any attitude change or persuasive strategy should give attention to several factors:

❏ the persuader;
❏ the message and its presentation;
❏ the audience or target individual or group; and
❏ other influences such as constituencies.

Persuaders

Persuaders are likely to be more successful if they have
prestige, attractiveness and credibility. These tend to be
rooted in their perceived knowledge, expertise, judgement,
past successes, good intentions and trustworthiness. Such
elements, of course, define the degree of power or control an
individual or team has over others in the social network
concerned.

If workers are ideologically committed to radical change
theory, then how trustworthy will they perceive managers to
be? If they acknowledge that certain managers have expertise,
for instance in finance or production, will they trust them to
utilise this expertise objectively or in their interests, or will
they reject them as inherently biased toward the interests of
shareholders or management? If a dominant group has established a long track record of racist action, will reform efforts
be seen as genuine or will they be seen as merely another
strategy?

Generally, effective persuaders are seen to share some
common values or interests with their audience. Politicians
inform voters that they are just like the voters — they too are
afraid of violence and rising crime rates; they too desire street

lighting and good educational facilities. They seldom expect to glean votes through honest statements of what is likely to happen, or through blunt promises that life is going to get harder. Potentially negative or neutral audiences then, can be swayed by the initial expression of opinions close to their own (Brager and Specht 1973). In other words, persuaders seek some convergence of values before embarking on efforts to change the thinking and feeling of others. This is basically an effort to convince the other that 'I am like you, I have similar concerns, needs and interests. You can trust me'.

Peers are believed to be more effective in value related situations, experts where factual knowledge is to be transmitted. The dividing line between these is very fine in practice. A factual presentation of the financial situation of an enterprise carries value- or interest-related information — returns to shareholders, amounts to be retained in the company, and wage gradients are ideologically laden issues. Thus a factual presentation may not be a simple task as it may always be conducted from a certain perspective, and accepted or rejected on the basis of this evaluative component rather than its mathematical aspects.

Personal characteristics are also important factors, even if they have little apparent relevance to the issue under discussion. In other words a persuader must be aware of the existing prejudices and attitudes of his target group, and consider whether he will in fact be the best person for the job. A male social work student who dressed in a flambuoyant manner, permed his hair and expressed himself in a sometimes effeminate manner was placed in criminal rehabilitation centre to work with hardened ex-cons many of whom had a history of street violence. He could not 'reach' these clients to establish a counselling relationship. Essentially he was too different to be useful for the change process envisaged. However much expertise he possessed it could find no avenue for expression as he was not accepted by the target group. Unfavourable impressions inhibit persuasion processes. It would be very naive of a negotiator to expect that values of tolerance and acceptance are held by those he is negotiating with simply because he holds them himself. It is clear that while a negotiator may conduct himself in a manner contrived to achieve perceptions of trustworthiness and values covergence, ultimately these characteristics are ascribed to him by the target group in question — and if they are not then he will struggle to persuade effectively.

Messages

The way in which issues are presented in negotiating forums has a direct bearing on whether effective attitude change will occur. Here such factors as the friendliness of the target group, their intelligence, and their existing attitudes on the matter under discussion should be taken into consideration.

Zimbardo and Ebbesen propose that where an audience is friendly or amenable to change, or the presenter's is the only position to be given, or when immediate though temporary change is desired, then only one side of an argument need be presented. If an audience starts out disagreeing with him, or if they will hear another view elsewhere, then both sides should be given.

Except in the case of an intelligent audience, opinion change is more likely to be successful when conclusions are explicitly stated. When opposing views are presented, the one presented last will probably be more effective. Thus effective negotiators might be expected to start with the arguments expected from the other side and deal with these before presenting his own perspective.

Brown (1977) proposes that all messages designed to modify attitudes occur in three stages:

❑ drawing attention and arousing interest;

❑ emotional stimulation; and

❑ showing how tension created can be relieved.

Issues that are important to a negotiator may simply not arouse much attention or interest in the other party which may have different priorities. Thus, the value of linking issues so that trading might take place ('I'll deal with your priorities if you respond to mine') makes my concerns important to you and vice versa.

A serious danger lies in creating tensions in another party without indicating how they might be relieved. Thus, a change agent may be able to induce feelings of guilt and a cognitive realisation in racially prejudiced persons that their stereotypes are inappropriate or wrong. Real feelings may however remain unchanged, resulting in feelings of internal conflict and tension. In order to deal with these as efficiently as possible they might well discharge their hostility against the original objects of their prejudice or the persuader himself (in effect for creating the tension, because they are easily identified and no major shake up occurs in the original attitudinal and behavioural set). The 'boomerang' effect here allows rejection of the persuader if he arouses too much guilt, tension or internal conflict in the target group.

Festinger's cognitive dissonance theory proposes that psychological inconsistency exists when an individual holds cognitive elements which are in conflict with another. For instance the National Serviceman may feel he is duty bound to serve his country, and be unwilling to 'let his family or community down', but at the same time believe that a war is an immoral one and disagree with his counrty's internal or foreign policies. This creates tension and the individual is motivated to reduce this. Three avenues present themselves:

❑ Change behaviour by not serving or resisting conscription.

❏ Change attitudes to become more consistent with behaviour, that is, by serving and convincing himself that this is really acceptable, often accompanied by selective information induction which serves to reinforce these rationalisations such as focusing on the atrocities of the enemy.

❏ Change the environment in some way so as to avoid the tension creating situation arising, for example, forming pressure groups to change government policies so that the war scenario is avoided (often too big a task for small lobby groups).

An important skill in bargaining then, is not only the capacity to raise tension in another party (that is, create the motivation for change) but also to make constructive, realistic and where possible, attractive alternatives which would allow reduction of tension. The skill is not only in applying pressure but also in knowing when and how to relieve it sufficiently for agreements to be signed. Agreements quite often depend on the 'loser' being given a face-saving way out — in other words, retaining sufficient dignity to sign an agreement. The final power of a party who has been defeated in a situation may simply be a refusal to sign an accord, thus denying the 'victor' a deal regardless of how rational, superior or more powerful he might be. This relates to the conflict entrapment discussed in chapter 2, where both parties spend far more of their resources and time on a matter than is rationally warranted — the one insisting on total victory, the other already beaten, but simply refusing to acknowledge this.

Several other factors influence the persuasion value of a message. The use of metaphors, active participation in the negotiation process via discussion rather than a passive (presenter-audience) process, the intensity of language used all help in effective message transmission. Another skill is that of 'expectation violation' where an audience's expectations or stereotypes are sharply contradicted by the reality of who they face. Instead of a hostile negotiator with radical suggestions, they are faced with an apparently mild person with fairly moderate proposals. All the marshalled defences and counterarguments are suddenly inappropriate. Similarly, when a reputedly quiet negotiator suddenly breaks into angry oration, a signal of real intensity and commitment is transmitted. Sudden shifts in style, or violations of expectations are then useful persuasion tools (Lewicki & Litterer 1985). The early meetings of the ANC in exile and visiting groups from South Africa were characterised by this to an extent — each wishing to convey impressions that they were not the monsters portrayed in their mutual stereotypes, but reasonable people anxious for a meaningful settlement.

Audiences and target groups

The effectiveness of any persuasive effort depends on the target group at which it is directed. People do not simply hear messages. They also avoid, misconstrue and distort them according to their needs and biases. Thus, if notice of a potential disagreement is provided ('you may not agree with me but . . .') the target group may lose attention in an effort to avoid a rise in emotional tension through hearing differing views.

Generally people with low self-esteem are more easily influenced than others, and more easily persuaded. A word of warning however — such people may be just as easily persuaded by the counter viewpoint when it is heard, and vacillate wildly in stances. This reduces their reliability as change agents in their own right (that is, with constituencies) and as allies on any particular issue.

Another important technique in persuading another party to adjust a position, is to get them to make a public commitment to a certain principle. Commitments of principle are of course powerful because everyone is aware that such statements would not be made unless the person is committed to a position. However they also lock people into positions and raise the risk of conflict entrapment.

The external factor — the constituency

People's attitudes are strongly influenced by the groups to which they belong and which are important to them — referent groups. Processes of conformity are important factors in understanding the behaviour of people in groups, and why they may adopt intransigent positions in the face of quite rational argument.

Negotiators may be able to sway the beliefs of each other in the negotiation process, but this may not mean much if they in turn cannot convince their constituencies. Apparently hopeful progress may be simply undone by the incapacity of a negotiator to persuade a constituency. Indeed instead of collective movement in a situation, constituencies may rather dismiss their negotiators and opt for others who will adhere to a tougher line.

7
MEDIATING CONFLICTUAL RELATIONS

Various efforts have been made to define the mediation process (Folberg and Taylor 1984; Zartman and Touval 1985; Pruitt and Kressel 1985; Moore 1986). While these have common elements, there are also clear differences of approach reflected. All perceive mediation as an intervention into a dispute by a third party whose task it is to assist disputants themselves to reach a settlement, but some differences emerge as to whether this third party should be neutral or impartial; how much power a mediator has or should wield, and what tasks or techniques may be used. For purposes of this work the following definition is proposed:

Mediation is a form of third-party intervention into disputes, directed at assisting disputants to find a mutually acceptable settlement. Although mediators may operate from a high or low power base, they are not accorded authoritative decision-making power, but are empowered to facilitate settlement searches through the use of the negotiation process.

Box 7.1
Mediation defined

Mediation is utilised in many dispute situations including international relations, community conflicts, hostage crises, domestic and divorce situations, environmental conflicts and labour–management relations. Several key debates exist in its use:

❏ Must the mediator be neutral and impartial?
❏ Is late entry to a dispute preferable to early intervention?
❏ On what basis does one judge the effectiveness of mediation?
❏ Does mediation change the power relations between the parties?
❏ What sources of power does a mediator have and how should these be exercised?
❏ What are the techniques used by mediators, and for what objectives?

Many of these questions are addressed, at least in part, in the debate surrounding mediator acceptability.

MEDIATOR ACCEPTABILITY

Mediator acceptability is crucial to successful intervention (Moore 1986; Kressel 1972; Kressel 1985). However, considerable debate surrounds the issue of what factors might contribute to this. On the one hand are those authors who propose that a mediator should be a disinterested party, whose salient characteristics are those of neutrality and impartiality (Folberg and Taylor 1984; Moore 1986). On the other are those who suggest that mediators are often interested parties who are in fact not neutral, but have a direct interest in the outcome of a dispute or in a particular network of social relations (Zartman and Touval 1985; Gulliver 1979). Gulliver (1979) clarifies the debate by distinguishing two types of mediator — those with disinterested status, and those with interests in a conflict.

Disinterested mediators

According to Gulliver(1979) disinterested status may arise from a number of sources;

❑ an institutionalised role in society, such as a mediation agency;
❑ acknowledged prestige or ability of an individual or agency not directly concerned with the issues or outcome of a dispute;
❑ expertise on the issues at stake;
❑ social status as a distinguished or socially eminent person;
❑ position in relation to the social network involved in a conflict.

Moore (1985) proposes that neutrality and impartiality are basic to mediator acceptability, the former referring to the relationship with the disputants, the latter to the attitude with which a dispute is approached. To remain neutral a mediator should not have had a relationship with either of the disputing parties, or at least not one in which they have directly influenced the rewards or benefits for one to the detriment of the other. No special favours, benefits or payments should be received as compensation for favours in the conduct of the mediation. Impartiality requires a capacity on the part of the mediator to separate from personal opinions to direct the parties to find a solution of their own to a problem. This is carried out by a focus on procedural rather than substantive elements of the process -by advocating fair process rather than a particular outcome.

The best example of an institutionalised mediation role in South Africa is that of the Independent Mediation Service of South Africa (IMSSA) which provides mediation and arbitration services. Until recently these services were provided solely in relation to labour–management disputes, but more recently some cautious entries have been made into the community arena, largely in the form of training, but also some

direct interventions. IMSSA is a private, non-profit organisation with a core of full-time staff who arrange mediations,
arbitrations, ballots and relationship by objectives programmes which are largely conducted by trained persons
drawn from its panels. These panelists are employed in a
variety of other fields including academia, law, and psychology. The organisation was established in 1983 in response to
a growing need for credible third-party assistance in the
country's rapidly developing industrial relations process.
The formal framework for collective bargaining under the
Labour Relations Act made provision for mediation, but
owing to suspicion of state structures and systems was seldom used. After a hesitant beginning use of IMMSA's services has grown dramatically.

Table 7.1
IMMSA mediations and arbitrations 1983–1990

YEAR	MEDIATIONS	ARBITRATIONS
1984	39	5
1885	60	24
1986	139	73
1987	199	162
1988	313	194
1989	475	222
1990 (1st half)	273	155

Interested mediators

While mediation may usually be carried out by low power
individuals with the status of neutrals, on some occasions it
is performed by a mediator with interests and influence in a
situation (Kressel 1985). Researchers in the fields of anthro-
pology (Gulliver 1979) and international relations (Zartman

and Touval 1985) vigorously challenge the emphasis on neutrality as a prerequisite for acceptability.

Gulliver(1979) argues that the roles and aims of mediators are far more varied in real life than traditional thought suggests, and that they turn dyadic disputes into triadic interactions introducing interests, values and perceptions of their own into the process which may not coincide entirely with those of the disputants.

> Therefore he is not, and cannot be, neutral and merely a catalyst. He not only affects the interaction but, at least in part, seeks and encourages an outcome that is tolerable to him in terms of his own ideas and interests. He may even come into conflict with one or both parties . . . the strong, Western, cultural stereotype and moral notion of the purely impartial mediator is neither invariably correct in practice in our own society nor valid crossculturally. (pp 213–4)

Gulliver suggests that mediators' own interests may be affected by the continuation of a dispute. In such instances a mediator may care less about the outcome of a dispute than about the termination of a disruptive conflict. The mediator may be directly participant in the network of social relations incorporating the adversaries, and may have known partiality. As a consequence of these factors the mediator may be able to intervene on the basis of a perceived ability to be able to influence one or both parties in the engagement. Alternatively the mediator may not be directly involved in the network of relations but be a community representative anxious to extend personal influence, or for opportunities to express a values system.

Zartman and Touval (1985) extend the argument of mediators as interested parties into the field of community relations, proposing that mediators are 'players' in the process. They posit two types of interest:

❏ defensive interests where continued conflict threatens the mediator's own interests; and

❏ influential interests where although not directly threatened by a conflict, a party may offer to intervene in order to extend influence over the parties concerned or in a particular region.

Zartman and Touval propose that:

> Mediators are seldom indifferent to the terms being negotiated . . . (they) are likely to seek terms that will increase the prospects of stability, deny their rivals opportunities for intervention earn them the gratitude of one or both parties, or enable them to continue to 'have a say'in the relations between the two adversaries . . . third parties are accepted as mediators only to the extent that they are thought capable of bringing about acceptable outcomes'.
> (p 33)

Adversaries may choose or accept an interested mediator for a variety of reasons:

❏ in the hope that a mediated outcome might produce an outcome more favourable in the balance than continued conflict or through direct negotiation;

❏ in the hope that mediation will reduce some of the risks inherent in concessionmaking;

❏ as a form of guarantor for the process and its outcome, that is,by reducing risks of violation of procedures or agreements by the adversary;

❏ in view of the risks to future relations with the mediator if intervention is not accepted and/or the conflict is not settled.

According to Zartman and Touval (1985), partiality does not mean that a mediator can push the interests of one party in a dispute while ignoring those of the other. His skill is to turn his partiality into an asset in the process by facilitating communications, developing creative proposals, converging positions and ultimately 'delivering' to the party to which he is closest. The mediator cannot be seen to be so close to one party as to preclude an agreement, but must, like disinterested mediators, be perceived as having a primary interest in achieving a settlement acceptable to both sides. In summary the argument from this perspective is that impartiality is not the central issue that renders the mediator acceptable, but a perceived capacity to provide an acceptable outcome.

Maintaining acceptability

The relevance of clarifying factors that contribute to mediator acceptability extend beyond identifying who might be invited to undertake the task, or who might be accepted to do it. The mediator must remain acceptable once the process has been initiated. The reasons why a mediator is acceptable to the parties provides an indication as to the type of influence that might be exercised in an intervention. It is proposed here that the criteria that the parties use to choose a mediator signal their expectations of the process and mediator behaviour within this.

Kressel (1972) indicates that mediators spend time in the opening phases of an intervention on what he terms 'reflexive' tactics which are designed to make the mediator an effective instrument for dispute resolution. Essentially the strategy is to:

❑ gain the trust and confidence of the parties;
❑ achieve rapport with them;
❑ discover the real issues in dispute; and
❑ get a feel for the dynamics of the situation.

Kolb (1985) indicates how this is done on the basis of her participant observation in a series of labour mediations. She concludes that mediators actively try to convey messages about themselves — expressive tactics — to the parties at this stage. They try to impress parties with their skills and abilities, their trustworthiness, experience, relevance, understanding and empathy, and contacts with significant others. In brief, mediators do not cease to be concerned about their acceptability once they have been agreed on by the parties in dispute. They must reassure them that the choice was a correct one, and build a power base from which to operate and orchestrate the process. The extent to which expressive tactics will be successful will be dependent on what is likely to impress the parties — which returns consideration to why they chose the mediator in the first place.

Disinterested mediators have little direct power over relations. They are temporary sojourners in the social network of the adversaries. Power then, is usually ascribed to them on the basis of the parties' perceptions of them as impartial, neutral, expert, prestigious or socially distant.

Expressive tactics should then be directed at maximising these sources of power or at least preventing their erosion.

Interested mediators may have some of those sources of power possessed by neutrals but are usually more powerful in terms of direct influence in a social network. Thus the parties may have a dependency relationship on the mediator, or subject to the mediator's capacity to reward or coerce their behaviour. As a consequence expressive tactics will be directed differently by interested mediators to those of their disinterested counterparts.

Dispute type and mediator acceptability

It is evident from the literature that the issue of mediator acceptability varies across fields. There is more evidence of interested mediation in the field of international relations for instance than in labour or family dispute situations where the emphasis is on the mediator's qualities of neutrality and impartiality than direct participation in network of conflict relations.

Research findings

Howells (1986) investigated the views of employers and union officers as to the attributes of the ideal mediator, to assess whether they have a stereotype of the role and whether their views coincide. Howells surveyed the perspectives of 116 employers and 102 union officers, covering most of the large corporations and sector unions in New Zealand. Respondents were asked to rate 36 variables on a Likert scale, the variables being based on previous research by Weschler (1949) and Landsberger (1960). The research indicated close agreement on the part of employer and union respondents as to the desireable attributes of a mediator. Both parties placed greater emphasis on intangible personality traits than on biographical variables such as sex, nationality, religion or marital status. Both parties valued experience in collective bargaining and a background knowledge of labour problems and labour law as more important than formal education. Employers placed greater emphasis than the unionists on a knowledge of business problems, and unionists a higher premium on the mediator's skills in chairing meetings and knowledge of committee procedures. The union respondents showed greater interest in the political affiliation of the mediator. Both agreed that the mediator should be physically fit. Perfect agreement was found for such qualities as honesty and integrity, trust, fairness and impartiality, and general reliability. The following were also closely rated by both: patience and persistence, abilities to grasp ideas and be good listener, tact and persuasiveness, self control, dignity and respect, intelligence, a sense of humour, firmness of action and originality of ideas. Of lesser importance but equally closely ranked by both were: sympathy, modesty, and 'being one of us'.

Howells suggests that the close correlation of union and employer views on the ideal mediator should make for easier choice of the third party. He proposes that mediation agencies should take care in their selection of mediators to ensure that the criteria valued by the parties are used in the assessment of recruits.

In my survey in the Eastern Cape (Anstey 1988) of unions' and employers' views of mediator acceptability, 25 unionists and 39 managers responded to the questionnaire which required ratings of 21 variables on a likert scale. Results indicated a high degree of agreement that the mediator should be trusted by both parties. Factors contributing to trust could be broadly ranked as neutrality and impartiality, followed by experience and expertise, a capacity to influence the parties and finally personal acquaintance. More specifically the following findings and tentative conclusions were drawn:

❏ Mediators must be trusted by both parties in a dispute.
❏ Mediators should be perceived as neutral in relations between labour and mangement. Parties may not reject a mediator who has served one of them, provided he usually provides services to both labour and management in the wider context, and provided he has not provided assistance to one of them on the issue actually in dispute. Managers were more concerned about the effects of service provision on mediator neutrality than unionists. In the light of a paucity of genuine neutrals in South Africa where services are provided by part-time panelists of IMSSA, perceptions of impartiality may override all these considerations.
❏ Mediators should be perceived as impartial, a quality that may be be related less to known sympathies for a side than to a capacity for objectivity on issues in dispute.
❏ All respondents agreed that a mediator should not be a government official.
❏ Nearly 90 %, both of managers and of trade unionists, felt a mediator should be experienced in mediating, and should be an expert in industrial relations generally.

❏ While almost 90 % of unionists felt that the mediator should have expertise in the issue under dispute, only 60 % of managers shared this view. This might be due to imbalances of information power between the parties, the union valuing the presence of the mediator as a guarantor for the process, his or her presence reducing any proclivities employers might have to abuse their usually stronger knowledge and information resources.

❏ Unions and employers both felt that it is more important that a mediator be able to influence their own side to move than that he should be able to induce such movement from the other side. This indicates the importance of a mediator recognising that the role of third-party assistance may extend within camps to helping negotiators with their own constituencies.

❏ Both parties ranked personal acquaintance with the mediator low, but interestingly those respondents with experience of mediation ranked this criteria far higher than those without.

It may be concluded that in South Africa there are indications that the parties share views on mediator acceptability and that they value qualities of disinterested third parties more than those of interested ones. It must be remembered, however, that acceptability criteria are always specific to the parties and the issues in dispute, and in this sense minority responses are as important as majority views for the disputes that those parties may be involved in.

OBJECTIVES OF MEDIATION

There is a tendency to assume that the sole purpose of mediation is to achieve a settlement, and that an intervention has failed if one has not been achieved. This is a crude measure of the effectiveness of third-party assistance. While it may be first prize, there are many other criteria against which to evaluate the usefulness of mediation. The range of objectives and criteria for an effective intervention include:

❏ achievement of a settlement;
❏ achievement of sufficient movement to allow the independent bargaining to continue;
❏ clearer definition of the issues at stake;
❏ removal of obstacles to bargaining;
❏ a broadened search for alternatives;
❏ tension reduction in the relationship;
❏ preparation of the parties to accept the consequences of continued conflict, that is, reality appraisal;
❏ assistance to the parties to improve their negotiation skills for future engagements;
❏ improved communications/understanding between the parties; and
❏ promotion of a clearer understanding of the power realities in a relationship.

MEDIATOR STRATEGIES AND TACTICS

The objectives of mediation are various, but there is agreement that settlement is the primary objective. What mediators do to achieve this, bearing in mind requirements to behave impartially, to treat information confidentially, and not to overcommit either party beyond a point of their choosing at any given moment in the process.

Kressel (1972) suggests three areas of concern for mediators entering a dispute — acceptability, timing, and the strategic implications of a request for assistance. The issue of acceptability has already been discussed. The question of timing is an intensely debated one in the field of dispute resolution.

Timing of entry

Moore (1986) states that as yet not enough is known to give an unqualified answer as to which circumstances favour early or late entry into a dispute. He suggests that the choice lies in the mediator's assessment as to whether an early entry would be more detrimental to the parties than delay.

Lewicki and Litterer (1985) propose that the timing of entry is an integral element in the success of an intervention, and the decision to embark on mediation should lie in the 'readiness' of the parties. If one or both parties believe that greater gains are possible through protracting a dispute, then mediation cannot work — the process is reliant on the cooperation of the parties. In other words, it demands a situation where the parties have softened their stances at least sufficiently to want to investigate alternatives in order to end the dispute.

Proponents of *late entry* believe that disputants are only psychologically prepared to use third-party assistance once they have reached impasse. This school proposes that conflicts must proceed through a developmental cycle in which the parties mobilise and test their strength, assess power realities, vent emotions and exhaust their own procedural and substantive options prior to seeking external assistance. It is the pressure of the deadlock that energises the mediation process. A premature intervention relaxes the parties and removes this vital motivational force. In a survey by Krislow and Mead (1971) labour as well as management respondents preferred that a mediator enter only once negotiations were well advanced. Pruitt (1981) suggests that parties seek assistance only when deadlock has been reached but the costs of further competitive behaviour are too high for both. Late entry advocates then base their arguments on the belief that highest levels of motivation are likely to be experienced in situations of interactive crisis — when the parties perceive themselves as being able to move neither forward nor back, where they have little time in which to negotiate a solution, and where negotiators have little flexibility in their mandates.

On the other hand, those proposing *early entry* into disputes suggest an effective mediator can promote parties' readiness for intervention without their having to test power relativities through actual use of coercive tactics. Early entry is effective, they argue, because it reduces positional rigidity, frustration and the build up of hostile emotions and exchanges of unproductive behaviour. This school agrees that the venting of emotions is useful, but not if it is prolonged and unstructured in expression, producing emotional barriers to effective problem solving.

Moore (1986) suggests that mediators delay entry in situations where parties have unequal power, or need a confrontation to test each other's strength and conviction before they become willing to bargain in good faith. Early entry is indicated in situations where the parties are informed of the power realities and do not need to actually exercise their power in order to understand the implications of a deadlock. Such a situation might arise in a labour–management relationship where the parties over a period of time in regular interaction learn to assess accurately each other's commitment, capacity, strategic moves and consequences of a confrontation. The imperative for settlement lies in the nature of the ongoing relationship and a mutual awareness of the consequences of conflict escalation and confrontation without having to test this in every negotiative exchange.

The assumption underlying these arguments is that mediation is wholly centred upon achieving settlement. It is proposed here that that disputants may also use the process for purposes other than settlement. For instance, they may seek, through the mediator, to assess how great the gap is between them on issues; to try to gain a sense of the other party's real priorities or intransigence; to communicate a signal of possible movement, concession or exchange more clearly; or to warn the other of seriousness of intent. Strategies aimed at goals other than settlement may run through the process then, complicating understanding of its use and analysis of the effectiveness of mediation. Some mediators believe that this is an abuse of the process by parties who use the mediator for strategic purposes other than settlement searches, for instance to convey incorrect information, or transmit false signals to evoke precipitate movement on the part of an opponent. It is my opinion that these fears are exaggerated. 'Abuse' of the process may occur in the final stages of negotiation in the same vein as in earlier ones. In addition the mediatory process is one which seeks to contribute to effective engagement between parties, and mediators may promote positive movement through assisting parties to assess accurately their circumstances and clarify communications. Intermediate contributions to effective engagement may be just as important as a late intervention of a more dramatic nature with regard to eventual settlement. Finally, mediators must recognise that they assist parties involved in a inherently strategic relationship. This awareness should serve to raise their sensitivity to abuse of the process and rapidly call a halt to it, or channel it in less destructive directions. It is my own experience that parties who enter without a willingness to genuinely consider movement or engage in settlement searches may be pulled into honest exchange despite their original intentions, if the other party moves in a way that gives hope of a settlement, or would leave them clearly exposed as having entered the process in bad faith.

Content and process tactics

Pruitt (1981) distinguishes between *process and content* mediation, the former being the means whereby mediators 'seek to develop conditions that will facilitate concession making and problem solving', and the latter with 'the third party developing suggested solutions or trying to persuade bargainers to move in a a particular direction'.

Kolb (1983) distinguishes between *strategy and tactics* in the mediation process, the former being an 'overall plan, approach or method a mediator has for resolving a dispute ... the way a mediator intends to manage the case, the parties and the issues' and the latter ' what the mediator actually does to bring the parties to settlement, to learn about the issues and priorities, and to encourage movement'. Tactics are the behavioural specifics of strategies and can only really be understood in their context, that is, what the mediator plans to do. She distinguished between 'dealmakers' who used directive information gathering and movement tactics early in the intervention to build acceptable packages from priority issues, and 'orchestrators' who used tactics to narrow the gap between the parties via consistent exchanges of increasingly refined proposals and counteroffers to the point of an acceptable package. As the responsibilty for the agreement lies with the parties, orchestrators would use directive tactics only late in the process, if at all.

Process tactics are essentially non-directive in nature designed to facilitate the parties capacity to evolve a settlement of their own. Content mediation, however, may be required where parties are struggling with substantive issues and deadlock seems entrenched. In such cases the mediator may be required to actively promote a solution, or pressure or manipulate parties directly into ending the dispute (Pruitt 1981).

Table 7.2 is an inventory of process strategy and tactics for mediators based on the work of Shulman (1968), Pruitt (1981), Kressel (1972), Moore (1986) and Kolb (1983).

TABLE 7.2
PROCESS MEDIATION SKILLS

MEDIATOR STRATEGY	ASSOCIATED TACTICS
1. Gain trust and confidence.	• Explain mediator's role. • State concern over dispute. • Speak language of the parties.
2. Achieve rapport with parties.	• Demonstrate competence. • Use humour effectively. • Demonstrate empathising under-standing of each side's case.
3. Discover the real issues.	• Listen actively. • Listen for real issues behind stated ones. • Use direct question. • Be sensitive to parties' real concerns. • Ask parties (jointly and separately) to explain stances and identify need, obliging them to think through positions and check out perceptions. • Establish factual vs. perceptual bases for further negotiations, i.e. avoid inferences. • Depersonalise issues — focus on problems rather than on people.
4. Understand the dynamics of the situation.	• Identify real issues. • Identify real leaders. • Grasp the relationship between the parties. • Grasp the pressures on each party. • Understand the influence of contextual variables, i.e., social, economic, political.
5. Promote a favourable climate for negotiations.	• A mutual agreement to seek mediational assistance gives each party the assurance that the other wants agreement, in the first instance. • Create favourable environmental conditions.

MEDIATOR STRATEGY	ASSOCIATED TACTICS
6. Promote inter-party relations.	• Improve inter-party empathy by stressing common ground and mutual payoffs, and by fostering beliefs that a mutually satisfactory solution is possible. • Promote understanding of the legitimacy of each party's needs/goals. • Promote feelings of commonality. • Focus on problems rather than on people. • Avoid inferences — promote active communication and checking out by the parties. • Get parties to agree on mutual confidentiality during negotiations. • Allow airing of grievances. • Allow but control expressions of anger. • Tackle less emotional issues first. • Promote active communications between parties. Assist 'listening' and clear expression of needs and objectives.
7. Improve inter-party communications.	• Identify communication problems: attitudes, prejudices, status problems, expressive problems, listening problems. • Establish a 'listening' environment. • Improve skills of message transmission. • Improve listening skills. • Demonstrate good listening behaviour. • Increase self-awareness of parties. • Understand defence mechanisms. • Tune in to purposes of communication.

MEDIATOR STRATEGY	ASSOCIATED TACTICS
	• Improve understanding of non-verbal and semi-verbal signals.
	• Improve communication networks.
	• Share own feelings and perspectives purposefully.
	• Mediate others' communications to promote understanding between parties.
	• Maintain dialogue between parties.
	• Promote empathy between parties.
8. Establish priorities.	• Help parties identify real needs; partialise issues and rankings in terms of priorities.
	• Get agreement on issues to be worked on.
9. Educate parties on the negotiation process.	• Teach communication/conflict resolution skills.
	• Promote searches for common ground.
	• Educate on the importance of such issues as third-party representation, mandates, pluralism, compromise, realism, trade-offs, linking, etc.
10. Promote searches for areas of compromise by the parties.	• Seek common ground.
	• Link priorities.
	• Promote solutions searches.
	• Establish criteria for acceptable agreements.
	• Keep problem-focused.
11. Demand reality orientation.	• Remind parties of costs.
	• Advise parties of similar agreements elsewhere.
	• Remind parties of needs and expectations of constituencies.
	• Remind parties of priorities.
	• Translate the realistic position of the other party to keep expectations realistic.

MEDIATOR STRATEGY	ASSOCIATED TACTICS
	• Avoid advocacy of a side — advocate reality orientation.
	• Remind parties of actual circumstances.
12. Pressurise settlement.	• Advocate settlement.
	• Make suggestions for settlement ('supposals').
	• Link.
	• Provide insights and relevant information.
	• Use time pressures to pace negotiation.
	• 'Sell' agreements to parties.
	• Narrow solution ranges.
	• 'Orchestrate' the negotiation by controlling agendas, meetings, time, 'bulking' issues, organising sub-committees, environmental conditions, etc.
	• Maintain the momentum of movement.
	• Precipitate deadlocks to increase motivation
	• Keep problem-focused.
	• Promote beliefs that more solutions may exist than originally envisaged by either party.
	• Clarify terms of the agreement.

Table 7.3 is an inventory of content mediation tactics based on the work of Pruitt (1981). (Source: Anstey 1986)

TABLE 7.3
CONTENT MEDIATION SKILLS

CONDITION	TACTICS
1. Parties are unwilling to concede to a viable alternative already under discussion because they believe the other will eventually concede beyond that option.	• Investigate true positions. • Impose deadlines to assess flexibility of parties. • Induce reality orientation by appraising parties of the other's genuine limits and strengths.
2. Parties are unwilling to make concessions owing to fears of loss of image.	• Elicit concession exchanges. • Provide alternatives. • Transmit concessions in disguised form (i.a. as own suggestions). • Announce parties' concessions simultaneously to disguise the fact of who moved first.
3. No viable alternatives exist but one can be found through integrative processes.	• Seek novel solutions. • Use problem-solving techniques, e.g. brainstorming, nomial groups, option surveys, cost cutting, compensation, logrolling, and bridging.
4. Parties unwilling to make concessions owing to positional commitments or adherence to principles.	• Seek means of decommitting parties honourably, i.e. changed circumstances. • Leave some areas unresolved while agreeing to others. • Relable an issue to circumvent it.

Effectiveness of intervention

Several researchers have addressed the complex issue of trying to ascertain under what circumstances mediation is most successful, and which mediator behaviours are most effective in achieving agreements.

Hiltrop (1985), in a study of 260 ACAS mediations in Britain found that there was an association between the *type of issue* under dispute and outcome of mediation. While 73 % of pay/conditions of work disputes were successfully resolved, only 55 % of disciplinary cases, 48 % of retrenchment cases and 33 % of union recognition matters were settled. In short, interests matters were shown to be more amenable to intervention than rights issues where options were more of an 'either-or' nature, and in which issues of principle or perceived prerogative served to entrench positions and make bargaining more difficult.

Hiltrop also found that settlements were achieved in 80 % of instances where there was *strike or lockout action* underway, 67 % of cases where such action was threatened, and only 53 % of cases where sanctions were neither threatened or in effect. This seems to confirm the late entry school's argument, but probably refers more to the conditions under which mediation took place than the timing of entry. A level of commitment to settle may well be more apparent in cases where there is some pain in the process.

Effectiveness and choice of tactics

Generally Hiltrop (1985) found that *non-directive rather than directive tactics* tend to be the most effective in settling disputes, but that where the latter were used they were more influential in non-pay disputes and in strike situations. She concluded that:

> . . . the effective mediator strategy appears to be predominantly one of go-between and prod. Successful mediators worked with the parties separately, acted as a communi-

cation link between them, intervened with their constituencies, and occasionally threatened to stop these actions when the parties failed to make satisfactory progress. (Hiltrop 1985, p 92).

Brett et al (1986) found that there were *differences of style* between five mediators and in four cases style differed across disputes. There was, however, no great variance in their effectiveness, all achieving a 79–90 % settlement rate. Nevertheless, style was related to type of settlement achieved, some (dealmaking or shuttle diplomacy) being more successful in facilitating compromise and others (pressing on the party) at getting either the trade union or management to drop their position. Brett et al (1986) proposed that mediators do a rough classification of grievance cases into potential outcomes categories, and then utilise strategies that move one or both parties to an outcome that they believe to be most efficacious.

This contingency approach by mediators was also investigated by Pegnetter et al (1985) to ascertain whether mediators do in fact tailor tactics to dispute circumstances. They found that where *bargainers are hostile*, mediators tend to use more directive tactics such as clarifying the other's needs, pressing for concessions, suggesting compromises, pointing out that the next impasse procedure was no better than mediation, trying to change expectations, and mentioning costs of continued disagreement. Also used in hostile situations was humour to lighten atmosphere.

Where *bargainer overoptimism* was assessed to be a central obstacle, mediators tried to lower expectations through discussing other settlements and patterns, mentioning costs of continued disagreement and directly telling parties that their expectations were unrealistic. In cases where problems arose out of negotiators *bringing too many issues* to the table, mediators used issue-related tactics, such as simplifying the agenda, developing a bargaining framework, keeping parties at the table and using long hours and sessions to facilitate compromise. In addition, more directive tactics of clarifying the other's needs, obliging a review of own needs and suggesting trade offs were also used.

In situations where *intransigent individuals* created problems, mediators used reflexive tactics of trying to gain trust, attempting to speak the same language, developing rapport and impartiality, and more directively, discussing costs of ongoing disagreement and pointing out that the next impasse procedure was no better than mediation.

Internal disagreements were dealt with by bargaining for long hours, educating parties about impasse process, expressing pleasure or displeasure according to progress, suggesting proposals and trying to settle simple issues first. *Lack of leadership* or *inexperience/lack of expertise* induced mediators to simplify the agenda, educate the parties as to the process, assist in prioritising issues and settle simple issues first, and in more difficult cases to point out the consequences of continuing the conflict.

MEDIATOR POWER

The issue of mediator power has already been introduced in the discussion of mediator acceptability. Here the issue is progressed in terms of the mediator's influence over the parties as they engage in a power exchange of their own in the course of a conflictual relationship. Moore (1986) states:

> Mediators, although neutral in relationship to the parties and generally impartial toward the substantive outcome, are directly involved in influence activities designed to move disputants toward settlement. (p 271)

Mayer(1987) observes that although power is often viewed in a negative light, it is a factor in all relationships, energising the process of conflict resolution. He states

> Mediators are also invested with a great deal of power by the mediation process. Whether or not they consciously

choose to exercise it, mediators inevitably use their influence at every point of the intervention. This is neither
good nor bad; rather it is a necessary consequence of the
structure of the intervenor's role in conflict resolution. What
mediators can choose is whether to use this power in a
deliberate way and with a specific purpose. (p 75)

Mayer proposes that an understanding of the nature of power
in the negotiation process is crucial for effective intervention.
Distinguishing between distributive and integrative approaches to conflict resolution, he points to a dilemma in the
use of power. On the one hand are those theorists who
propose that conflict situations are defined at root by a power
struggle, that is, the ability of one side to inflict more damage
on the other than it incurs. From this perspective a good
negotiator is one who is capable of assessing the power
realities of an exchange and selecting the best alternative
when his power is at its height. On the other hand are those
theorists, such as Fisher (1983), who propose that while
power is an essential part of negotiation, it ought not to be
associated solely with a capacity to inflict damage, but rather
with the ability to influence the decisions of others, residing
in principle, persuasiveness, relationship, and creative problem solving as well. A principled approach to negotiation
then recognises that appropriate use of tactics can change
power relationships. A dilemma arises then, in perspectives
on the nature of power in relationships. Mayer (1987) proposes that it is not merely a means to an end in an exchange,
but also often an end in itself — parties seek not only to
achieve substantively to satisfy their interests but also to
increase or preserve their power over others in relationships.
Hobbes, in his thesis on authority in *Leviathan* in 1651 recognised this:

. . . in the first place, I put for a general inclination of all
mankind, a perpetual and restless desire of power after
power, that ceaseth only in death. And the cause of this, is

not always that a man hopes for a more intensive delight,
than he has already attained to; or that he cannot be
content with a moderate power: but because he cannot
assure the power and means to live well, which he hath at
at present, without the acquisition of more. (Curtis 1981, p
330)

Mayer (1987) concludes that power has a role in both distributive and integrative exchanges, but that it is 'hard to understand how to reconcile its impact with the principled basis on
which collaborative negotiations are assumed to rest' (p 77).
The fact is that negotiators often do not bargain in a principled
way, desireable as this may be, and therefore that a wider
sensitivity to the place and use of power is required in conflict
situations.

A contingency approach to understanding power is suggested which recognises a wide range of sources of influence
in interpersonal and intergroup exchanges, and considers
which would be the appropriate form to use in given situations. The characteristics of the participants in a conflict, the
process and the desired outcome of an exchange are factors
critical to this decision-making process.

The issue of power in relationships has already been
discussed in this work. Here attention is given to the sources
of power available to mediators, their usage and limitations.

Mediator power

Moore (1986) suggests twelve forms of influence that mediators might use to move parties toward agreement, and expands on how they might be utilised:

❑ *Management of the negotiation process*: by conscious influence over the sequence of steps to be followed in the
   process, to separate the parties or hold joint meetings, to
   propose solutions or exchanges or concentrate on tactics
   designed to narrow gaps.

❑ *Communication between and within parties* via control over the sharing of information, the manner of exchange, the reframing of demands.

❑ *Physical setting*: arranging seating, room size, caucus facilities, meeting places.

❑ *Timing*: starting times, duration of meetings, imposition of deadlines for settlement, timing of offers, concessions and communications.

❑ *Information exchange*: control over the type of information sought or conveyed, suggestions, proposals or referral to information resources.

❑ *Associational influence*: mediators exercise power simply by virtue of the factors that made for their choice as third party, but also sometimes by influence over others who have influence over the disputing parties themselves.

❑ *Expert power*: mediators may exercise influence through their expertise or knowledge in a particular area, or by referring parties to people with such skills or knowledge.

❑ *Authority influence*: on occasion mediators may have legitimate power through their position in an agency with authoritative power or their capacity to call on other parties with power to exert influence on the disputants.

❑ *Habits of disputants*: longstanding relationships usually see the evolution of norms of behaviour and habitual approaches to problem resolution that can be appealed to for purposes on conciliation.

❑ *Parties doubt and unintended consequences*: mediators use doubt about the viability of a position in one or both of the parties, and obliges them to consider potential outcomes.

❑ *Rewards or benefits*: with the exception of international disputes mediators tend not to have the power to reward parties for movement, these powers are vested in the parties themselves. They may however be able to offer indirect rewards such as respect, interest or by identifying positive results of a settlement.

❑ *Coercive influence*: the voluntary nature of mediation tends to limit a mediator's power in this sphere, but it may be exerted indirectly via displays of impatience, threats to pull out or withdrawal of approval.

Moore points out that mediators seldom enter relations of *symmetrical power relations* (power balance) where one technique would be to ask the parties to assess their own and the other's power potentials and the costs and benefits of utilising it. Accurate and considered assessment would lead logically to efforts to find a settlement. Equal power tends to produce more cooperative behaviour and limit the use of coercive tactics. In such situations mediators might concentrate their efforts on trying to help the parties to make an accurate assessment of the power realities, or how they might satisfy each other's interests. Where there is an inaccurate assessment of power realities, a process of testing of each other's stregth may be obliged wherein the parties seek to use coercive tactics for a period before they recognise the need to seek more cooperative modes of resolving their differences.

In *asymmetrical power relations* there may be actual or real power imbalances, and the weaker party may use bluff to convince the other of strength while the more powerful may simply believe that a negotiated settlement will not be as rewarding as one achieved through defeating the other. Power imbalances tend to escalate conflicts as they result in rigidity of stances, the powerful party believing it can crush opposition, the less powerful recognising the odds often resorting to intransigence rather than capitulation. In such situations the stronger party often sees no benefits to a negotiated settlement, while the weaker one is not in position to offer one and certainly not in a position to use leverage to oblige one (Pruitt and Rubin 1986).

Mayer (1987) observes:

> Power imbalances occur when one party has a great deal
> more real or perceived power than another. This may be
> characteristic of the parties' total relationship or relevant
> only to a particular negotiation or to the specific type of
> power being utilised. Power inequities cause problems
> because they lead to rigidity on the part of both the stronger
> and weaker parties, because they lead to a breakdown in
> the collaborative process, or because they cause unprin-
> cipled agreements to be reached. (p 79)

Moore (1986) suggests that mediators in such cases work with
both parties to attempt to minimise the effects of unequal
power. The techniques he suggests are helping the weaker to
recognise the costs of bluffing, especially where bluffs are
characterised by threats, and to cause doubt in the parties'
minds as to their assessments of the power balance, thus
inhibiting any exploitative use of influence. He proceeds to
point out that in cases of extremely unequal power relations
the mediator is faced with ethical and role dilemmas and
must resist the temptation to become an advocate for the
weaker party while adhering to the task of assisting them to
seek an acceptable settlement. Mayer (1987) states that situations of power imbalance present real tests to the mediation
process, and addresses the question of whether it is possible
or appropriate for a mediator to redress imbalances where
they exist. Drawing on the work of Davis and Salem (1984) he
suggests that mediation is appropriate for dealing with such
situations to the extent that it ensures a measure of fair
process within the context of existing structural realities:

> . . . handling the imbalances means ensuring that each
> party's point of view gets a fair hearing and that no party is
> coerced into agreeing to something that is not in his or her
> interests . . . however . . . a proposed settlement, although
> unequal, may really be the best option for the weaker party.
> Thus, the underlying power relations may dictate an un-
> equal result. Mediation in other words, can provide proce-

dural equality but cannot usually alter the division of resources or the structural conditions that determine the basic
power relations between the parties . . . [it] is not able to
correct basic social ills, create social policy where none
exists, or make resources available that do not exist. (p
81–4)

Critics of mediation have suggested that it not only fails to
equalise power, but that it entrenches inequality by preemp-
ting the use of advocates by weaker parties. Some sceptics
expressed this sentiment on the establishment of IMSSA. The
argument is negated to a large extent by the fact that *mediation
is a voluntary process* — mediators only intervene at the express
invitation of the parties, including the weaker in the relationship. The mediator did not create this situation, and may even
perceive the imbalance as undesireable. This is not the issue
to be addressed, however. Rather the mediator is usually
invited to assist in the search for a settlement of a given
dispute within the context of a larger ongoing relationship,
not to determine the broader ongoing conflict that may
underlie the relationship. Mayer (1987) observes:

Mediation is not a substitute for institutional safeguards that
protect the interests of the public, the unrepresented, or the
disempowered. When safeguards exist, mediators should
see to it that they are not bypassed or subverted. When
they do not, mediators should be clear that their services
cannot substitute for the procedures and policies that protect individual rights and the public interest . . . perhaps the
most that should be expected of mediation is that it does
not exacerbate inequities or prevent people from obtaining
support, redress, or assistance that might otherwise be
available to them. (p 84–5)

Clearly the issue of power is one that will evoke values
dilemmas for mediators — procedural fairness may not
necessarily produce a fair outcome from a substantive point
of view from the perspective of either the weaker party or that
of the mediator. This would narrow mediation in some cir-

cumstances then to assisting a weak party make the best out of a poor set of options, or simply avoid a defeat by overt coercion, that is, find a face saving means of retreat from an impasse.

Mayer(1987) proposes that there is no escaping the ethical dilemmas inherent in such a situation, and that essentially mediation is about helping parties to apply their power more constructively in relationships. The mediator has power in the conflict but this is limited by his role, the mediation contract, the wider social network within which the mediation occurs and self-imposed ethical considerations. The combination of these constraints acts generally to confine mediator behaviour to those of an impartial nature, and deviation from this role may well give rise to the termination of the process as parties withdraw their support.

As indicated earlier, Mayer(1987) proposes that the mediator most appropriately addresses the power relations of the parties, and exercises his own by means of the pursuit of procedural fairness. This, he suggests, would strengthen the bargaining process itself, empowering the parties to negotiate more effectively in the future with the objective of achieving more integrative solutions to problems. Thus mediators could exert their power by, inter alia:

❑ ensuring access by the parties to relevant data;
❑ ensuring an opportunity by each to be heard;
❑ assisting to articulate feelings, perceptions, and values and to identify all relevant interests;
❑ helping to develop creative sets of options that maximise individual and collective interests;
❑ helping parties to evaluate identified options;
❑ formulating selected solutions in a way that increases its effective implementation;
❑ assisting in the design of an implementation procedure;

❑ reminding parties of long term interests as well as immediate or short term objectives.

He points out that almost anything a mediator does in an
intervention is an exercise of influence over the parties in a
dispute, and suggests the following principles to guide ethical practice:

❑ Use power consciously rather than deny its reality.
❑ Use questions and reframe statements to apply pressure
rather than make direct assertions or opinion statements.
❑ Support the process rather than either of the parties, empowering parties through procedural means to speak for
themselves when it is necessary to support them in a
power imbalance situation.
❑ Provide information to exert influence on substantive
issues rather than voice an opinion.
❑ Allow parties to find their own solutions rather than
pressurise one of the mediator's own.
❑ Impartiality is only lost when influence is exerted in favour of one party at the expense of the other.
❑ Be clear on the purpose of mediation to assist parties to
achieve settlements of their own, rather than correct basic
social ills or create new social policy.
❑ Support process rather than any particular outcome.

Mediator assertiveness

Kressel and Pruitt (1985) in a review of research into mediation note that while the popular conception of a mediator is
that of a non-assertive facilitator, there is evidence that this is
not always the case in reality. They state that mediator assertiveness seems especially likely when:

❑ A mediator's own values or interests are at stake.
❑ The dispute involves very high levels of tension and hostility.

❑ The mediator is exposed to strong institutional pressures
    to avoid the costs of adjudication.

While mediators may be assertive in 'forcing an entry' to
a dispute when their interests are at stake (Zartman and
Touval 1985), or in obtaining information in an exchange it
appears that they are most likely to exercise such an approach
on substantive issues when they may directly pressurise a
party to agree to specific proposals (Kressel and Pruitt 1985).
Further, assertive intervention is positively associated with
settlement under certain circumstances. Hiltrop (1985) proposes that directive actions such as threatening to quit or
suggesting arbitration are most effective in situations of high
conflict intensity (for example during a strike) or where issues
of principle are at stake (for example union recognition). On
the other hand such interventions appear to be ineffective in
interests disputes, such as wage bargaining. Kolb (1983) cautions that directiveness may negatively affect a mediator's
acceptability for future disputes, and Kressel and Pruitt
(1985) warn that the long term effects of assertiveness are
unknown, but warn that it may reduce the psychological
ownership parties have over an agreement and result in
non-compliance.

THE CONFLICT DYNAMIC

Mediators require sensitivity to a variety of levels of possible
conflict in entering a dispute situation, especially where the
parties in direct interaction are representative of larger constituencies.

The *presenting dispute* is the one faced by a mediator upon
entry to a situation. Typically it is the issue that negotiators
at the table have stalled on, and is the issue for which they
invite the mediator's assistance. Not uncommonly this is the
focus of much of the mediator's activities. However, many
disputes have more complex roots than this. Quite often there

are *disagreements within the bargaining teams,* which may be the real reason for failing to achieve movement between the parties at the table. It is my experience that teams often attempt to conceal this from the mediator — it is seen as a domestic matter, and certainly not the issue for which the mediator was asked in. Although such internal disputes may be the real obstacle to progress then, there may be resistance to the mediator uncovering or discussing these. The need to present a unified front prevails over the search for settlement.

There is an added dimension, however, that of the *constituency.* Constituencies are not at the table, they are not confronted with all the facts and pressures that their representatives face. As a consequence their expectations may remain unrealistic as to what might actually be achieved in the bargaining process. Bargaining representatives may be hampered in their efforts to achieve agreements by intransigent constituencies, producing tensions between these and their own negotiation teams, and an enormously complex and risky process for all concerned. Nelson Mandela, for instance, has been accused of making contradictory statements about the talks process with government. This might be ascribed to the fact that he is talking to two or more constituencies. Firstly he is faced with his own constituency whose expectations may not equate with what can actually be achieved at the table — the task is to keep them satisfied that their team is not selling them out, mobilised in order to keep the necessary tension in the process, and at the same time realistic in order that a settlement might be 'sold' to them when and if one is achieved. If he appears too placatory or seems to be weak in the negotiation he may lose constituency to other more radical groups who harbour doubts about the process. If he does not appear reasonable he may frighten off the constituency of the team with which he is bargaining. So he must talk concurrently to several constituencies with conflicting interests — as must De Klerk.

Appearing to have integrity, strength, a capacity to meet expectations and be realistic all at the same time clearly presents some problems — some inconsistency is not entirely surprising.

Other problems arise in cases where there is a *tenuous relationship between a constituency and its representatives*. This may arise for several reasons — factions within the constituency with competing views as to goals or strategies, may render clear mandates impossible and settlements reached difficult to implement with any consistency. Alternatively a unified constituency may begin to believe that its representatives are operating beyond their mandate, or getting 'too close' to the opposition team producing tensions.

Thus mediators need to be aware of the dimensions of the conflict dynamic, and to assess whether the problem on the table is really the issue at stake. If not, how open are the parties to dealing with problems arising at other levels, and how amenable are they to trying to grips with these?

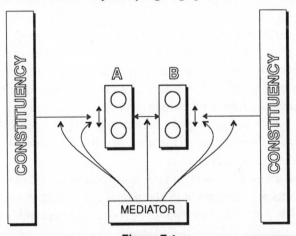

Figure 7.1
Dimensions of the conflict dynamic

In a labour–management dispute where the union was negotiating for the first time with management having only recently achieved a majority representation, the mediator became aware that the union organiser was asking for the kind of information and impressions that he would already have had and discussed with union members: 'Why do you think the group personnel manager has flown all the way from Johannesburg to this meeting?' 'What do you think the likelihood is that the company will improve its offer?' 'What would happen if no agreement is reached?' The mediator became aware that the organiser was probably asking for confirmation of impressions he had already imparted to the members himself, either because he had been unable to convince them or because a second opinion would act to confirm their validity. When management put forward a final offer, the personnel manager suggested to the mediator that they both leave the situation so as to convey to members that this was the final offer, and that no further negotiations would be pursued. The mediator turned down the suggestion, not wanting to be used as part of management's strategy in the process, but also because the shopstewards had asked that he come to the reportback meeting where a similar process was followed with the representatives asking him in front of those present why the personnel manager had left, what the significance of a 'final offer' was, and so on. The mediator thus performed a role in this situation of assisting the union representatives to convey a message clearly to their members — in effect a form of internal mediation between representatives and their constituency.

An interesting finding in my study (Anstey 1988) was that more respondents on both the management and the union side felt that a mediator should be able to persuade their side than the other. This would seem to reflect an acknowledgement that often frontline negotiators find the mediator helpful in getting their team or constituency to move where they have been unable to. This internal persuasion process may follow unusual lines. After a deadlock had been reached in a mediation wherein management was demanding that it retract a food allowance in a hostel in exchange for improved wages, the mediator contacted the group industrial relations manager in head office. He pointed out that the union had indicated that it might accept the retraction if it was carried out over a period of time, but that the company team had stated that it had no mandate for this — only to retract the allowance. The mediator suggested staggering the withdrawal of the allowance over say a three year period. The group industrial relations manager stated that this was categorically unacceptable. When the mediator phoned the company some weeks later, the number two negotiator advised that the chief negotiator had had a brainwave that settled the matter — he had suggested staggering the withdrawal of the allowance over a three year period, and the union had accepted! The chief negotiator had obviously claimed the idea as his own, having obtained it from the group industrial relations manager who no doubt claimed it as *his* own! A shift of this sort allowed everyone to retain a semblance of dignity in the change of stance, to own the idea and appear good in front of their subordinates. Again a form of internal mediation away from the negotiation table to allow flexibility into a dispute situation. Sometimes mediation requires some hard swallowing in terms of idea ownership, but agreements are more likely if parties own the process and the outcome.

MEDIATING COMMUNITY DISPUTES

Community disputes are quite different to labour disputes in many respects. In labour disputes the parties are defined and usually accorded a level of mutual legitimacy by each other, the relationship is structured, the negotiators are accountable to defined constituencies with known procedures for mandating and reportbacks as well as for their election or appointment as representatives. The areas of dispute that arise between the parties are relatively clearly identified, and mediators tend to have a recognised expertise in the field in which they operate.

These characteristics are often not evident in community disputes. Often it is not clear who the parties are that should be involved in dispute settlement. Because disputes often arise in an ad hoc way, there is no trackrecord of negotiation or mutual problem solving to fall back on. Parties often do not give each other legitimacy — even arguing that to negotiate would ascribe acceptance of the existence of the other party or an acknowledgement of the legitimacy of their problem. If one negotiates with squatters, is one not ascribing them some sort of right to discuss their presence in an area, moving the debate from whether they should be there at all to one wherein the conditions of their presence are ironed out? Leaders may arise who have not been formally elected, operate under no constitutions, and have no clear mandating or reportback structures. Community disputes then often lack many of the factors that facilitate dispute resolution, and are far more complex and difficult to deal with. It may difficult to locate acceptable mediators — often those with some expertise are not seen as acceptable to the parties or even known to them. Conversely, acceptable persons may lack the expertise. One way to deal with this problem is to provide training for those in communities who might be acceptable mediators in conflict-torn communities, and provide back-up resources for them. In a seriously conflictual community, comprising people deeply suspicious of each other and outsiders, how does one gain entry to the situation? (Pretorius 1990)

Mika (1987) proposes several defining features of community conflicts:

- ❑ They are often multi-party and complex in character.
- ❑ Violence is often a factor.
- ❑ They are often centred in racial, ethnic, religious or ideological differences.
- ❑ They often have protracted histories.
- ❑ The violent character of the relationship often demands state intervention.
- ❑ State intervention often protracts the conflict, merely adding another dimension to its already complex character.
- ❑ All the characteristics of escalated conflict are evident with parties having low trust in each other, deindividuation, loss of belief that solutions are possible, rigid stands of principle and threats and applications of violent sanctions.

The applicability of this American-based set of observations to South Africa is self-evident. Mika also provides some hints to community mediators for tackling disputes (box 7.2).

Problems in community mediations: some experiences

In a factional dispute in a township, the problems of power imbalance and absence of bargaining structures was evidenced when one side kept sending different negotiation teams to each session. No consistency could be maintained and there was serious doubt about mandating procedures — every session started from scratch. The fact that it was the more powerful of the two parties that played this game led to some suspicion that there was a deliberate effort to scuttle the negotiation process while at the same time appearing to be interested in the search for a settlement. There was no formal procedure for bargaining, no history of negotiation to call on in respect of normative behaviour, and only one side really needed an agreement. The other simply wanted to look as if

- Focus on dispute settlement rather than trying to resolve the whole conflict — *an issue by issue approach.*
- *Target less complex disputes first* — get the parties on a roll of settling matters to improve their attitude to the process and the possibilities of settlement through negotiation generally.
- Aim for a process of *incremental reconciliation.*
- Link parties with *community resources.*
- *Proactive interventions* may act to limit conflict escalation rather than reactive responses.
- Establish an *advisory committee/ use a mediation team*
- Establish *procedural ground rules.*
- Establish *an agreed agenda* to focus energies and keep the process on track.
- *Write down and sign agreements*
- Have *clear implementation plans* and progress evaluations/monitoring processes.

Box 7.2
Hints for community mediators

it was playing in good faith. Eventually the mediators withdrew from the process, suspending it until the negative party showed good faith in the process. Within a week the leaders of this group were involved in a shootout with the other group and then the police — a subsequent conviction seeing them off to jail.

Another experience served to illustrate problems in community bargaining when an intervention was attempted in a black taxi dispute. Two rival factions had experienced a crisis when their drivers refused to convey passengers until they had consummated a unity. The drivers claimed that they would no longer tolerate being at shot at, knifed, or attacked as part of their duties, or arrested by police because owners of the vehicles would not licence them timeously or ensure their roadworthiness. The taxi faction fights in South Africa are rooted in a complexity of reasons — a struggle for territory in terms of routes and ranks; historical relations between groups of owners; ideological issues (some claiming to be the 'peoples' taxis' and accusing the others of exploitative fares); a power imbalance with one group having established good relations with vehicle producers, insurance houses, and the authorities, and being perceived as closing out opportunities for others. On entering the dispute at half an hour's notice, and with the urgency being that no taxis would run the following day unless an accord could be achieved, the mediator established that some of the problem lay in a previous attempt to settle the matter which had been poorly handled.

When faced with protesting drivers the two groups had agreed to attempt a unity. One of the parties (the more powerful) was particularly angry that the other appeared to have joined forces with the drivers in forcing the matter through — they had been publicly targeted in a march to their offices. At a meeting a chairman (from the weaker group) was elected to control the proceedings which included the proper election of a unity sub-committee with representatives from both sides. This chairman was also chosen to be an additional member of the sub-committee, but not its chairman — a post achieved by a member of the stronger group. At the meeting a provisional new name was agreed but it was determined that this would not be made official until each had reported to their national bodies. In the interim, the subcommittee convened, and impressed by the way the chairman of the first meeting had handled matters, determined that he would be a better chairman of the subcommittee as well and duly appointed him — an act never reported to the wider consti-tuencies. With no decisions having been made as to the secrecy of the meeting, this chairman proceeded to discuss the proposed new unity and its name with the press. When the stronger party read the newspapers, their suspicions about a conspiracy were confirmed—a person from the other group claiming to be chairman (contrary to the election process) was making public the whole issue before the national meetings. An urgent meeting was convened with the mediator invited to attempt to achieve a settlement.

In the course of this meeting during which the mediator met with each group in separate caucus, it became clear that the stronger group was worried that the weaker was conspiring a unity to gain access to its funds; the drivers were demanding payment from a common fund as the sign of a *de facto* unity; the weaker group's major concern was not the idea of unity, or access to funds, but the trustworthiness of the other owners; the members of the unity committee complained that they had been given no terms of reference or rules of behaviour and felt they were being set up by the larger groups to carry blame for whatever went wrong. Drawing on these fears and interests, the mediator compiled an agreement which acknowledged the complexity of the dispute, and the fact that each party operated under articles of association which made a simple disbanding and immediate new unity impossible. Both parties agreed to contribute to a common fund — known as the unity fund — on an interim basis, from which the drivers would be paid. An elected interim committee would be charged with investigating the obstacles to unity in terms of funding, articles of association, legal aspects and to report back to all at a common meeting to be held in month's time. No access to each other's funds would be allowed, and routes and ranks would be shared. The sub-committee was not to make any public statements. In this way an agreement based in the fears and interests of the parties was evolved — the agreement was an interim one; the subcommittee was given clear tasks, time periods and guidelines and empowered to seek any advice it needed from expert sources; the funds of each group were protected; the drivers would be paid from a common fund.

Everyone liked the agreement — until the mediator suggested writing it down and signing it! Then the resistance emerged. This was not a usual practice (to which the other groups responded by suggesting a lack of intention to live out the agreement honourably), elected representatives were not given powers to sign agreements, why can't we just do it, why do we have to sign a written agreement? The mediator suggested that perhaps problems had arisen in the past owing to the failure to live out agreements and the lack of clarity in such agreements. Writing the settlement down would provide everyone with a factual record. It emerged that not only were representatives unwilling to sign, but so were their electorates unwilling to let them. Eventually everyone in the meeting signed — over eighty signatures! A brief period of peace was experienced before matters fell apart again.

A lack of good faith, an absence of bargaining experience, a history of distrust, no clear mandating procedures or empowered negotiating teams, an unwillingness to utilise societal structures such as courts, complex collections of issues threaded with deep interpersonal and factional differences bedevil such interventions. In others the sheer power imbalance between the parties renders constructive negotiation almost impossible. Squatter communities attempting to negotiate with the authorities have little power — they have nowhere to stay, are not recognised as formal communities, are illegally occupying land, distrust and are alienated from mainstream resources of legal and social assistance. All they may have to trade with is their capacity to make relocation an orderly and peaceful process or a difficult resistant one, and the power of embarrassment over the authorities through use of the press. They cannot negotiate with local authorities for land which they are not empowered to grant. While interim measures such as use of the media, trading off good behaviour in exchange for temporary basic services such as water and latrines is possible in some instances, until the land issue has been redefined their bargaining prospects are bleak. It is a matter which must be dealt with at a national policy level — at local levels it is often a matter of holding action on a temporary basis.

BUILDING RELATIONSHIPS BY OBJECTIVES

A different approach to tackling deeply fractured labour–management relationships using third-party assistance is the Relationships by Objectives (RbO) programme. Introduced by the Federal Mediation and Conciliation Service in the USA in 1975, the technique was introduced to South Africa in 1984. It specifically precludes substantive bargaining, focusing its attention on open discussion of problems in a relationship, and targeted jointly devised ways of improving matters.

The roots of the RbO

The RbO draws its values and techniques from three bases -traditional dispute mediation, organisation development (OD), and Management by Objectives (MbO). Values of a developmental and humanist character underpin the RbO as they do OD, but unlike OD the role and power of a trade union in an enterprise as a legitimate agent of employee interests is acknowledged. Like MbO it places emphasis on clear goal identification, action plans, deadlines and regular evaluation of progress, but again, unlike MbO it is conducted through employee representatives rather than individual employees. The collective power base makes for a different level of relations in the engagement. Finally, like traditional mediation it makes use of third-party assistance, but extends the process beyond attention solely on issues in dispute to the relationship itself and the daily experiences of managers and workers in places of work. Attitudes, behaviours, communications and perceptions are the issues of concern.

Key elements of the RbO

Several elements are mooted in the literature (Young 1982; Popular undated):

❑ Its use is confined to exceptionally *stressed relationships* — it is not an everyday intervention.

❑ The parties must *recognise the need for and want assistance.*

❑ *Top level commitment* from management and the union is required.

❑ A full spectrum of *key personnel* from top management to supervisors, and union officials and shopstewards should participate.

❑ The intervention is carried out in a *retreat setting* over a period of four days, with regular follow-ups. Current thinking in South Africa questions this tradition. It has been proposed that RbOs should be conducted closer to workplaces to enable regular feedback to union members, and fresh mandating. This might prevent the discreditation of worker representatives which could occur within the context of a retreat setting where representatives are removed from direct interaction with workers.

❑ A *team of facilitators* is required to deal with the numbers of persons involved and cope with the level of administrative and facilitative tasks required.

Stages in the RbO process

Several descriptions of the RbO phases are evidenced in the literature. It is proposed here that five major stages are distinguishable:

❑ the pre-RbO phase;

❑ the ice-breaker phase;
❑ the problem analysis phase;
❑ the action planning phase; and
❑ the implementation and follow-up phase.

Pre-RbO phase

Prior to undertaking an RbO it is essential that the parties have a clear grasp of what the process entails — its steps, the nature of the intervention, its risks and the fact that it is not a 'magic wand' but rather the first step in a long-term process of building a more effective relationship between them. Ideally the mediators should make separate presentations to the company management team and the labour team on the process, deal with questions and provide information on its method and objectives to ensure that neither party enters the RbO with any illusions. It is particularly important that the parties understand that the intervention is *not* to be used for *negotiation of substantive issues* (wages and conditions of employment) nor to *renegotiate the recognition/procedural agreement*, although experience shows that the parties may assume tasks during the course of the RbO which do result in amendments or additions to such agreements eg a new strike code.

Ice-breaker phase

Existing tensions, communication problems and distrust may make it difficult for the parties to engage directly with the central tasks of the RbO. In addition the adversarial nature of the relationship may have polarised the parties into us–them attitudes and stances. Icebreakers are then used to engender a joint ethos of problem solving, sharing and openness. These are usually carried out in mixed labour–management teams, although this practice has not been strictly adhered to in South Africa.

Commonly, the parties in small groups address the question: 'What do I expect to get out of this programme?'

It appears that in the USA this process is usually conducted in small joint labour–management subgroups. In South Africa we have tended to address the question in separate caucuses prior to bringing the parties together to exchange their views. One reason is to allow the parties a feeling of room to develop and expand on their ideas in their own caucuses before entering exchanges with the other, where further discussion can take place. However, in recent times the mixed caucus has been utilised and has worked well for all concerned.

Some typical trade union and management responses are shown in box 7.3. Early experience would indicate that labour hopes and expectations are largely *value-instrumental and affectual* in nature expressing needs for recognition, understanding, equity and opportunity, while managerial expectations although having some of this tone are largely *instrumental-rational* in nature, being centred in a desire to improve communications and understanding, clarify mutual roles, achieve greater cooperation and promote procedural adherence for purposes of improved organisational effectiveness. In a sense this reflects the nature of the 'trade-off' in the process: an exchange of greater acknowledgement of employees as human beings for improved organisational functioning.

In the USA a further icebreaker is commonly used. The parties, again in mixed groups, view a film portraying a supervisor–subordinate interaction of a problem nature. The groups then analyse the film giving particular attention to the attitudes of the individuals in the film, their relationship problems and finally suggestions for improving matters. In this way the parties are warmed to the impending task of grappling with their own pain, by tackling a parallel problem in someone else's relationship. The experience of joint problem solving on a parallel problem is a useful groupwork

Trade unions expect:

- management to obtain a *grassroots* understanding of the lives of workers;
- to discuss and change racial practices in the company;
- to obtain equitable opportunities and treatment of people in the organisation regardless of race or union membership;
- to ensured that management does not use police in dispute situations; and
- greater management respect for trade unions' rights, and for workers.

Management expects:

- to achieve better understanding between the union and management;
- to clarify the role and power of shop stewards;
- to impart a clearer understanding of management functions, powers and responsibilities to the union;
- to achieve a clearer understanding of cultural differences;
- to achieve greater cooperation between workers and managers;
- to ensure adherence to agreements; and
- to improve communications between parties.

Box 7.3
Expectations of the RbO

technique for improving people's problemsolving skills without invoking the deep anxieties that may accompany a premature demand that they deal with their own interactional troubles (Anstey 1988).

In South Africa the film has not been used in every intervention and some debate surrounds its appropriateness, and beyond this the amount of time required for the exercise especially as the RbO seems to take longer here than in the

USA. This is the product of a variety of unique variables including language and the amount of caucus time used by unions in the internal consensus seeking process.

The objectives phase

This phase comprises several substeps. The labour and management parties are separated and asked to identify *what they believe each of them should be doing to improve and maintain a constructive relationship*. Each side addresses the following:

> To improve and maintain constructive relations, management should . . .

> To improve and maintain constructive relations the trade union should . . .

Each side is assisted to compile lists of objectives by the mediators who act to clarify and record items, and then to draw up four lists of preliminary goals:

❑ Management thinks the union should (MU).
❑ Management thinks management should (MM).
❑ Union thinks management should (UM).
❑ Union thinks union should (UU).

Limited experience in South Africa indicates (not surprisingly perhaps) that the parties tend to make many more proposals for the other party than for their own (table 7.4). This clearly reflects how perceptions of blameworthiness tend to be projected onto the other party with a corresponding minimisation of own culpability in conflictual, polarised interactions.

Table 7.4
Number of proposals to improve relations
by management and unions in RbOs

	MM	MU	UM	UU	TOTAL	Consolidated to
RbO 1	6	22	20	2	50	21 items
RbO 2	27	24	34	4	89	44 items

This process may take a day as the parties wrestle with the tasks of concretising sometimes vague feelings of grievance into more operational statements — the emphasis is on what the parties should *do* to improve relations, rather than what is wrong between them. This obliges a task oriented, remedial orientation rather than the generalised catharsis of a 'gripe group'. The mediators' participation is to ensure the groups remain 'on track' in this exercise.

It is important that this step be thoroughly and openly performed as it lays the foundations for the action steps that are to follow. The clearer the proposals generated here, and the more comprehensive and honest the lists compiled the sounder the base from which to continue the intervention. It becomes difficult later during action planning for instance, if the parties keep adding to the list of proposals and thereby lengthening the agenda, producing 'surprise' grievances at inopportune moments and obstructing a clear focus on issues under discussion.

Once these four lists have been compiled by the mediators, labour and management *convene to discuss them and to clarify terms and meaning.* This initial exchange has shown itself to be an emotive interaction as the parties enter their first meaningful exchange on their relationship. Hurt, anger and confusion accompany some of the surprise (or shock) of expressing and listening to previously unspoken perceptions. The parties may want to extend the exchange beyond that of mutual clarification and it is the task of the mediators to confine discussion to this end at this point in time. Certainly items are not removed from the lists merely because they evoke anger, if anything such items demand open exploration if progress is to be made, but this is yet to come. In one RbO the union suggested that the personnel and IR functions be separated, and an IR Director be appointed in a poorly disguised expression of mistrust and hostility towards the personnel manager. Management responded angrily to the 'attack' on an individual within its ranks insisting the item be withdrawn if the exercise was to be continued. A lengthy and sometimes angry exchange eventually saw the item tabled but not withdrawn, that is, held over for further discussion in a subsequent meeting.

In another intervention management suggested that it actively improve its communications with all employees. This apparently benign, common-sense suggestion evoked resistance from the trade union, to which managers responded angrily. They felt their deepest fears of an attack on managerial 'prerogative' were being realised and that a clear effort to establish worker control was in evidence. How could an employer be prohibited from speaking with his employees?

While not retreating from their position, the shop stewards pointed out that over the years a practice had been established whereby the foreman would issue instructions through the shop steward. Any change in this would be likely to create industrial unrest. In other words managerial practice had deviated from the ideal in managers' minds. This demanded some serious review of issues of control, communication systems, roles of foremen, supervisors and shop stewards, past practices, future concerns, and simply 'what works' in terms of production requirements.

Once the clarification process is completed, the parties are adjourned while the mediators compile a *consolidated list of objectives*. In this exercise they attempt to synthesise the lists compiled by the teams and to produce a less daunting set of objectives for the parties to engage around. However, the mediators assume no rights to arbitrarily dispense with items — each item on the consolidated list is carefully crossreferenced or sourced to its place on the original lists so that the labour–management teams can check that nothing has been omitted or distorted. The consolidation process extends the mediators' day, usually being carried out overnight so that the parties can start a new day with the synthesised list. Further exchange takes place on the list as the parties endure their concerns are embodied satisfactorily in the new working document. Box 7.4 reflects a typical objective off consolidated lists compiled in this manner.

The consolidated list may for purposes of convenience and organisation be subdivided into subcategories, the most common being:

❑ training
❑ communications
❑ management attitudes and practices
❑ union attitudes and practices
❑ management-union relations
❑ supervisory relations
❑ other

In the interventions I have been involved in, this exchange and the debate surrounding each objective tends to carry through to the end of the third day, and the days are not short. About 40 hours of work is involved over this period. Unlike the US model, we have quite often adjourned the parties for a week or so at this stage before meeting to establish joint action plans for each objective on the consolidated list. This would appear to be useful temporal separation of tasks as the parties are often tired as a consequence of some cathartic debate. The interim period between meetings allows a rejuvenation of energies, some time to reflect on what has emerged in the process, a period to 'settle into' or 'cool off' on more contentious proposals and to give thought to constructive action plans.

UU2 Comply with and abide by the joint agreement.
UM12 Comply with the recognition agreement and not use 'pol-
      icy' as a means of avoiding it.
MU14 Encourage common understanding and interpretation of
      the recognition agreement.

CONSOLIDATED LIST OF OBJECTIVES	SOURCE
1 Encourage common understanding and mutual interpretation of the recognition agreement to promote compliance with it.	UU2 UM12 MU14

Box 7.4
An example of items in a consolidated objectives list

The action planning phase

In this phase labour and management jointly, either in smaller sub-groups or the main caucus depending on the size of the group, address the question of action steps to achieve the objectives already identified. While the parties may have initially spent time in separate caucus identifying problems in, and objectives for the relationship, this is very much a joint endeavour. It is now that objectives must be translated into feasible tasks, that the interaction moves beyond identifying what people want, to what they must do to achieve it.

As in the MbO, objectives are addressed through the joint agreement of action steps the assignment of responsibilities for performing these steps and agreement as to deadlines for completion of tasks. The following format is utilised:

Objectives	Action steps	Responsibility	Date
1			
2			
3			
4			

Managements have undertaken:

- to audit workforce qualifications, survey interest and establish costs of providing educational assistance to assist employees to advance their training and education;
- to consult with the shopstewards' committees on vacancies and short- and long-term planning affecting training and job advancement on a standard monthly meeting basis;
- to recognise criteria such as experience rather than just qualifications for promotions, and to advertise opportunities internally first;
- to eliminate separate facilities for different race groups;
- to improve worker facilities;
- to publish and distribute the recognition agreement core policies and procedures in relevant languages;
- to involve shop stewards on safety matters;
- to draw up and distribute organisational charts to clarify management structures and functions;
- to implement a more equitable system for the use of telephones by all employees;
- to respond more timeously to worker problems and grievances;
- to provide facilities to assist shop stewards fulfil their tasks;
- to improve communications to all levels of management;
- to treat workers with greater respect, and engage them on levels other than discipline alone;
- to improve industrial relations skills of all line managers;
- to disclose information manning levels, production changes and financial circumstances; and
- to consult and involve the union in changes to production targets, while the union recognises its right to set such targets.

Box 7.5 (a)
Selected examples of action steps undertaken
by management in RbOs

Trade unions have undertaken:

- to arrive punctually and prepared for negotiations at agreed times;
- to carry reasonable, company-specific/relevant demands from workers to negotiations (as opposed to stereotyped, standard union positions);
- to give more notice to management with regard to the release of shop stewards for union training courses;
- to respond to issues more timeously;
- to confine shop stewards' activities to those outlined in relevant agreements;
- to articulate true aspirations of workers to management;
- to ensure swift use of procedures to bring matters to management's attention;
- to ensure complete and accurate conveying of information to members; and
- to respect the foreman's role of first line manager.

Unions and managements have agreed jointly:

- to introduce an induction programme involving a demonstration of the whole production process and the significance of each employee's role in it;
- to address methods and requirements for information disclosure purposes;
- to negotiate a code of conduct for strike and protest action;
- to negotiate all decisions affecting union members;
- to consult on overseas codes of practice;
- to oppose intimidation and discrimination in the workplace;
- to establish a committee to address housing needs of employees and frame a company response to these;
- to improve social and welfare facilities;
- to issue joint statements of good intent prior to the start of negotiations and cooperate in issuing joint statements of positions after each negotiation session; and
- to regulate expression of political protest in the workplace.

Box 7.5 (b)
Selected examples of action steps undertaken by labour, and jointly by labour and management in RbOs

Some examples of agreed action steps are reflected in box 7.5.

Care must be taken to ensure that the parties establish realistic time frames for task completion. Early experience indicates that in the enthusiasm of engaging positively over action steps the parties sometimes overload themselves or misjudge what is possible in given time periods. This can lead to feelings of disillusionment with the process and with each others' good intent.

Follow-up and implementation phase

The mediators undertake the task of covering the parties every 3–6 months initially, to review progress and assist the parties to overcome obstacles that arise in the process. As discussed earlier, feedback on the parties' feelings of satisfaction with the process has to date been largely positive, and some demonstrable changes in practices and attitudes have been evidenced as a consequence of RbO. American experience warns that not all interventions are successful, and certainly more recent interventions may be experiencing something of a honeymoon phase in the first flush of a new beginning.

The crisis at Mercedes Benz where 500 workers occupied the factory to pressurise for decentralised bargaining, has been held up as a symptom of failure of the RbO conducted there shortly beforehand. This I believe is an erroneous assessment. The RbO does not guarantee a comfortable outcome for all players. Sometimes problems in factories are the product of internal tensions in a team. No progress may be possible until these have been dealt with. The process may simply act to bring a boil to a head in order that it might be lanced. In the Mercedes case 500 workers defied the company and their union in their demands and were eventually dismissed. In other RbOs managers have been dismissed or left an organisation following the process when their activities

were identified as the cause of discontent. If the parties use
the process honestly they can identify problems in their relationship — the action choices that must follow are often
painful. Nevertheless, meaningful change has been achieved
where the parties committed themselves to the process and
hopefully the new trackrecord of successful engagement built
up through the RbO will be sufficient to develop an ongoing
commitment to more effective ways of relating between labour and management in places of work.

RBO: AN EARLY ASSESSMENT

The paucity of experience with RbO in South Africa must act
to temper any definitive statements as to its effectiveness and
potentials. However, the few interventions conducted to date
have largely left the parties satisfied with the outcomes and
there is certainly room to feel positive about the technique.

Positively, both labour and management have reported
improved communications, greater levels of trust and openness in relations and improved understanding of each others'
needs, pressures and roles. Some of the rhetoric, posturing,
stereotyping and distancing that characterise deeply conflictual relations has diminished. Beyond this it seems that improved relations on a daily shopfloor level have had a
positive influence on the parties' engagement in substantive
bargaining. In effect, the RbO provides a means for parties
desirous of moving out of self-reinforcing cycles of mutual
attack to establish a new relationship base for future interaction.

Some important cautionary notes are necessary at this juncture:

RbO is no panacea
It cannot be expected to 'magically' resolve all the issues,
undo embittered histories or remedy all poor relationships on

a one-off basis. It is a *process technique,* providing a framework within which the parties might engage to improve their realtionship. It guarantees no outcomes or answers — these are dependent on the commitment of the parties to seeking a more effective engagement.

RbO is not an alternative to collective bargaining

It is not a aprocess to undermine trade unions, or to evade adversarialism as a component of labour–management. RbO acknowledges the pluralist notion of an ongoing interaction between employers and organised labour characterised by an ongoing tension of divergent interests and mutual dependence. It does not seek to supplant substantive or contractual negotiations — the adversarial component of the relationship. It does seek to improve the cooperative relations required in an enterprise to be successful. An improved effectiveness in adversarial exchanges may well be a spinoff consequence of improved daily relations between the parties but this must be understood in perspective. Issues underlying the conflictual component of the relationship remain. In improving the climate of wider relations, a carryover *may* occur into negotiations over distributive issues — but this does not obscure these as distributive issues.

RbO has an uncertain place in South Africa's evolving IR system

Countries have evolved different systems to accommodate the dynamic of adversarialism and cooperation in labour–management relations. In an established system such as that of the USA intensive techniques acceptable to both parties can be evolved within relatively secure ideological boundaries. South Africa is in a more volatile stage of development. Its 'system' is subject to the interaction of sharply divergent interests and ideologies, its future shape and form are uncertain in many senses. Adversarial roles are safer than cooperative ones for parties engaged in a debate over fundamental power related issues. If any of the parties feel that their interests might be compromised through work on 'cooperatively toned' endeavours the commitment required for the RbO may be eroded.

The above debate does not address all the issues that the introduction of the RbO to South Africa raises. It should, however, serve to caution against a 'flavour of the month' implementation of the technique. An overexcited, careless introduction of the intervention could act to discredit it. The RbO should be applied in appropriate situations with parties who are committed, appraised as to the process and realistic in their expectations, with the assistance of mediators/facilitators experienced in the collective bargaining process and a good grasp of group dynamics and organisation development.

As a technique RbO offers a meaningful 'bridge' between the collaborative techniques of OD, the adversarialism of dispute mediation between employers and organised labour, and the clear task-directed focus of MbO. It offers a framework within which the parties might jointly establish the boundaries of adversarialism and cooperation in their engagement, and a means to redefining embittered relationships towards a new beginning. It offers process rather than outcomes, opportunities rather than answers. A proper introduction of the technique giving attention to its voluntarist character, the requirement of a 'knowledgeable' commitment on the part of the parties prior to embarking on the exercise and the importance of using jointly acceptable mediators will hopefully act to limit inappropriate implementation of RbOs in South Africa.

8
CHECKLISTS FOR PRACTICE

This book has sought to introduce readers to the dynamics of conflict relations, and to the theory and practice of effective negotiation and peacemaking. It is clear that knowledge and skills in negotiation are not sufficient to ensure that this is the method parties will choose in attempting to resolve or regulate their differences. Many other factors influence whether negotiation or problem solving will be the alternative of choice for the parties -past relations, perceptions of each other's sincerity or trustworthiness, beliefs that more confrontational approaches will produce more rewarding outcomes, ideological rigidity, constituency pressures, available resources, experiences of other negotiations to mention but a few.

The approach adopted here then, is not a simple advocacy of negotiation as the palliative for all ills. History is littered with examples of failed negotiations, rebellions, authoritarian repression and confrontational exchange at enormous cost to human life and liberty. It must be acknowledged that, however desireable the negotiation option might be, it is not the only one available to parties in conflict — it is the consequence of *strategic choices* between such parties, and a wide range of historical and current environmental influences. There seems to be a human tendency towards competitive rather than cooperative interactive behaviour, even where the latter is clearly indicated by rational criteria; to become entrapped by conflict process; and perhaps to negotiate out of a base of 'enlightened self-interest' rather than altruism or a blind commitment to the process as having inherent worth.

The intention here is in the first instance to provide a basic understanding of conflict, its sources and dynamics. Then an attempt has been made to provide some criteria that might be used to assess the potentials for negotiation in conflict situations, in the recognition that parties have other options available to them in such situations. Where negotiation *is* the process of choice for the parties, a practical framework for effective negotiation and problem solving is provided. A range of original works have been drawn on for this purpose, with the objective being less to introduce new thinking than to present available knowledge and experience in a reachable form. Finally, a chapter on aspects of mediation as a process concerned with facilitating and promoting the efficacy of negotiation in conflict and relationship building is presented as a vehicle to assist peacemakers and users of third-party assistance to think through practice-related issues.

The substance of the book obviously lies in the preceding chapters, but it is perhaps appropriate in a work of this sort, whose intention is to provide practical guidelines and debate, to finish with a short set of reminders of some of the key issues, criteria and guidelines raised.

Several reminder categories are addressed here to help parties in conflict, negotiators and mediators achieve clearer understanding of the situations they find themselves in, and to assess problems and potentials in the use of negotiation and third-party assistance. Specifically, 'ready reckoners' are provided for:

❏ assessing the source of the conflict;
❏ determining how the conflict is being expressed/which conflict handling tactics are in evidence;
❏ assessing symptoms of conflict escalation;
❏ considering reasons for the escalation;
❏ assessing whether stalemate has been reached or is imminent; and

❏ determining whether a conflict is de-escalating or might be de-escalated?

Beyond providing some means for understanding the conflict process some criteria for considering the potentials for negotiation in a situation are outlined.

Where negotiation is underway but problems are being experienced, some checklists for assessing what these might be are presented:

❏ What are the obstacles to effective distributive negotiation?

❏ What are the obstacles to effective problem solving?

❏ Are there communication problems?

❏ If we use mediation, what would be the objectives for the process? What should we consider with regard to acceptability? What issues are relevant to the timing of entry?

❏ What are some of the activities required to do it right?

ASSESSING CONFLICT SITUATIONS

It is proposed that conflict exists in relations whenever parties believe that their aspirations cannot be met simultaneously, or perceive a divergence in their values, needs or interests. It remains latent until the parties use their power purposefully to defeat, neutralise or eliminate each other in order to protect or further own interests in the interaction. The emphasis on beliefs and perceptions does not deny that real differences may exist, but lays emphasis on how people understand their relationships and matters arising within these. Seeking to grasp the parties' perceptions, beliefs, assumptions, fears, needs and interests is a critically important element in understanding a conflict situation, the legitimacy the parties accord each other and ascribe to the conflict process, and whether they see it as being functional or dysfunctional in nature. Understanding conflicts requires attention to their structural features (underlying conditions promoting hostilities) and process elements (internal dynamics).

WHAT IS THE SOURCE OF THE CONFLICT?

In seeking to grasp the sources of any conflict it is important to remember that it is the beliefs and perceptions of the actors involved that is significant. Do they perceive the conflict to be rooted in:

❑ differing goals,
❑ structural imbalances,
❑ differing values,
❑ ambiguity,
❑ coordination,
❑ information, or
❑ some other cause?

Are their understandings of the situation the same or different — are they operating out of the same frame of reference?

HOW HAS THE CONFLICT BEEN EXPRESSED/HANDLED TO THIS TIME?

Understanding of conflict situations requires attention not only to sources of strife in a relationship, but also to how it expresses itself or how the parties have dealt with it. Have they used confrontational methods or is negotiation the normative means? Insight into this area may provide information about the knowledge, skills, and motives of the parties. It will provide a grasp of their history of relations and their experience with a range of dispute handling methods. Typical categories of experience include:

❑ Coercion   repressive rules/laws
                                          acts of deterrence

	use of authorities
	restrictions
❏ Insurrection	physical attacks on opposition groups
	generalised violence
	violent attacks on authorities
	violent attacks on property
	civil disobedience
❏ Disruption	protests
	demonstrations
	boycotts
	stayaways
	fasts
	conscientious affirmation
❏ Negotiation	distributive bargaining
	problem solving
	bargaining on the merits
❏ Litigation	legal representation
	arbitration
	use of the courts

IS THE CONFLICT ESCALATING?

An important consideration in assessing any conflict is whether it is escalating. It would seem that during escalation processes, relationship dynamics emerge which make it difficult for effective settlement searches to occur. People often become entrapped in the process until a stalemate is reached or countervailing de-escalation processes emerge.

Symptoms of conflict escalation include:

❏ proliferation of issues;
❏ inefficient communications;
❏ selective information induction;
❏ negative stereotypes/demonisation;

❑ motives of blame and retribution;
❑ zero-sum/all or nothing perceptions;
❑ deindividuation;
❑ increase in contentious tactics;
❑ increased commitment of resources to the conflict;
❑ demands for in-group conformity; and
❑ emergence of autocratic/'hawkish' leaders

WHAT ARE THE REASONS FOR THE ESCALATION IN CONFLICT?

The reasons associated with conflict escalation processes have a cause and effect nature — in other words they are not only symptoms but act in their own right to lock parties into confrontational attitudes and behaviour. In attempting to understand why a conflict is growing, the following should be considered:

❑ expanding agendas;
❑ poor communications;
❑ incorrect assumptions/information;
❑ mutual demonisation/negative stereotypes;
❑ motives of blame and retribution;
❑ zero-sum perceptions;
❑ increased use of contentious tactics;
❑ increased commitment of resources to the conflict;
❑ emergence of 'hawkish' leaders;
❑ constituency pressures;
❑ the belief that conflict escalation acts to unite/cohere/mobilise a party;
❑ the belief that conflict escalation removes dissidents from a group;
❑ the belief that conflict escalation consolidates leadership;
❑ the belief that conflict escalation divides or weakens adversaries;

❏ the belief that conflict escalation removes focus from own problems (internal dissent);
❏ the belief that conflict escalation attracts attention to own problems (external sympathies);
❏ the belief that conflict escalation triggers creativity/ efficiency drives;
❏ the belief that greater gains are possible than through settling or defusing the conflict;
❏ gratification of mobilisation process;
❏ refusal to legitimate alternative interest groups;
❏ absence of acceptable conflict regulation mechanisms;
❏ absence of shared conflict limiting norms;
❏ absence of crosscutting group memberships;
❏ large grievances/large threat;
❏ entrapment

ARE THE PARTIES ENTRAPPED IN THE CONFLICT ESCALATION PROCESS?

Understanding of the entrapment dynamic demands some further consideration as it gives parties an understanding of how they might lock themselves into a dispute, and also some clear indicators about what might be required to defuse a situation. Appropriate questions might include whether parties have entrapped themselves:

❏ by their own ultimatums and deadlines;
❏ by public statements;
❏ by their strategies and actions;
❏ by acts of provocation;
❏ by undisciplined actions of constituencies;
❏ by refusals to legitimate/recognise each other as negotiating partners;
❏ by ideological rigidity;
❏ by perceived threats to their survival

IS THERE A HIGH POTENTIAL FOR VIOLENCE?

A matter of key concern in scenarios of escalating conflict is the extent to which they contain the potential for violence. Theory would indicate that the following factors indicate a higher potential for violence:

❑ high frustration/high threat;
❑ absence of trusted forums, procedures, third parties;
❑ alienation from societal regulation;
❑ violence ideologically acceptable;
❑ group legitimation of violence in relations/normative violence;
❑ poor social controls;
❑ breakdown of group norms;
❑ absence of perceived alternatives;
❑ perceived unfairness/system 'rigged';
❑ perceptions of lessened responsibility;
❑ situations promoting anonymity in groups;
❑ dehumanisation of adversaries;
❑ deindividuation of others; and
❑ track record of violence in relations.

HAS A STALEMATE BEEN REACHED/ CAN THE CONFLICT BE DE-ESCALATED?

Conflicts tend not to escalate in an ongoing way but reach points of stalemate or show signs of de-escalation owing to shifts in relations or internal dynamics in the parties. These often represent 'strategic moments' for exploring alternative means of regulating conflict in future relations or for resolving the issues that caused the confrontation. In other words they represent moments when the negotiation process may have some potential.

Typically the following conditions or activities precipitate stalemates:

- ❏ failure of contentious tactics;
- ❏ exhaustion of necessary resources;
- ❏ loss of social support;
- ❏ unacceptable costs;
- ❏ mutual recognition of a grinding conflict plateau into the future;
- ❏ a conflict crisis/precipice;
- ❏ internal division/competition for leadership;
- ❏ organisational conservatism;
- ❏ new relations between adversaries;
- ❏ coercion; and
- ❏ third-party intervention

WHAT ARE THE POTENTIALS FOR NEGOTIATION?

As indicated earlier, negotiation may not always hold attraction for parties in conflict, they may lack the knowledge or skills to utilise the process effectively; residual effects of past relations may hinder effective use of the process; or appropriate social conditions may not exist for its implementation. The following issues/criteria need attention in considering the potentials for negotiation in any conflictual relationship:

- ❏ Is there a stalemate or de-escalation of the conflict?
- ❏ How do the parties perceive the legitimacy of each other's interests?
- ❏ Are there signals of willingness to accommodate or compromise or problem solve?
- ❏ Is there legitimation of differing interests:
  - − formal legitimation of diverse interest groups;
  - − freedom to associate;
  - − freedom to bargain collectively;

- freedom to protest/campaign; and
- protection of rights under law vs. government edict?
❏ Are there institutionalised mechanisms jointly acceptable for purposes of conflict regulation:
  - negotiation forums;
  - third-party assistance;
  - judicial access; and
  - legitimation of lobby/pressure group activities?
❏ Are these mechanisms seen as:
  - fair;
  - within reach and usable; and
  - having a successful track record?
❏ Is there a norm or successful track record of negotiation/cooperation in relations?
❏ Are there ideological obstacles to negotiation?
❏ Do the parties have the skills (know-how) to negotiate, or do the perceive themselves as having these skills?
❏ Do the parties perceive negotiation as having as much potential as other approaches for the achievement of desireable objectives?
❏ Do the available rewards have valence for the parties?

CHOOSING AN APPROPRIATE NEGOTIATION APPROACH

There is a tendency to define an appropriate negotiation approach by the issues at stake, that is, whether these are substantive or scarce resources issues (distributive tendency); values or procedural issues (integrative tendency); or rights (litigatory) issues. These guidelines tend to be somewhat superficial and academic on their own, however — other factors, for example the history of relations, previous tactics, and ideologies of the parties, can also be important influences in the choice of approach.

Some relevant questions to be addressed here include:

- ❏ Have the parties accurately identified the issues in dispute?
- ❏ What is the nature of the issues?
  - – substantive, fixed sum, variable payoff (distributive tendency);
  - – procedural,values based, potential for mutual benefit (integrative tendency); or
  - – rights dispute (litigation, arbitration).
- ❏ What knowledge and skills do the parties have?
- ❏ What are the parties' ideological commitments?
- ❏ What were their past relations and trust levels?
- ❏ What tactics were used in previous conflicts?
- ❏ In what stage of escalation or de-escalation is the conflict?
- ❏ Are negotiation forums and procedures available, and do the parties have trust in them?

Once negotiation is underway, problems may arise in utilising an approach effectively. The competitive character of distributive bargaining may lead to a wide range of problems in the use of tactics, misjudgement of power realities, and closure. In other instances parties may attempt to implement a more integrative problem-solving approach inappropriately — however desireable cooperative endeavour may sound, certain prerequisites exist if it is to be used effectively, and if those pushing its introduction are not to be discredited by the way in which they attempt to do so.

ASSESSING OBSTACLES TO EFFECTIVE DISTRIBUTIVE BARGAINING

Distributive bargaining is usually associated with situations where parties with competing interests are faced with dividing a limited resource amongst themselves. Bargaining tends to centre around substantive issues with fixed-sum, variable pay-off characteristics. The approach where it is employed poorly, or from a base of rigid positional play and confrontational tactics may lead to problems of brinkmanship, misjudgements of power, and power abuse in relations. This extremely competitive approach has been termed 'positional bargaining' by advocates of alternative needs-based approaches to negotiation. Distributive bargaining may, however, be quite pragmatically employed, without power abuses or rigid positional adherence and in a positive climate. Simply, the parties may recognise that the issues between them are distributive, and that some competitive tactics are required if their substantive interests are to be furthered or protected. They may at the same time recognise the importance of the longer-term relationship and the maintenance of a positive bargaining climate, and utilise their power and choose their pressure tactics in a manner that does not unduly threaten these.

Distributive bargaining should therefore not be understood simplistically — it offers a range of alternatives and thus strategic choices to its users. How they choose to implement the approach is the critical question.

Where problems arise in distributive bargaining, these are often rooted in one or more of the following:

❑ Refusal to legitimate the other in negotiation.
❑ Poor planning (effective planning demands consideration of *both parties'* issues, priorities and ranges):
   - failure to identify issues and their priority;
   - failure to partialise issues;
   - failure to plan for movement;
   - failure to consider fallbacks properly;
   - poor assessment of power realities; and
   - failure to consider possible concessions/common ground.
❑ Extreme/unrealistic positions.

- ❏ Rigid positions/brinkmanship.
- ❏ Lack of clarity on positions/demands/offers.
- ❏ Hidden agendas.
- ❏ Not enough items to trade meaningfully.
- ❏ Too many items to focus negotiation.
- ❏ Rigid/unrealistic mandates/constituency expectations.
- ❏ Absence of mandates.
- ❏ Absence of trust in relations.
- ❏ Tactics that damage relations.
- ❏ Tactics that inhibit movement.
- ❏ Failure to explore interests and needs behind stated positions.
- ❏ Refusal or failure to defend, motivate, justify demands/offers.
- ❏ Absence of acceptable procedures/forums.
- ❏ Stresses in wider social network.
- ❏ Missed signals/failure to transmit signals.
- ❏ Brinkmanship at close.
- ❏ Absence of genuine desire to settle.
- ❏ Escalation in conflict.
- ❏ Entrapment.
- ❏ Misjudgement of capacity to move.
- ❏ Zero-sum perceptions/absence of apparent alternatives.
- ❏ Concessions not valued by the other party.
- ❏ Poor packaging and linking.
- ❏ Communication problems.

ASSESSING OBSTACLES TO/POTENTIALS FOR INTEGRATIVE RELATIONS

Critics of distributive bargaining propose that it locks parties into positions, their commitment to these growing as they try to defend them and convince the other to move. Grudging compromise, rigidity in thinking, attacks on ideas rather than building on them, and a denial of underlying needs and interests are seen to be the consequence. In other words, it is seen as inherently confrontational in character. Several theorists have proposed alternative approaches which they base on techniques designed to promote flexible and creative thinking; a problem orientation rather than a position or person orientation; and fairness and the establishment of sound relationships. These are sound in themselves, and lend themselves particularly to matters of a procedural or values-based nature where there is not such heavy emphasis on substantive reward. However, they may fail to fulfil their promise if certain favourable conditions do not exist, or if the the parties utilise them insincerely as a means of reducing the power of others rather than engaging them as equal and legitimate players in the long-term search for solutions and settlements.

The following conditions and behaviours promote effective integrative approaches:

- ❏ Mutually acknowledged common objectives.
- ❏ Shared beliefs that mutually acceptable solutions are possible and desireable.
- ❏ Beliefs in cooperation rather than competition.
- ❏ Beliefs that everyone is of equal value.
- ❏ Acceptance of difference as legitimate.
- ❏ Acceptance of other while not necessarily accepting values or behaviour.
- ❏ Beliefs that differences of opinion are helpful.
- ❏ Mutual trust.
- ❏ Signals of openness.
- ❏ Free flow of relevant information.
- ❏ Flexible constituencies.
- ❏ Reality based approach in situations of scarce resource.
- ❏ Parties have the skills to use the approach.
- ❏ Parties separate people from problems.

❑ Parties work at understanding each other's needs and interests.

❑ Relations and statements that are empathic rather than blame oriented.

❑ Willingness to be constructive regardless of reciprocity.

❑ Sensitivity to emotions in the process.

❑ Reliable behaviour.

❑ Reasonable trust.

❑ No premature commitments to positions.

❑ Multiple options approaches.

❑ Avoidance of premature option evaluation.

❑ Evaluation of options against agreed criteria.

❑ Emphasis on fairness rather than on power.

❑ Avoidance of threats and sanctions.

❑ Use of techniques to promote lateral thinking.

ASSESSING AND IMPROVING COMMUNICATIONS

The communication process is basic to all approaches to negotiation and problem solving. Negotiation is in effect a process of persuasive communication. Several reminders are presented here as to means of improving communications and persuasive capacity.

Persuasion reminders:

Is the intended *persuader*:

❑ prestigous in terms of perceived knowledge and expertise;

❑ credible in terms of track record of trustworthiness, past successes, position, perceived good intentions; and

❑ attractive in terms of values convergence?

Is the *message*:

❏ pitched at the level of the audience (metaphors, life experiences, education);

❏ structured according to existing audience prejudices values and beliefs;

❏ designed to arouse interest, raise emotional stimulation, show how tensions might be reduced; and

❏ designed to alter/contradict preconceptions?

Has the *target group* been accurately assessed as regards existing attitudes, openness to persuasion, self-esteem, constituency pressures, competing attitudinal influences?

Communication reminders

Are communication styles influencing the negotiation climate?

Punitive/defensive	*Supportive/accepting*
Communications are evaluative, controlling and strategic.	Communications are descriptive, spontaneous and problem oriented.

Are there listening problems?

Problems in listening	*Improve listening behaviour*
– Overstimulation	– show attention and
– Preparing to answer	interest
before understanding	– avoid interruptions
– Distractions	– avoid immediate
– Prejudices	counterproposals
	– reach for facts
	– respond empathically
	– wait out feelings
	– paraphrase messages
	– withhold evaluation

- improve understanding
  of verbal and non-verbal
  behaviour
- check understanding

Are there problems in message transmission?

*Problems in message
transmission*
- poor verbal skills
- poor control over
  non-verbals
- poor listening by other

Improve message transmission
- make messages complete
  and specific
- ensure congruency of
  message behaviour/
  content
- adjust messages to other's
  frame of reference
- ask listeners to repeat
  understanding
- label behaviour
- avoid double bind
  messages
- mediate other's
  communications/unravel
  content-emotion
  confusion/redirect signals

Use questions to:
- cause attention
- obtain information
- give information
- start thinking
- bring matters to
  conclusion

Handle difficult questions by:
- leaving impression
  answered
- incomplete answer
- inaccurate answer
- leaving other without
  desire to pursue the
  matter further

Other useful techniques
- Understand communication networks
- Use of humour
- Threat-free apology
- Purposeful expression of feelings

THINKING THROUGH SOME ISSUES IN THE USE OF MEDIATION

Mediation is a form of third-party assistance in disputes directed at helping parties negotiate their own settlements. Mediators don't assume the authoritative decision-making power associated with arbitration, but rather help parties to make better use of the negotiation process. Mediators and mediation users need to think through several issues in employing the process, including objectives for the process, the choice of mediator, timing of entry and the use of mediator power in the process.

Objectives for mediation

Objectives for mediation may include:
❑ achievement of a settlement;
❑ achievement of movement sufficient to allow negotiations to continue independently;
❑ clearer definition of issues at stake;
❑ removal of obstacles to bargaining;
❑ broadened solution searches;
❑ reality appraisal;
❑ assistance with use of the negotiation process; and
❑ improved communications/understanding between the parties

Reasons for choosing a mediator

Disinterested status
❑ Institutionalised role (agency)

- ❏ Prestige/ability of individual/agency
- ❏ Expertise on issues
- ❏ Social status
- ❏ Position in relation to conflict network
- ❏ Perceived neutrality
- ❏ Perceived impartiality

Interested status
- ❏ Desire by mediator to extend influence
- ❏ Desire by mediator to end a conflict owing to threat to own interests
- ❏ Parties perception of mediator's capacity to deliver an agreement
- ❏ Perception of mediator as a guarantor for the process and as likely to reduce the risks of concessionmaking
- ❏ Desire by one or more of parties to build future relations with the mediator

Timing of entry
Late entry considerations
- ❏ Parties psychologically ready to use the process owing to impasse
- ❏ Acknowledgement of developmental cycle of conflict process — deadlock energises the process
- ❏ Exhaustion of alternatives promotes motivation to settle

Early entry considerations
- ❏ Prevents necessity of having to test power realities
- ❏ Reduces positional rigidity
- ❏ Reduces emotional frustration/hostility

MAKING NEGOTIATIONS WORK

Having provided checklists for the assessment of problems in negotiation, a list of dos for effective negotiation are provided as a short reminder of the types of action that assist process and the achievement of settlements. Negotiation approaches are not entirely mutually exclusive, and an integrated model would allow for flexibility and acknowledge that many skills are usable across approaches, and that depending on issues and relationships several approaches may be used in the course of a single negotiation. Skills listed here represent a mix from the various schools and are suggested in this form to allow for maximum flexibility in practice.

Planning and preparation:
❑ Plan for all parties involved.
❑ Identify issues and priorities for all parties.
❑ Plan your bargaining range under different scenarios.
❑ Assess likely bargaining ranges for the others.
❑ Identify the needs and interests underlying your demands or offers.
❑ Identify the needs and interests underlying possible positions by others.
❑ Consider power relativities.
❑ Identify common ground possibilities.
❑ Consider possible concessions and their value in the others' terms for trading purposes.
❑ Identify possible pressure tactics you might use and the consequences of their use.
❑ Identify pressure tactics they might use and how you might deal with them.
❑ Assess whether appropriate conditions exist for an integrative approach.
❑ Determine which approach might be used — distributive or integrative.

Effective distributive negotiation requires:
❑ clear bargaining boundaries;
❑ informed debate — stances that can be motivated, defended, justified;

❏ reality-based opening positions;
❏ a willingness to explore each other's positions;
❏ a willingness to move;
❏ clear signals of willingness to move if reciprocity evident;
❏ clear proposals to break argument cycles;
❏ willingness to explore proposals;
❏ patience — don't force the pace;
❏ concessions valued by the other;
❏ linking and packaging — conditions before concessions;
❏ creativity;
❏ sound judgement of what is possible;
❏ skills in closure;
❏ use of pressure tactics that do not violate norms in the relationship/damage relations; and
❏ use of tactics to promote movement/seek settlement vs attack the other party

Effective integrative bargaining requires:
❏ appropriate attitudes;
❏ common objectives;
❏ trust;
❏ constituency flexibility;
❏ information exchange;
❏ clear and accurate communications;
❏ acknowledgement of a joint problem;
❏ exploration of understandings, assumptions, needs and interests;
❏ joint definition of the problem;
❏ separation of people from the problem;
❏ focus on interests rather than on positions;
❏ identification of criteria for a solution acceptable to everyone;
❏ delayed solution searches or evaluation of ideas;
❏ generation of ideas/solutions;
❏ efforts to invent options for mutual gain;

- ❏ appropriate use of experts, surveys, brainstorming;
- ❏ use of structured exercises to promote effective solution searches;
- ❏ evaluation of solutions using identified criteria; and
- ❏ clear action steps

All negotiation is facilitated by:
- ❏ acceptance of others as legitimate negotiation partners;
- ❏ understanding of others needs, interests, emotions;
- ❏ empathy;
- ❏ exploration of assumptions, perceptions and fears;
- ❏ effective listening skills;
- ❏ effective message transmission skills;
- ❏ sensitivity to emotions;
- ❏ reliability;
- ❏ trustworthiness/integrity;
- ❏ problem attacks rather than people attacks;
- ❏ fair/acceptable standards and procedures;
- ❏ supportive rather than punitive bargaining climates;
- ❏ insight as to dynamics of the conflict/constituency pressures/problems in bargaining teams;
- ❏ confidentiality;
- ❏ reality orientation;
- ❏ consideration of consequences of progressing disputes;
- ❏ movement/signals of movement;
- ❏ flexibility/willingness to explore options; and
- ❏ use of questions to check out assumptions, improve understanding, acquire information

Ideas for dealing with specific situations
Unwillingness to move owing to belief that other will concede further
- ❏ Use of realistic deadlines.
- ❏ Use of information.

❑ Use of trusted third parties to convey real positions/capacities.

Unwillingness to move owing to fears of loss of face
❑ Elicit simultaneous concession exchanges.
❑ Provide alternatives.
❑ Use of mediator's suggestions.

Unwillingness to move owing to entrapment
❑ Seek means of decommiting parties honourably.
❑ Argue changed circumstances.
❑ Relabel issues to circumvent.
❑ Leave some issues unresolved while agreeing to others.
❑ Moratoriums on public statements.
❑ Acknowledge a joint problem to shift from 'us vs. them' tone.

Absence of apparent alternatives
❑ Use problem solving techniques.
❑ Obtain expert advice.
❑ Survey alternatives.

Hostile bargainers
❑ Maintain a problem focus.
❑ Explore consequences of conflict escalation.
❑ Humour.
❑ Act in a way that contradicts fears or prejudices.
❑ Insist on fair criteria.

Unrealistic expectations
❑ Refer to other settlements or patterns.
❑ Explore consequences of escalated conflict.
❑ Provide information on other's limits and pressures.
❑ Provide information on resources.

Overloaded agendas
❑ Simplify agendas.

❏ Sort priorities.
❏ Use side-caucuses/delegated joint task groups.

Poor use of bargaining process.
❏ Educate parties by discussing implications of intended moves, timing, signals, proposals, pressure tactics.
❏ Apply pressure to plan properly.
❏ Mention other cases where creative solutions have been used/parallel cases
❏ Refer to colleagues or trusted others who have been through the experience.
❏ Discuss implications/consequences of certain tactics or behaviours.

Intransigence
❏ Consider consequences of continued conflict.
❏ Explore expectations of the process.
❏ Separate issues and get agreement on some before reconsidering position on others.
❏ Explore fears and underlying needs.
❏ Explore constituency pressures.
❏ Communicate directly with significant players in constituencies.

In complex situations
❏ Adopt an issue-by-issue approach.
❏ Target less complex disputes first.
❏ Aim for incremental reconciliation.
❏ Set up bodies that work on issues in an ongoing manner rather than in a crisis intervention manner.
❏ Establish ground rules.
❏ Use experts and resources.
❏ Have clear action plans.
❏ Write down and sign agreements.

BIBLIOGRAPHY

Adam H 'Engineering Compliance: The Management of Dissent in South Africa' in Hund J (ed) *Law and Justice in South Africa* Cape Town, Centre for Intergroup Studies, 1988

Albertyn CJ 'Freedom of Association and the Morality of the Closed Shop' *Industrial Law Journal* Vol 10, 6, 1989 pp 981–1005

Anstey M 'I.R. in Transition: Challenges for South Africa' *IPM Journal* Vol 9 No 3, Oct 1990 pp 13–19

Anstey M 'Relationships by Objectives: Some Early Observations of Theory and Practice in South Africa' *Industrial Relations Journal of South Africa* Vol 9 No 3, 1989 pp 47–60

Anstey M 'Mediator Acceptability: A Pilot Survey of Labour and ManagementPerceptions in South Africa' *Industrial Relations Journal of South Africa*, Vol 8 No 4 1988pp 1–14

Anstey M 'The Living Wage Debate' *IPM Journal* Vol 6 No 6, 1987

Anstey M 'Mediation in South African Industry Concepts, Skills, Approaches and Problems' *SA Journal of LabourRelations* Vol 10 No 1, March 1986 pp 31–52

Anstey M *Working With Groups* Cape Town, Juta & Co, 1983

Argyle M *The Psychology of Interpersonal Behaviour*, Harmondsworth, Pelican Books 1967

Atkinson GGM *The Effective Negotiator* (3rd ed) London, Quest Publications 1980

Barker LL, Cegala DJ, Kibler RJ & Wahlers KJ *Groups in Process: An Introduction to Small Group Communication* Englewood Cliffs, New Jersey, Prentice Hall Inc 1979

Bartos OJ *Process and Outcome in Negotiation* New York, Columbia University Press, 1974

Berger PL *The Capitalist Revolution: Fifty Propositions About Prosperity, Equality, and Liberty* New York, Basic Books, 1986

Bottomore T (ed) *A Dictionary of Marxist Thought* Cambridge, Harvard University Press, 1983

Boulle L *South Africa and the Consociational Option* Cape Town, Juta & Co Ltd, 1984

Brager G & Specht H *Community Organising* New York, Columbia University Press, 1973

Brett JM, Drieghe R & Shapiro DL 'Mediator Style and Mediation Effectiveness' *Negotiation Journal* Vol 2 No 3, July 1986 pp 277–87

Brown JAC *Techniques of Persuasion* Hammondsworth, Middlesex, Penguin Books Ltd, 1963

Budlender D 'A Critique of Poverty Datum Lines' (monograph) Cape Town, SA Labour and Development Research Unit, Working Paper No 63 August 1985

Buraway M 'Painting Socialism in Hungary' *South African Labour Bulletin*, Vol 15, No 3, 1990, pp 75–85

Burton JW *Resolving Deep-rooted Conflict: A Handbook* Lanham, University Press of America, 1987

Buzuev A *What is Capitalism?* Moscow, Progress Publishers 1987

Cameron E, Cheadle H & Thompson C *The New Labour Relations Act: The Law After the 1988 Amendments* Cape Town, Juta & Co Ltd, 1989

Carkhuff R & Pierce RM *The Art of Helping: Trainers Guide — An Introduction to Life Skills* Amherst, Massachusetts: Carkhuff Institute of Human Technology, Human Resource Development Press 1975

Carnevale PJD & Pegnetter R 'The Selection of Mediation Tactics in Public Sector Disputes: AContingency Approach' *Journal ofSocial Issues* Vol 41 No 2, 1985 pp 65–82

Clegg H 'Pluralism in Industrial Relations'*British Journal of Industrial Relations* Vol 19 No 2, 1975, pp 309–16

Cohen M 'Violence in the Workplace' *Industrial Relations Journal of South Africa* Vol 10 No 3, 1990 pp 30–9

Commerce Clearing House *Labour Law Reporter* Chicago 1987

Coser L *The Functions of Social Conflict* New York; Free Press 1956

Coser L 'Social Conflict and The Theory of Social Change' *British Journal of Sociology* Vol 8, 1957 pp 190–297

Curtis M (ed) *The Great Political Theories: Volume 1* New York, Avon Books 1981

De Bono E *Conflicts: A Better Way To Resolve Them* Middlesex, Penguin Books, 1986

Dessler G *Organisation Theory: Integrating Structure and Behaviour* Englewood Cliffs, Prentice Hall 1980

Deutsch M *The Resolution of Conflict: Constructive and Destructive Processes* New Haven, Conn, Yale University Press 1973

Deutsch M & Krauss RM 'The Effect of Threat upon Interpersonal Bargaining' *Journal of Abnormal and Social Psychology* Vol 61 1960 pp 181–9

Douglas T *Group Work Practice* London, Tavistock Publications 1976

Eastern Province Herald 4 January 1991

Filley A *Interpersonal Conflict Resolution* Glenview, Illinois; Scott, Foresman & Co, 1985

Fisher R & Ury W *Getting To Yes* London, Hutchinson 1981

Fisher R & Brown S *Getting Together: Building a Relationship that gets to Yes* Boston, Houghton Mifflin Co, 1988

Folberg J & Taylor A *Mediation* San Francisco, JosseyBass, 1984

Fox A 'Industrial Relations: A Social Critique of Pluralist Ideology' in Barrett B, Rhodes E & Beishon J (eds) *Industrial Relations in the Wider Society* London, Collier MacMillan 1975

Frescura F 'The Freedom Charter: land redistribution and social conflict' in Polley JA (ed) *The Freedom Charter and the Future* Cape Town, IDASA 1988

Fukuyama F 'The End of History' *The National Interest* Summer 1989, pp 3–18

Gallagher AM 'Social Identity and the Northern Ireland Conflict' *Human Relations* Vol 42 No 10, 1989, pp 917–35

Gaw BA & Sayer JE *May I Join You? An Interpersonal Needs Approach To Small Group Communications* Sherman Oaks, California: Alfred Publishing 1979

Giliomee H & Schlemmer L *From Apartheid to Nation Building* Cape Town, Oxford University Press, 1989

Gorbachev M *Perestroika* New York, Harper & Row Publishers, 1987

Grossman G *Economic Systems* Englewood Cliffs New Jersey, Prentice Hall Inc, 1974

Gulliver PH *Disputes and Negotiations: A Cross Cultural Perspective* New York, Academic Press 1979

Habib A & Andrews M 'Disinheriting the heritage of Stalinism' *South African Labour Bulletin* Vol 15 No 3, 1990 pp 86–93

Hague R & Harrop R *Comparative Government and Politics* (2nd ed) London, MacMillan 1987

Hanf T 'The Prospects of Accommodation in Communal Conflicts' in Giliomee H & Schlemmer L *Negotiating South Africa's Future* Johannesburg, Southern Book Publishers, 1989

Hiltrop JM 'Mediator Behaviour and the Settlement of Collective BargainingDisputes in Britain' *Journal of Social Issues* Vol 41 No 2 1985 pp 83–100

Himes JS *Conflict and Conflict Management* Athens, University of Georgia Press, 1980

Hodder-Williams R *An Introduction to the Politics of Tropical Africa* London, George Allen & Unwin 1984

Howells JM 'Employers' and Union Officers' Views on the Ideal Mediator' *Journal of Industrial Relations* Vol 28 No 3 September 1986 pp 428–435

HSRC *The South African Society: Realities and Future Prospects* Pretoria, Human Sciences Research Council 1985

Hughes H & Merret C 'Detentions' in Robertson M (ed) *South African Human Rights and Labour Law Yearbook 1990* Cape Town, Oxford University Press 1990

Human Rights Commission 'Violence in Detention' in McKendrick B & Hoffmann W (eds) *People and Violence* Cape Town, Oxford University Press 1990 pp 405–35

Hyman R *Industrial Relations: A Marxist Introduction*, London, MacMillan 1975

Indicator SA 'Select Indicators of Political Violence' *Indicator SA* Vol 5 No 2, Summer 1988 pp 20–1

Jack A 'Towards a Living Wage — Workers' demands over sixty years' *South African Labour Bulletin* Vol 12 No 3, 1987

Johnson P *A History of the Modern World: From 1917 to the 1980's* London, George Weidenfeld & Nicholson Ltd, 1983

Johnston RW 'Negotiation Strategies: Different Strokes for Different Folks' *Personnel*, March–April, 1982

Johnson DW & Johnson FP *Joining Together* Englewood Cliffs New Jersey, Prentice Hall, 1975

Jordan P 'Crisis of Coinscience in the SACP' *SA Labour Bulletin* Vol 15 No 3, Sept 1990, pp 66–74

Karrass CL *The Negotiating Game* New York, World
    Publishing Co 1970

Kennedy G *Everything is Negotiable: How To Negotiate and
    Win* London, Arrow Books, 1982

Kennedy G, Benson J & McMillan J *Managing Negotiations*
    (3rd ed) & London, Hutchinson Business, 1987

King L 'Three Cheers for Conflict' *Personnel* Jan–Feb 1981,
    pp 13–22

Kolb DM 'Strategy and Tactics of Mediation' *Human
    Relations Journal* Vol 36 No 3, 1983 pp 247–268

Kolb DM 'To be a Mediator: Expressive Tactics in
    Mediation' *Journal of Social Issues* Vol 41 No 2 1985
    pp 11–26

Kraybill R 'Negotiating Deep-rooted Conflicts'*Industrial
    Relations Journal of South Africa* Vol 10 No 3, 1990
    pp 52–61

Kressel K 'Labour Mediation: An Exploratory Survey'
    Albany NY: Association of Labour Mediation Agencies

Kressel K & Pruitt DG 'Themes in the Mediation of Social
    Conflict' *Journal of Social Issues* Vol 41 No 2 1985
    pp 179–198

Kriesberg L *The Sociology of Social Conflicts* Englewood Cliffs
    New Jersey, Prentice Hall 1973

Krislow J & Mead JF 'Labour–management Attitudes
    Toward Mediation' *Personnel* Vol 51 No 2, 1972

Laue J Personal communication 1988

Leavitt HJ 'Some Effects of Certain Communication
    Patterns on Group Performance' *Journal of Abnormal and
    Social Psychology* Vol 46, 1951, pp 38–50

Lewicki RJ & Litterer AL *Negotiation* Homewood Illinois,
    Irwin 1985

Lion Publishing *The World's Religions* Herts, Lion
    Publishing 1982

Mayer B 'The Dynamics of Power in Negotiation and Mediation' *Mediation Quarterly* No 16 Summer 1987 pp 75–86

McColm RB 'The Comparative Survey of Freedom' *Freedom Review* Vol 22 No 1 1991

McLellan D *Marxism: Essential Writings* Oxford, Oxford University Press, 1988

Moore CW *The Mediation Process: Practical Strategies for Resolving Conflict* San Francisco, Jossey Bass 1986

McDonald F 'Disclosure of Information: A Prerequisite for Bargaining in Good Faith' *Information Sheet* No 78, Institute for Industrial Relations May 1985

McKendrick BW & Hoffmann W *People and Violence in South Africa* Cape Town, Oxford University Press, 1990

Mika H 'Neighbourhood Conflict: A Critical Appraisal of The Forms, Processes, and Social Structural Linkages of Multi-Party Conflict and Resolution' Washington, Society of Professionals in Dispute Resolution: 1986 Proceedings of the Fourteenth International Conference (1987)

Morley IE & Stephenson GM *The Social Psychology of Bargaining* London, George Allen & Unwin, 1977

Mulder M *The Daily Power Game* Leiden, Martinus Nihoff Social Sciences Division, 1977

Nattrass J 'Political Change and Capitalism in South Africa' in Butler J, Elphick R & Welsh D (eds) *Democratic Liberalism in South Africa: Its History and Prospect* Cape Town, David Phillip, 1987

Nel J 'Developing a Systematic Approach to Disclosure of Information Requests From Trade Unions' in *Key Issues in Collective Bargaining* Johannesburg, Institute for Industrial Relations 1985

Newall I *The Demand for a Living Wage* Constantia, Zebra Publications, 1989

Nierenberg GI *The Complete Negotiator* New York,
    Nierenberg & Zeif Publishers, 1986

Nierenberg GI & Calero HH *How to Read a Person Like a Book*
    Wellingborough, Thorsons Publishers, 1973

Olivier N 'A Bill of Rights' in Schrire R (ed) *Critical Choices
    for South Africa* Cape Town, Oxford University Press
    1990

Palomares U & Logan B *A Curriculum on Conflict
    Management* Human Development Training Institute
    1975

Parfitt J 'Industrial Relations Trends in the Eastern Cape:
    Strikes and Stayaways' *IR Research and Topics Series No 3*
    IR Unit, University of Port Elizabeth 1989

Parfitt J 'Industrial Relations Trends in the Eastern Cape:
    Strikes and Stoppages in 1989' *IR Research and Topics
    Series No 6* IR Unit, University of Port Elizabeth 1990

Pondy LR 'Organisational Conflict: Concepts and Models'
    Administrative Science Quarterly Vol 12 No 2, Sept 1967
    pp 296–320

Potgeiter JF *Background and Interpretation of the Household
    Subsistence Level* Port Elizabeth, Institute for Planning
    Research, University of Port Elizabeth, undated

Power DF 'Target-specific Bargaining' *IPM Journal* Vol 9 No
    8, April 1991 pp 15–20

Pretorius P 'Questions on the Expansion of IMSSA into
    Fields other than Labour' IMMSSA National Seminar
    1990

Pruitt DG *Negotiation Behaviour* New York, Academic Press,
    1981

Pruitt DG & Kressel K 'The Mediation of Social Conflict:
    An Introduction' *Journal of Social Issues* Vol 41 No 2 1985
    pp 1–10

Pruitt DG & Rubin JZ *Social Conflict: Escalation, Stalemate,
    and Settlement* New York, Random House, 1986

Rackham N 'The Effective Negotiator' *People and Profits* March 1979, pp 7–10

Raven BH & Kruglanski AW 'Conflict and Power' in Swingle P (ed) *The Structure of Conflict* New York, Academic Press 1970

Richardson RC *Collective Bargaining By Objectives: A Positivist Approach* (2nd ed) Englewood Cliffs; New Jersey; Prentice Hall Inc, 1985

Riekert J *Basic Employment Law* Cape Town, Juta & Co 1987

Riordan R 'Putting FW in the Picture' *Eastern Province Herald* 31 December 1990

Riordan R 'In Search of the Source of Strife' *EP Herald* 27 August 1990

Rubin JZ & Brown BR *The Social Psychology of Bargaining and Negotiation* New York, Academic Press, 1975

Ruble TL & Thomas KW 'Support for Two-dimensional Model of Conflict Behaviour' *Organisational Behaviour and Human Performance* Vol 16 1976, pp 143–55

Rycroft A & Jordaan B *A Guide to South African Labour Law* Cape Town, Juta & Co Ltd, 1990

SA Barometer 'Rightwing Attacks 1988–90' *SA Barometer* Vol 4 No 11 June 22, 1990, pp 169–75

Sabirov KH *What is Communism?* Moscow, Progress Publishers 1987

Sandbrook R *The Politics of Africa's Economic Stagnation* Cambridge, Cambridge University Press, 1985

Savage M 'An Anatomy of the South African Economy: Ownership, Control and the Interlocking Directorate' *Industrial Relations Journal of South Africa* 2nd Quarter 1987 pp 4–29

Savage M 'Poor Track Record' *Finance Week* March 7–13, 1985

Schein E *Organisational Psychology* (2nd ed) Englewood Cliffs, New Jersey; Prentice Hall 1970

Schmidt S & Kochan T 'Conflict: Toward Conceptual Clarity' *Administrative Science Quarterly* Vol 17 No 3, Sept 1972 pp 359–70

Scott B *The Skills of Negotiation* Hampshire, Gower Publishing Co 1981

Shulman L *A Casebook of Social Work With Groups* New York Council on Social Work Education, 1968

Simkins C 'Population Policy' in Schrire R (ed) *Critical Choices for Spouth Africa* Cape Town, Oxford University Press, 1990

Sloane & Whitney GG *Labor Relations* (4th ed) Englewood Cliffs, Prentice Hall, 1981

Slovo J 'Has Socialism Failed?' *South African Labour Bulletin* Vol 14 No 6, 1990, pp 11–28

Solzhenitsyn A *The Gulag Archipelago* Glasgow, Collins, 1974

Specht H 'Disruptive Tactics' in Kramer RM & Specht H (eds) *Readings in Community Organisation Practice* Englewood Cliffs New Jersey, Prentice Hall Inc 1969

Star 24 October 1990

Stepan A 'Paths Toward Redemocratisation: Theoretical and Comparative Considerations' in O'Donnell G, Schmitter PC, Whitehead L, *Transitions From Authoritarian Rule* Baltimore, The John Hopkins University Press, 1986

Tedeschi JT & Lindskold S *Social Psychology* New York, John Wiley & Sons 1976

Thomas K 'Conflict and Conflict Management' in Dunette MD (ed) *Handbook of Industrial and Organisational Psychology* Rand McNally Publishing Co, 1976, pp 889–935

The Democrat 'Target Black Councils' Dec 1990 p 1

Time Magazine 9 January 1989 & 10 October 1988

Van den Berg S 'Long term economic trends and development prospects in South Africa' Paper delivered at a conference on *Southern Africa: Crucial Issues* Munchen, 15–17th May 1987

Van Gundy AB *Techniques of Structured Problem Solving* (2nd ed) New York; Van Nostrand Reinhold Co 1988

Vogelman L 'Strike Violence: Some Factors to Consider' *South African Labour Bulletin* Vol 14 No 3, 1989 pp 47–56

Von Holdt K 'Marxism, Leninism, and Stalin' *South African Labour Bulletin*, Vol 15 No 3, 1990, pp 94–6

Walton RE & McKersie RB *A Behavioural Theory of Labor Negotiations* New York, McGraw Hill, 1965

Walton RE & Dutton JM 'The Management of Interdepartmental Conflict: A Model and Review' *Administrative Science Quarterly* Vol 14 No 1, March 1969 pp 73–84

Whitney GG 'Before You Negotiate, Get Your Act Together' *Personnel* July/August 1982 pp 13–26

Wilson F & Ramphele M *Uprooting Poverty: The South African Challenge* Cape Town, David Phillip 1989

Yemin E 'Comparative Survey' in *Workforce Reductions* Geneva, ILO 1984

Young HA 'The Cause of Industrial Peace Revisited' *Human Resources Management* Summer 1982, pp 50—57

Zartman IW *Ripe for Resolution: Conflict and Intervention in Africa*, Oxford, Oxford University Press, 1985

Zartman IW & Touval S 'International Mediation: Conflict Resolution and Power Politics' *Journal of Social Issues* Vol 41 No 2 1985 pp 27–46

Zimbardo P & Ebbesen E *Changing Attitudes and Behavior* Phillipines, Addison Wesley Publishing Co 1970

UNIVERSAL DECLARATION OF HUMAN RIGHTS

On December 10, 1948, the General Assembly of the United Nations adopted and proclaimed the Universal Declaration of Human Rights, the full text of which appears in the following pages. Following this historic act the Assembly called upon all Member countries to publicize the text of the Declaration and 'to cause it to be disseminated, displayed, read and expounded principally in schools and other educational institutions, without distinction based on the political status of countries or territories'.

PREAMBLE

Whereas recognition of the inherent dignity and of the equal and inalienable rights of all members of the human family is the foundation of freedom, justice and peace in the world,

Whereas disregard and contempt for human rights have resulted in barbarous acts which have outraged the conscience of mankind, and the advent of a world in which human beings shall enjoy freedom of speech and belief and freedom from fear and want has been proclaimed as the highest aspiration of the common people,

Whereas it is essential, if man is not to be compelled to have recourse, as a last resort, to rebellion against tyranny and oppression, that human rights should be protected by the rule of law,

Whereas it is essential to promote the development of friendly relations between nations,

Whereas the peoples of the United Nations have in the Charter reaffirmed their faith in fundamental human rights, in the dignity and worth of the human person and in the equal rights of men and women and have determined to promote social progress and better standards of life in larger freedom,

Whereas Member States have pledged themselves to achieve, in co-operation with the United Nations, the promotion of universal respect for and observance of human rights and fundamental freedoms,

Whereas a common understanding of these rights and freedoms is of the greatest importance for the full realization of the pledge,

Now, Therefore,
THE GENERAL ASSEMBLY proclaims

This universal declaration of human rights as a common standard of achievement for all peoples and all nations, to the end that every individual and every organ of society, keeping this Declaration constantly in mind, shall strive by teaching and education to promote respect for these rights and freedoms and by progressive measures, national and international, to secure their universal and effective recognition and observance, both among the peoples of Member States themselves and among the peoples of territories under their jurisdiction.

Article 1
All human beings are born free and equal in dignity and rights. They are endowed with reason and conscience and should act towards one another in a spirit of brotherhood.

Article 2
Everyone is entitled to all the rights and freedoms set forth in this Declaration, without distinction of any kind, such as race, colour, sex, language, religion, political or other opinion, national or social origin, property, birth or other status. Furthermore, no distinction shall be made on the basis of the political, jurisdictional or international status of the country or territory to which a person belongs, whether it be independent, trust, non-self-governing or under any other limitation of sovereignty.

Article 3
Everyone has the right to life, liberty and security of person.

Article 4
No one shall be held in slavery or servitude; slavery and the slave trade shall be prohibited in all their forms.

Article 5
No one shall be subjected to torture or to cruel, inhuman or degrading treatment or punishment.

Article 6

Everyone has the right to recognition everywhere as a person before the law.

Article 7

All are equal before the law and are entitled without any discrimination to equal protection of the law. All are entitled to equal protection against any discrimination in violation of this Declaration and against any incitement to such discrimination.

Article 8

Everyone has the right to an effective remedy by the competent national tribunals for acts violating the fundamental rights granted him by the constitution or by law.

Article 9

No one shall be subjected to arbitrary arrest, detention or exile.

Article 10

Everyone is entitled in full equality to a fair and public hearing by an independent and impartial tribunal, in the determination of his rights and obligations and of any criminal charge against him.

Article 11

(1) Everyone charged with a penal offence has the right to be presumed innocent until proved guilty according to law in a public trial at which he has had all the guarantees necessary for his defence.
(2) No one shall be held guilty of any penal offence on account of any act or omission which did not constitute a penal offence, under national or international law, at the time when it was committed. Nor shall a heavier penalty be imposed than the one that was applicable at the time the penal offence was committed.

Article 12

No one shall be subjected to arbitrary interference with his privacy, family, home or correspondence, nor to attacks upon his honour and reputation. Everyone has the right to the protection of the law against such interference or attacks.

Article 13

(1) Everyone has the right to freedom of movement and residence within the borders of each state.

(2) Everyone has the right to leave any country, including his own, and to return to his country.

Article 14

(1) Everyone has the right to seek and to enjoy in other countries asylum from persecution.
(2) This right may not be invoked in the case of prosecutions genuinely arising from non-political crimes or from acts contrary to the purposes and principles of the United Nations.

Article 15

(1) Everyone has the right to a nationality.
(2) No one shall be arbitrarily deprived of his nationality nor denied the right to change his nationality.

Article 16

(1) Men and women of full age, without any limitation due to race, nationality or religion, have the right to marry and to found a family. They are entitled to equal rights as to marriage, during marriage and at its dissolution.
(2) Marriage shall be entered into only with the free and full consent of the intending spouses.
(3) The family is the natural and fundamental group unit of society and is entitled to protection by society and the State.

Article 17

(1) Everyone has the right to own property alone as well as in association with others.
(2) No one shall be arbitrarily deprived of his property.

Article 18

Everyone has the right to freedom of thought, conscience and religion; this right includes freedom to change his religion or belief, and freedom, either alone or in community with others and in public or private, to manifest his religion or belief in teaching, practice, worship and observance.

Article 19

Everyone has the right to freedom of opinion and expression; this right includes freedom to hold opinions without interference and to seek, receive and impart information and ideas through any media and regardless of frontiers.

Article 20

(1) Everyone has the right to freedom of peaceful assembly and association.
(2) No one may be compelled to belong to an association.

Article 21

(1) Everyone has the right to take part in the government of his country, directly or through freely chosen representatives.
(2) Everyone has the right of equal access to public service in his country.
(3) The will of the people shall be the basis of the authority of government; this will shall be expressed in periodic and genuine elections which shall be by universal and equal suffrage and shall be held by secret vote or by equivalent free voting procedures.

Article 22

Everyone, as a member of society, has the right to social security and is entitled to realization, through national effort and international co-operation and in accordance with the organization and resources of each State, of the economic, social and cultural rights indispensable for his dignity and the free development of his personality.

Article 23

(1) Everyone has the right to work, to free choice of employment, to just and favourable conditions of work and to protection against unemployment.
(2) Everyone, without any discrimination, has the right to equal pay for equal work.
(3) Everyone who works has the right to just and favourable remuneration ensuring for himself and his family an existence worthy of human dignity, and supplemented, if necessary, by other means of social protection.
(4) Everyone has the right to form and to join trade unions for the protection of his interests.

Article 24

Everyone has the right to rest and leisure, including reasonable limitation of working hours and periodic holidays with pay.

Article 25

(1) Everyone has the right to a standard of living adequate for the health and well-being of himself and of his family, including

food, clothing, housing and medical care and necessary social services, and the right to security in the event of unemployment, sickness, disability, widowhood, old age or other lack of livelihood in circumstances beyond his control

(2) Motherhood and childhood are entitled to special care and assistance. All children, whether born in or out of wedlock, shall enjoy the same social protection.

Article 26

(1) Everyone has the right to education. Education shall be free, at least in the elementary and fundamental stages. Elementary education shall be compulsory. Technical and professional education shall be made generally available and higher education shall be equally accessible to all on the basis of merit.

(2) Education shall be directed to the full development of the human personality and to the strengthening of respect for human rights and fundamental freedoms. It shall promote understanding, tolerance and friendship among all nations, racial or religious groups, and shall further the activities of the United Nations for the maintenance of peace.

(3) Parents have a prior right to choose the kind of education that shall be given to their children.

Article 27

(1) Everyone has the right freely to participate in the cultural life of the community, to enjoy the arts and to share in scientific advancement and its benefits.

(2) Everyone has the right to the protection of the moral and material interests resulting from any scientific, literary or artistic production of which he is the author.

Article 28

Everyone is entitled to social and international order in which the rights and freedoms set forth in this Declaration can be fully realized.

Article 29

(1) Everyone has duties to the community in which alone the free and full development of his personality is possible.

(2) In the exercise of his rights and freedoms, everyone shall be subject only to such limitations as are determined by law solely for the purpose of securing due recognition and respect for the

rights and freedoms of others and of meeting the just requirements of morality, public order and the general welfare in a
democratic society.

(3) These rights and freedoms may in no case be exercised contrary
to the purposes and principles of the United Nations.

Article 30

Nothing in this Declaration may be interpreted as implying for any
State, group or person any right to engage in any activity or to
perform any act aimed at the destruction of any of the rights and
freedoms set forth herein.

THE FREEDOM CHARTER

We, the people of South Africa, declare for all our country and the world to know:

That South Africa belongs to all who live in it, black and white, and that no government can justly claim authority unless it is based on the will of the people;

That our people have been robbed of their birthright to land, liberty and peace by a form of government founded on injustice and inequality;

That our country will never be prosperous or free until all our people live in brotherhood, enjoying equal rights and opportunities;

That only a democratic state, based on the will of the people, can secure to all their birthright without distinction of colour, race, sex or belief;

And therefore, we, the people of South Africa, black and white, together — equals, countrymen and brothers — adopt this FREEDOM CHARTER. And we pledge ourselves to strive together, sparing nothing of our strength and courage, until the democratic changes here set out have been won.

The people shall govern
Every man and woman shall have the right to vote for and stand as a candidate for all bodies which make laws.

All the people shall be entitled to take part in the administration of the country.

The rights of the people shall be the same regardless of race, colour or sex.

All bodies of minority rule, advisory boards, councils and authorities shall be replaced by democratic organs of self-government.

All national groups shall have equal rights
There shall be equal status in the bodies of state, in the courts and in the schools for all national groups and races;

All national groups shall be protected by law against insults to their race and national pride;

All people shall have equal rights to use their own language and to develop their own folk culture and customs;

All apartheid laws and practices shall be set aside.

The people shall share in the country's wealth

The national wealth of our country, the heritage of all south Africans, shall be restored to the people;

The mineral wealth beneath the soil, the banks and monopoly industry shall be transferred to the ownership of the people as a whole;

All other industries and trade shall be controlled to assist the well-being of the people;

All people shall have equal rights to trade where they choose, to manufacture and to enter all trades, crafts and professions.

The land shall be shared amongst those who work it

Restriction of land ownership on a racial basis shall be ended, and all the land redivided amongst those who work it, to banish famine and land hunger;

The state shall help the peasants with implements, seed, tractors and dams to save the soil and assist the tillers;

Freedom of movement shall be guaranteed to all who work on the land;

All shall have the right to occupy land wherever they choose;

People shall not be robbed of their cattle; forced labour and farm prisons shall be abolished.

All people shall be equal before the law

No one shall be imprisoned, deported or restricted without a fair trial;

No one shall be condemned by the order of any Government official;

The courts shall be representative of all the people;

Imprisonment shall be only for serious crimes against the people, and shall aim at re-education, not vengeance;

The police force and army shall be open to all on an equal basis and shall be the helpers and protectors of the people;

All laws which discriminate on grounds of race, colour or belief shall be repealed.

The preaching and practice of national, race or colour discrimination and contempt shall be a punishable crime.

All shall enjoy equal human rights

The law shall guarantee to all their right to speak, to organise, to meet together, to publish, to preach, to worship and to educate their children;

The privacy of the house from police raids shall be protected by law;

All shall be free to travel without restriction from countryside to town, from province to province, and from South Africa abroad;

Pass laws, permits and all other laws restricting these freedoms shall be abolished.

There shall be work and security

All who work shall be free to form trade unions, to elect their officers and to make wage agreements with their employers;

The state shall recognise the right and duty of all to work, and to draw full unemployment benefits;

Men and women of all races shall receive equal pay for equal work;

There shall be a forty-hour working week, a national minimum wage, paid annual leave, and sick leave for all workers, and maternity leave on full pay for all working mothers;

Miners, domestic workers, farm workers and civil servants shall have the same rights as all others who work;

Child labour, compound labour, the tot system and contract labour shall be abolished.

The doors of learning and of culture shall be opened

The government shall discover, develop and encourage national talent for the enhancement of our cultural life;

All the cultural treasures of mankind shall be open to all, by free exchange of books, ideas and contacts with other lands;

The aim of education shall be to teach the youth to love their people and their culture, to honour human brotherhood, liberty and peace;

Education shall be free, compulsory, universal and equal for all children;

Higher education and technical training shall be opened to all by means of state allowances an scholarships awarded on the basis of merit;

Adult illiteracy shall be ended by a mass state education plan;

Teachers shall have all the rights of other citizens;

The colour bar in cultural life, in sport and in education shall be abolished.

There shall be houses, security and comfort
All people shall have the right to live where they choose, to be decently housed, and to bring up their families in comfort and security;

Unused housing space to be available to the people;

Rent and prices shall be lowered, food plentiful and no one shall go hungry.

A preventive health scheme shall be run by the state;

Free medical care and hospitalisation shall be provided for all, with special care for mothers and young children;

Slums shall be demolished and new suburbs built where all have transport, roads, lighting, playing fields, creches and social centres;

The aged, the orphans, the disabled and the sick shall be cared for by the state;

Rest, leisure and recreation shall be the right of all;

Fenced locations and ghettos shall be abolished, and laws which break up families shall be repealed.

There shall be peace and friendship
South Africa shall be a fully independent state, which respects the rights and sovereignty of all nations;

South Africa shall strive to maintain world peace and the settlement of all international disputes by negotiation — not ware;

Peace and friendship amongst all our people shall be secured by upholding the equal rights, opportunities and status of all;

The people of the protectorates — Basutoland, Bechuanaland and Swaziland — shall be free to decide for themselves their own future;

The right of all the peoples of Africa to independence and self-government shall be recognised, and shall be the basis of close co-operation.

Let all who love their people and their country now say, as we say here:
'these freedoms we will fight for, side by side, throughout our lives, until
we have won our liberty.'

NOTES FOR LABOUR NEGOTIATORS

It is not the purpose of this work to attempt a full discussion of the content of the labour–management relationship. Its focus has been on process and approach rather than content issues. Nevertheless some notes are provided here on selected issues of core concern to both parties. These cover:

❑ basic features of the Labour Relations Act 28 of 1956 relating to collective bargaining, dispute settlement and the unfair labour practice
❑ approaches to union recognition,
❑ the duty to bargain and good faith bargaining,
❑ key arguments used in wage negotiations, and
❑ termination of contract.

COLLECTIVE BARGAINING AND DISPUTE RESOLUTION

Collective bargaining and dispute resolution in South Africa occur both in terms of a formal system under the Labour Relations Act 28 of 1956, and in terms of various voluntary systems which the parties may contract between themselves in terms of the common law.

THE LABOUR RELATIONS ACT

The Labour Relations Act 28 of 1956 (as amended) seeks essentially to provide means for preventing and settling disputes between employers and employees, to provide for the establishment of a National Manpower Commission, to provide for the establishment of an industrial court and a labour appeal court, and to control the activities of labour brokers. The Labour Relations Act promotes a system of self-governance in industry through the process of collective bargaining between employers and their associations, and employees and their representatives.

It *applies* to every industry, occupation and undertaking except for persons employed in domestic service in private households, farming operations, the public service, teachers in institutions receiving public funds, and employees working for charitable bodies without payment.

The Act makes provision for the *registration* of trade unions and employer organisations. To be registered these bodies must operate according to a constitution containing provisions detailing membership, procedures for meetings, the use of funds, the powers and duties of office bearers and officials and their election by ballot. No political affiliation, party political activity or financial assistance for political parties is permitted. Audited books of account must be maintained, and these along with details of membership and office bearers and officials must be submitted to the registrar annually. Registration is not compulsory but it carries the benefit of permitting participation in industrial councils and thus the opportunity to negotiate agreements which can be gazetted to become legally binding.

The Labour Relations Act protects *freedom of association,* individuals having the right to join unions of their choice, and makes victimisation for reasons of union membership or activity a criminal offence. Under certain conditions the Act makes provision for the deduction of union membership fees compulsory on employers.

The Act defines an *unfair labour practice* as:

'any act or omission other than a strike or a lockout which has or may have the effect that

(i)   any employee or class of employees is or may be unfairly affected or that his or their employment opportunities or work security is or may be prejudiced or jeopardised thereby;

(ii) the business of any employer or class of employers is or may be unfairly affected or disrupted thereby;

(iii) labour unrest is or may be created or promoted thereby;

(iv) the relationship between the employer and employee is or may be detrimentally affected thereby.

This definition excludes strikes and lockouts from the unfair labour practice jurisdiction, but the industrial court may nevertheless interdict strikes or lockouts that are illegal in terms of section 65 of the Labour Relations Act.

Provision is made for the formation of *industrial councils* which are permanent bodies established by agreement between representative, registered trade unions and employers organisations for purposes of negotiating and monitoring the application of industrial agreements, as well as a dispute resolution function. Industrial councils have equal representation from employers and unions. Like employer organisations and trade unions they must register under the Labour Relations Act, operate under a constitution, and submit various particulars to the registrar annually. Industrial councils are registered in terms of specific areas and industries, limiting their function to these. New parties may only be admitted to the council by way of a consensus agreement between the existing parties, but if an applicant is rejected an appeal to the industrial court can be lodged.

Industrial councils may negotiate agreements on such matters as wages, conditions of service, hours of work, overtime, benefits — indeed any matter pertaining to the employment relationship. Agreements reached in the council may be submitted to the Minister of Manpower who may gazette them to make them legally binding on the parties, and extend them to govern employment relations between other employers and employees in the industry who are not party to the industrial council. Industrial councils may grant exemption from provisions of their agreements to employers under certain conditions, and there is provision for appeal to the Minister if there is dissatisfaction with a decision. They must administer their own agreements and may appoint agents to do so.

Industrial councils also have a dispute settlement function, being required to deal with all disputes that arise in the industry and area for which they are registered. The dispute must be referred in writing to the industrial council by the party declaring the dispute. This party must state in the reference that relevant provisions of the constitution have been complied with, and it must be signed by an office bearer or official of the organisation. A copy of the reference must be sent to the other party and the industrial council must be satisfied that this was received before it can consider the dispute.

In cases where there is no industrial council in an industry the Labour Relations Act makes provision for the establishment of a *conciliation board* upon application to an inspector of the Department of Manpower. This is an ad hoc body established solely for the purpose of resolving the dispute in question. In cases of disputes in essential services, the Minister can of his own accord establish a conciliation board. A conciliation board comprises the parties to the dispute and a chairman appointed by the inspector acceptable to the parties involved.

Where the parties in an industrial council or conciliation board are unable to settle a dispute they may refer it to mediation or voluntary arbitration, except in cases of essential services where they must refer it to arbitration (i.e. compulsory arbitration). Where they decide not to pursue these routes they may embark on procedures leading up to strike or lockout action.

Where a dispute concerns an unfair labour practice a period of 180 days from the date the practice commenced or ceased is allowed for referral to an industrial council or conciliation board. Where these bodies are unable to settle the matter within 30 days or a further period agreed by the parties, any party may refer it to the industrial court for determination.

Mediation is provided for under the Labour Relations Act. The parties may apply to the Minister to appoint a mediator acceptable to them or the Minister may do so of his/her own accord if of the opinion that this will assist settlement of the dispute. Such an appointed mediator has no decision-making powers over the parties.

Arbitration may be resorted to when parties feel that they are unable to resolve the dispute through negotiation, and is chosen jointly as a course of action, i.e. both parties revoke the option of strike or lockout action to resolve the matter. In voluntary arbitration the parties may choose a single arbitrator, an equal number of arbitrators with an umpire, or refer the matter to the industrial court. The arbitrator's decision is final and binding upon the parties.

In certain essential services defined by the Labour Relations Act, strike and lockout action is prohibited and arbitration is compulsory, e.g. local authorities and suppliers of sanitation, water, light, power, passenger transport and fire-fighting services, and by ministerial declaration food canning operations. In such cases an industrial council or conciliation board unable to resolve a matter in 30 days must report the matter to the Minister and it must be referred to arbitration.

Strikes and lockouts are comprehensively defined under the Labour Relations Act. Strikes essentially must involve collective action in pursuance of a demand which pertains to the employment relationship. Likewise lockout action must involve an action in pursuance of a demand by an employer pertaining to the employment relationship. In terms of section 65 of the Labour Relations Act a strike or lockout may not occur during the operation of an agreement award or determination governing the matter giving rise to the dispute, within one year of a wage board determination, or pending an arbitration award. Further, a strike or lockout is not legal unless the matter has been referred to an industrial council or conciliation board. Action may not be embarked on until the prescribed 30 days for such bodies to resolve the dispute has elapsed, or a conciliation board has not been established within 30 days of application. No strike action may be embarked on unless the majority of union members in good financial standing have voted by ballot in favour of such action. Essential service employees are prohibited from industrial action, as are certain other employees under other statutes, such as doctors, nurses and hospital employees.

The industrial court established in 1979 comprises a president and deputy president and a number of permanent and additional members whose numbers are determined by the Minister from time to time. Its functions include *inter alia* the determination of unfair labour practices, the conduct of arbitrations, the determination of section 43 (*status quo*) applications, the granting of urgent interdicts and deciding on appeals relating to membership of industrial councils.

Section 43 provides for the granting of temporary orders by the industrial court to restore circumstances to those which existed before an unfair labour practice dispute, e.g. reinstatement or at least payment of a dismissed worker in the case of a dismissal alleged to be an unfair labour practice. Such an order is temporary (up to 90 days with provision for short extensions) lasting until the court has made a final determination in terms of the unfair labour practice definition (section 46), or the parties settle the matter between themselves. Application for a section 43 order must be made to the court within 10 days of referral of the dispute to an industrial council or application for a conciliation board and within 30 days after the alleged unfair labour practice was introduced.

While the industrial court cannot interdict strikes or lockouts on the basis of their fairness, it can interdict those which contravene section 65 of the Labour Relations Act, i.e. unlawful action. All courts now require 48 hours notice to the other of a party's intention to apply for an interdict, and even where shorter periods may be permitted for good reason, the other must have had a reasonable opportunity to prepare and be heard. Where 10 days or more notice has been given of a party's intention to embark on a strike or lockout, then the other if it intends applying for a restraining interdict, must provide at least 5 days notice of its intention to do so. No restrictions apply in the case of interdicts prohibiting unlawful actions such as intimidation, violence, factory occupations, interference with trade or damage to property.

In cases where parties are dissatisfied with an unfair labour practice determination of the industrial court, they may appeal to the labour appeal court. All decisions or judgements of the industrial court may be taken on review to the labour appeal court.

COLLECTIVE BARGAINING OUTSIDE INDUSTRIAL COUNCILS

Collective bargaining does not only take place in industrial councils but at enterprise, company and plant levels as well. Usually this takes place in terms of what is commonly known as a Recognition Agreement. The first recognition agreement was signed in 1974. Today there are over 1 000 such agreements in existence. The first recognition agreements represented efforts by trade unions representing black workers and employers to regulate their relations, before the 1979 labour reforms gave access to such unions to participate in industrial councils. Even then, however, most unions viewed industrial councils as unholy alliances between employers and white unions, and perceived registration requirements as state interventionism. Recognition agreements provided a means for institutionalising relations with employers without having to enter industrial councils from a weak base while they gathered strength through recruiting drives. In addition the new unions serving the interests of black workers believed it important to develop grassroots structures for purposes of democracy and to remain closely in touch with members in places of work, i.e. to avoid distancing between leadership and union members. As they grew in size, however, this became an unwieldy system and a return to industrial councils occurred with the registration requirement being complied with. At present these unions dominate in many industrial councils. While this return to centralised negotiations has occurred, recognition agreements remain in place to regulate company level relations and quite often for purposes of substantive bargaining as well. A two-tier wage bargaining system has developed in many industries, the minima being established in industrial councils, and larger increases being negotiated at company level.

Typically recognition agreements contain clauses pertaining to scope of recognition, bargaining units, shopstewards' elections, functions, rights and facilities, constituencies, access to the plant by union officials, access to notice boards, meeting procedures, negotiation and dispute settling procedures, strike procedures, and procedures relating to grievance handling discipline and retrenchment.

THE DUTY TO NEGOTIATE AND GOOD FAITH BARGAINING

The concepts of a duty to negotiate and good faith bargaining are rooted in the US labour relations system, where employers *must* bargain collectively with unions representing a majority of their employees in a bargaining unit. Such unions have sole bargaining rights, and are duty bound to represent all employees fairly.

> The duty to bargain is, basically, a duty to bargain in good faith. The law does not require either unions or employers to make concessions; their duty is only to approach negotiations with an open mind and a real intention to reach an agreement wherever possible. If an agreement is actually reached, there is a duty to set it out in a written contract.' (para 1200)

In the USA, the law distinguishes between three categories of bargaining subjects:

- ❑ *Mandatory items* are those over which the parties must bargain if they are introduced by either to the bargaining table. These include wages, rates of pay, hours and other conditions of employment such as tenure, discipline and grievance procedures and practices, promotion, demotion, transfer, health and safety, leave and sick leave, union security and contracting out. The Court and the National Labour Relations Board have declared about 70 basic items as mandatory for bargaining purposes (Richardson 1985).
- ❑ *Illegal items* are those forbidden by law such as a closed shop, or a union security clause in a right-to-work state.
- ❑ *Permissive items* are those which are neither mandatory nor illegal. Such items can become part of negotiations only through the joint agreement of the parties, i.e. one party may refuse to do so and

the signing of an agreement may not be held up on the basis of a
refusal to bargain on a voluntary item.

Having defined what an employer and a trade union must bargain
on, the National Labour Relations Act also expressly requires that
the process must be conducted in good faith. The National Labour
Relations Board and the courts have given definition to what good
faith bargaining is.

To meet the requirements an employer:

- must meet with employee representatives on mandatory bargaining items;
- cannot flatly reject a union's proposal without considering it and
  should make counterproposals and attempt to reconcile differences;
- must make his own representatives available for bargaining at
  reasonable times and places
- must accept the union's representatives;
- must bargain on questions arising out of collective agreements
  (e.g. grievances);
- is not excused from bargaining by virtue of competitive disad-
  vantages, economic hardship or labour strife;
- may not demand of a union that it give up any rights as a
  pre-condition to bargaining;
- may not substitute collective contracts with individual contracts;
- may not employ dilatory tactics, anti-union actions or mislead
  employee representatives;
- may not refuse to set down an agreement in writing;
- must provide the union with information it needs for bargaining
  purposes;
- may not take unilateral action in regard to wages or working
  conditions where this action will discredit a majority union or
  impair its position;
- may not grant a unilateral wage increase where this is greater
  than that offered to the union in negotiations.

Duties to bargain in good faith are not confined to employers, but
extend also to trade unions. A trade union:

- must as sole collective bargaining agent fairly represent all employees in a unit;
- cannot refuse to bargain with an employer;

❑ must bargain in good faith in the same way as an employer is
   obliged to.
(Commerce Clearing House Inc, Labour Law Reports 1987 paras
1200–1212)

The duty to bargain in South Africa
In South Africa the duty to bargain has been equivocally dealt with
by the legislation and by the courts. Although the Labour Relations
Act has as its central purpose the promotion of collective bargaining
and prevention of industrial unrest, and to this end protects freedom
of association, and provides extensive machinery for negotiation
and dispute resolution purposes, it is silent on the duty to bargain.

No obligation is placed on the employer to recognise a representative union. Rather, this has been left implicit in the Act. For
instance, a registered union might claim recognition by virtue of
stoporders which a company is legally obliged to deduct for it if it
requests such a service; or a union might oblige a meeting with an
intransigent employer simply by declaring a dispute with it and
setting in motion the legal machinery which would oblige meetings
between the parties, i.e. in conciliation boards and industrial councils. Such implicit or confrontationally obliged pressures are hardly
sufficient to meet the purposes of the Act. The duty to bargain and
to bargain in good faith have found support in the courts, but this
was, at least initially, equivocally granted — the court vacillating
between two stances:

❑ *voluntarism* whereby it stated that, while collective bargaining
   was desirable, it had no competence to compel parties to engage;
   and
❑ *a duty to bargain* whereby it has stated that it does have such
   competence.

The voluntarist stance
In *Building and Allied Construction Workers Union* v *Johnson Tiles (Pty)
Ltd* (1985) 6 ILJ 210 IC the court, on being asked to make an order
requiring the company to negotiate in good faith with the union,
determined that findings in previous cases were of no authority and
concluded that it could not order a company to negotiate in good
faith with a union. Similarly in *Metal and Allied Workers Union* v *Hart
Ltd* (1985) 6 ILJ 478 IC the court in dealing with a question of
appropriate levels of bargaining, referred to a passage from the

International Labour Conference (No 5 (i) of 1980: Promotion of Collective Bargaining):

> The Committee on Freedom of Association has had occasion to examine a number of cases relating to the obligation to negotiate. In the decision that it has taken on the subject, the Committee has pointed out 'the importance which it attaches to the principle that both employers & trade unions should bargain in good faith making every effort to come to an agreement'. It must however also be emphasised that a 'refusal by an employer to bargain with a particular union has not been regarded by the Committee as an infringement of Freedom of Association appropriate for consideration by the Committee; it has adopted this attitude on the basis of the principle that collective bargaining must, if it is to be effective, assume a voluntary character and not entail recourse to measures of compulsion which would alter the voluntary nature of such bargaining.

In not granting application by the union the court in this instance did state however that its determination was case specific and that it would not be averse to granting an order to bargain in good faith in all instances.

The duty to bargain stance
In a number of important cases both preceding and following the 'voluntarism determinations' the industrial court has taken a different view — that it does have a competence to compel good faith bargaining.

In *Bleazard & Others* v *Argus Printing and Publishing Co Ltd* (1983) 4 ILJ 60 IC the industrial court ordered the employer to return to participate in a long established bargaining forum from which it had withdrawn and to bargain in good faith. From this early stage the court indicated that where a bargaining relationship had been in existence over a period that it was empowered to order either party to resume the relationship as a labour practice.

In *Metal & Allied Workers Union* v *Stobar Reinforcing (Pty) Ltd & Another* (1983) 4 ILJ 84 IC the court in similar vein held that the employer's failure to consult with the union on the matter of a retrenchment, where the parties had established a practice of mutual consultation, was unfair.

In *United African Motor & Allied Workers Union of South Africa & Others* v *Fodens (SA) (Pty) Ltd* (1983) 4 ILJ 212 IC the company was alleged to have carried out a number of unfair labour practices, including a refusal to negotiate with a representative, registered trade union. Carefully emphasising that its determination was case specific, the industrial court nevertheless stated:

It would seem that the legislature had intended that a representative trade union should act on behalf of its members in matters concerning their relationship with their employer and that employees should avail themselves of the services of their trade union in this respect. One might as a result infer on the other hand that where the majority of the employees should elect to be represented by a registered trade union the employer could be fairly expected to deal with that union in connection with matters concerning the relationship with its employees . . .

and ordered the employer forthwith to commence negotiations in good faith with the union with regard to its recognition and several other matters.

Thus, determinations on the duty to bargain emanating from the industrial court were confusingly at odds with each other in the first half of the eighties. However, in 1988 and 1989 the court came down strongly in favour of a compulsion to bargain in good faith.

In *Food and Allied Workers Union* v *Spekenham Supreme* (1988) 9 ILJ 628 IC the court stated:

. . . I do not believe that voluntarism has any further right of existence in a system which is principally intended to combat industrial unrest . . . having regard to the fact that fairness is now the overriding consideration in labour relations in South Africa, it is time for the court to find firmly and unequivocally that in general terms it is unfair for an employer not to negotiate bona fide with a representative trade union. . . . The duty to bargain in good faith reinforces the obligation of an employer to recognise the bargaining agent and fosters rational, informed discussion, thereby minimising the potential for unnecessary industrial conflict' (pp 636–7)

In this case the court was also at pains to point out that in exercising its duty to enforce collective bargaining this would not imply interference in the power exchange of the parties or a determination of the outcome of their engagement, i.e. it may not arbitrate unless requested by the parties to do so.

It would seem then, that the industrial court has overcome its initial hesitancy and moved strongly to a position where it perceives itself as having a duty to compel, and if necessary, enforce fair collective bargaining as part of the overall objectives of the Labour Relations Act to promote collective bargaining and avoid industrial unrest. It may be reasonably safely concluded that an enforceable duty to bargain in good faith now exists in South African industrial relations. A determination which confirms this conclusion but extends it somewhat controversially is that of *Natal Baking and Allied Workers Union* v *BB Cereals & Another* (1989) 10 ILJ 870 IC wherein the court held that an employer has a duty to negotiate with a minority union. This is based in the view that individuals with the right to associate have a general right to negotiate through agents of their choice even though these may be in a minority in a workplace, and that a majority union cannot properly represent these interests. This wide interpretation of the allcomers approach may obviously lead to a hopelessly complicated process wherein unions representing miniscule interests demand full negotiation rights.

The elements of good faith bargaining
If the duty to bargain in good faith has been established its defining elements are less easily identifiable.

In *Metal & Allied Workers Union* v *Natal Die Casting Co (Pty) Ltd* (1986) 7 ILJ 520 IC the court used the guidelines proposed by Richardson (1977) who proposed that relevant criteria for good faith bargaining might be:

❑ Did one party merely go through the motions without any real interest in arriving at an agreement?
❑ Were concessions made which are indicative of good faith?
❑ Were proposals made which are indicative of good faith?
❑ Were dilatory tactics used?
❑ Were onerous or unreasonable conditions imposed by a party?
❑ Were unilateral changes in conditions made? was a representative by-passed?
❑ Was sufficient information provided, upon request, to enable a party to appreciate and properly discuss the issues involved?

In the case at hand the court determined that the company's timing of offers, use of concessions and proposals, it use of dilatory tactics and imposition of certain conditions in negotiation reflected a failure to negotiate in good faith which, in the circumstances, constituted an unfair labour practice.

In *Nasionale Suiwelkooperasie Bpk* v *Food & Allied Workers Union* (1989) 10 ILJ 870 IC the employer alleged that the union had bargained in bad faith by *inter alia*:

❑ failing to motivate an unrealistic wage demand;

❑ failing to disclose sufficient information in support of its demands;

❑ failing to make concessions in the course of bargaining;

❑ resorting to dilatory tactics.

The court in favouring a view that it had a duty to compel good faith bargaining, stated that the failure to do so falls within the 'catch-all' phrase of the unfair labour practice definition, i.e. would create or promote labour unrest, detrimentally affect the employer–employee relationship and impair labour relations between an employer and employee. The onus is on the applicant to show that bad faith bargaining has been practised. In this case the court found that the employer had not met this requirement — the union had moved substantially from its opening position (an 85,7 % demand) during negotiations, and *most importantly* had eventually accepted the employer's offer, although it had failed to fully explain its demands correctly. Postponement of 3 out of 19 meetings over a six-month negotiation period was not sufficient evidence to conclude the use of dilatory tactics. On the balance, with a mind to the fact that the central purpose of collective bargaining is to achieve an agreement, and that this had in fact been achieved, the court found that no unfair labour practice had been committed.

Another important case relating to good faith bargaining, and centring on the purposes of collective bargaining was *East Rand Gold & Uranium Company Limited* v *National Union of Mineworkers* (1989) 10 ILJ 103 IC heard in the Transvaal Division of the labour appeal court. The industrial court had determined that the employer's refusal to backdate its 1987 wage increment to employees who had unsuccessfully struck was an unfair labour practice because it penalised these employees. Non-striking employees had accepted the wage offer and received their increase at the time of acceptance. The chairman of the labour appeal court held that the union had not negotiated in good faith on the following grounds:

❑ personal insults against the employer's bargaining team which went beyond levels of abrasiveness which should be tolerated in negotiations;

❑ a failure and refusal to motivate its demands and indicate its bottomline;

❑ indications to the employer that an improved offer might settle the dispute and that settlement was close, and then contemptuously rejecting the improved offer;

❑ setting preconditions to the commencement of negotiation which
    were tantamount to a refusal to negotiate;
❑ a failure to explain its conduct to the court and to call witnesses
    justifying the inference that it had bargained in bad faith.

The chairman further found that the employer's offer to all employees (ie that employees who did not strike and accepted its final
offer would receive wage increases backdated to 1st June 1987 and
those striking would not receive backdated increases) had to be seen
against:

❑ the union's lack of good faith bargaining leading to the deadlock;
    and
❑ the sit-in, disruption and damage of the previous year's negotia-
    tion with the consequent concern of the company to prevent a
    recurrence of this.

The union argued that the offer had undermined the union as the
sole collective bargaining agent and the company could not bypass
it in this way. The chairman found:

❑ The bad faith bargaining coupled with an impasse and the possi-
    bility of illegal action constituted a sufficient cause to bypass the
    acknowledged collective bargaining agent.
❑ The sole collective bargaining agent had shown bad faith accept-
    ing its position, those employees who it represented and the
    employer.
❑ The union had broken the rules and it was inappropriate for it to
    suggest that the employer must adhere to them.
❑ The employer's behaviour was akin to self-defence and not un-
    fair.
❑ The bad faith coupled with the impasse and threat of disruption
    and damage, in fairness, released the company, if only tempo-
    rarily, from its obligation to negotiate solely through the union
    which had only itself to blame for the state of affairs.

The assessors concurred with the chairman that the employer's offer
had not been discriminatory when it was made as it was made to all
employees. Those employees who chose not to accept it and strike
had not been victimised or penalised by the employer's later refusal
to extend the benefit of the offer to them — the offer had been made
to all and there was no intention to penalise. Differentiation of
treatment did not imply a motive to punish — employees were not

all treated equally but those who struck did not render an equal service to those who did not.

❏ The assessors felt that it was necessary to define the crux of the concept of good faith bargaining, stating:

> In our view, it is clear that an important element of the obligation to bargain in good faith is to meet and to negotiate with an honest intention of reaching an agreement, if this is possible.
>
> Negotiations which are conducted with any other purpose in mind will not usually satisfy the requirements of good faith bargaining. If the purpose with which a party enters into negotiations is to draw out or protract the negotiations, in order to achieve some object other than reaching agreement, he will not be bargaining in good faith . . . a party not intending to reach agreement, at all, will not be bargaining in good faith. We should also draw a distinction between unfair bargaining tactics and the failure to bargain in good faith . . . Although certain tactics, such as insulting the representative of the other party, are to be deprecated, the mere fact that a tactic is unacceptable does not automatically mean that the bargaining is not being conducted in good faith. One can only decide whether bargaining is not being conducted in good faith on the totality of the evidence. (pp 697–8)

The assessors argued that in cases of impasse in negotiations (i.e. a final deadlock or breakdown) it is not in the interests of the parties to leave a matter unresolved, and the only course of action open to them is unilateral action. The purpose of such action must be to attempt to resolve the impasse rather than to destroy or weaken the other party *unless* it has bargained in bad faith for instance by acting without a mandate, failing or refusing to renew its mandate, or putting an offer to a consistuency when this could be reasonably expected.

> . . . where the impasse is caused by one party's lack of good faith in bargaining, the other party may enjoy greater freedom of action than would be the case where the impasse occurs after good faith bargaining. (p 698)

Further, the assessors, stated their belief that an employer would act fairly in implementing unilaterally an offer *already on the bargaining table* when the union intends resorting to industrial action to resolve the impasse. However, the implementation of terms not offered during the course of negotiation would indicate an attempt to use the impasse to bypass the union (as bargaining agent of its employees), which would be unfair.

Such an implementation would have to be made without distinction to all employees in the bargaining unit. Acceptance of the offer would introduce a binding agreement and employees would waive their right to industrial action to further improve terms for the bargaining period.

In Ergo's case the assessors added that the employer was entitled to make an offer directly to members of the bargaining unit once impasse was reached, the offer was the same as that already made to the union.

> Secondly, the union members were also employees and stood in that relationship to Ergo. Because of their dual capacity, an offer to the employees was just as much an offer to the union as an offer to the union was an offer to employees. (p 700)

The union had known an offer was to be made to employees and if it had had the necessary support could have withstood it:

> if it could not do this it cannot seek to hold the employer responsible for this failure. (p 700)

In the event, the assessors agreed with the chairman's decision that the employer had not committed an unfair labour practice, albeit for different reasons.

In another case, involving unilateral implementation *HARWU* v *Karos Hotels* (unreported) NH 12/3/151 30 September 1988 IC, the union tried to interdict the employer against putting into effect its offer. The parties had exhausted internal procedures to reach deadlock in negotiations, and no case was made that the employer had bargained in bad faith. The court held that while the wage increase was unilaterally implemented it was not unfairly performed, but in the circumstances reflected that

> the change contemplated was not of an unconscionable kind — the employer was merely seeking to increase wages, while the union was holding out for a better deal ... It was a wholly legitimate and timely exercise of economic power. (Thompson 1989 p 105)

In conclusion it would seem that:
- □ an enforceable duty to negotiate does exist in South Africa; and
- □ some progress has been made in identifying what constitutes good faith bargaining in the eyes of the court.

APPROACHES TO UNION RECOGNITION

Two major approaches exist as regards union recognition:

❑ *the allcomers approach,* and
❑ *the majoritarian approach.*

In terms of the allcomers approach an employer recognises any union with significant representation in a bargaining unit for collective bargaining purposes. Depending on the size of the workforce this is often around 25–30 % as a minimum. In terms of the majoritarian approach an employer recognises a trade union only if it has representation of 50 % + 1 in a bargaining unit for collective bargaining purposes.

The majoritarian approach, if used consistently, means that only one union may be recognised for collective bargaining purposes in respect of a given bargaining unit. It has been argued that this has advantages in limiting negotiations to one round per year, and that it reduces disruptive union competition in places of work. Opponents of the approach argue that it does not allow full expression of the freedom of association; that a union with 49 % membership may not achieve bargaining rights; that it fails to deal with a multi-union situation where a workforce is 80 % organised but no union has a majority; and that it does not effectively reduce inter-union conflict, especially where two are vying for majority and both have about 40 %. On the other hand the allcomers approach is seen as allowing full expression of freedom of association and allowing open and tolerant acknowledgement of the range of competing interests in a workplace. It has been criticised as lacking clear cutoffs; as promoting racial unionism/sectionalism; as leading to endless bargaining with a succession of unions catering for similar interests and therefore as unlikely to lessen inter-union rivalry.

The basis upon which the first recognition agreement is entered into sets criteria for all future union relations if an employer is to be consistent — it would hardly be fair to base recognition of one union on different criteria to recognition of others. Some propose that majoritarian recognition applies only to collective matters and that the principle should not preclude individuals from exercising their rights to belong to a union of their choice or appropriate representation by such a union on individual grievances or rights matters. This is, of course, different from the US system wherein the majority union has sole rights of representation but is enjoined to represent non-members fairly.

A related issue is that of the *closed shop* whereby employees must by agreement between the employer and a union, belong to that union in order to remain in employment, i.e. it is a condition of employment. At present provision for such agreements is restricted to industrial councils, and there seems every chance that private closed shops would not be favourably looked on by the industrial court. In *Mazibuko & Others* v *Mooi River Textiles Ltd* (1989) 10 ILJ 575 IC the court held that an extra-statutory closed shop is an infringement of the right to associate or not to associate and accordingly an unfair labour practice.

Critics of the closed shop state that it is a violation of the freedom of association. Proponents argue that no rights are absolute and in this instance institutions which strengthen collective bargaining as a social stabiliser should prevail over individual rights. If strong single union situations promote industrial peace then this should be the paramount consideration. In addition, the closed shop is proposed to prevent free riders gaining the benefits of union efforts without contributing towards its activities; allowing a union the freedom to consider long-term issues rather than becoming bogged down in the short-term successes demanded in union rivalry situations; as stabilising employment; as more effectively regulating wage negotiations by eliminating leapfrogging by unions; and as contributing to greater union unity and discipline. Scabbing in strikes would not be possible and violence would therefore also be less likely.

The pro-closed shop school argues that the inclusionary arrangements are more fair than exclusionary closed shops, i.e. apply to all rather than a selected few, and that through regular elections, democratic constitutions and fair representation the abuses of freedom of association might be limited. Closed-shop unions would not be allowed to hold particular political affiliations, and individuals would be allowed to belong to other unions as well, should they wish, but not to have this organisation represent them. (Albertyn 1989) It is difficult in South Africa to see how a closed shop might prevent union rivalry or that it would necessarily prevent violence in strikes if there was disagreement within the ranks of a closed shop union for instance. The hidden agendas of political affiliation and rivalry in a deeply cleavaged society would be more difficult to deal with than through simple unitary structures.

KEY ARGUMENTS IN WAGE BARGAINING

Various methods exist internationally for fixing wages:

- decision by employer and individual agreements;
- minimum wage determined by boards;
- national minimum wages;
- collective bargaining; and
- voluntary or compulsory arbitration.

Except for a national minimum wage all the other forms of wage fixing are evidenced in South Africa. Many employees undertake employment allowing individual negotiation over wages and conditions with employers. The less skilled the employee the more the employer retains decision-making power over these terms and conditions. The Wage Act provides for Wage Boards which, in the absence of industrial councils in an industry, may set minimum wages and conditions in the form of wage determinations for that industry after hearing argument from labour and employer interests. The Labour Relations Act provides for collective bargaining between employers and organised labour as a means of determining wages and conditions at sectoral levels through industrial councils. Enterprise or company level wages and conditions of service may be negotiated through recognition agreements. Provision is made for compulsory arbitration in cases of dispute involving employees in public service and for voluntary arbitration in cases where the parties are unable to resolve their dispute but are unwilling to utilise the strike or lockout mechanisms.

Discussion here is limited to the major arguments used in collective bargaining situations, i.e. in the negotiation process. Three issues are of concern — determining the wage level, the wage structure and individual wages (figure C.1). The wage level is concerned with the establishment of the base wage in an organisation or across an industry; the wage structure is concerned with issues such as the wage gradient, differentials between grades and therefore with the equity of various job evaluation systems; and the individual wage is centred in debate around how individual wages might be determined if they are to differ from the norm, and is therefore concerned with issues of performance appraisal. Discussion here will be limited to typical arguments used in the determination of wage levels.

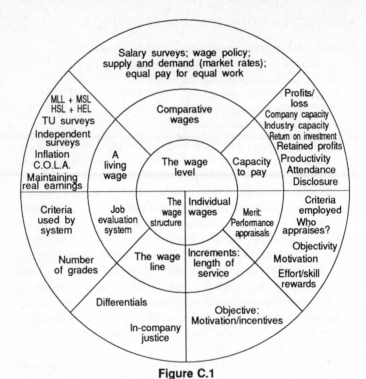

Figure C.1

Arguments used by labour and management in determining wage
levels, wage structures and individual wages

WAGE LEVELS

Labour and management representatives tend to utilise three main
areas of argument to negotiate wage levels: the living wage debate,
comparative wages, and the capacity to pay. Each party, of course,
uses arguments that strengthen its position. Thus companies in
financial straits tend to argue incapacity to pay; while unions facing
such companies will probably push living wage or comparative
wages arguments. On the other hand, where companies are very
profitable and already paying comparatively high wages, unions
will tend to push capacity to pay arguments, while the employer
will argue that living wage criteria have been surpassed and that it
pays at a level beyond its competitors.

THE LIVING WAGE DEBATE

Sloane and Whitney (1977) propose that the concept of a living wage reflects the ethical values of a society as regards the elimination of exploitation. The living wage debate is central to union approaches to collective bargaining in South Africa. Jack (1987) plots the history of the living wage demand from Makgatho's Presidential address for the S.A. Native National Congress in 1919, through the demand for a five pound a month minimum by the Industrial and Commercial Workers Union in 1928, through SACTU's demand for a pound a day in the 1950s, to FOSATU's campaign in 1980 and more recently the living wage campaign initiated by COSATU in 1987.

Newall (1989) notes several characteristics of the living wage demand:

- ❑ a rejection of poverty datum levels;
- ❑ the use of a round figure around which to rally workers; and
- ❑ the emotive connotations of impugning that employers pay less than a living wage.

Poverty datum levels

Poverty investigations have their roots in the work of Booth (1889 and 1891) and Rowntree (1901 onwards) in Britain. Rowntree distinguished between primary poverty where people did not have enough money to maintain physical efficiency, and secondary poverty where income would be sufficient for this purpose were it not that some is always absorbed by other expenditure either useful or wasteful. This distinction recognised that man's needs are not only physical but social as well. Bowley developed the concept of the *poverty datum* line at around the turn of the century, and Batson introduced it to South Africa in the 1930s, defining it as 'an estimate of the income needed by an individual household if it is to attain a defined minimum level of health and decency'. The concept of an *effective minimum level* was developed in recognition of the idea of secondary poverty and in recognition of the fact that people in poverty would be unlikely to purchase only those bare essentials defined in the PDL. Batson defined the EML as 150 % of the PDL.

The PDL was never envisaged as a 'norm', for wage setting purposes — it was a measure of poverty. Two modern surveys are conducted nationally and regularly, those of UNISA's Bureau for Market Research which produces figures for a Minimum Living Level (MLL) and and Higher Living Wage (HLL), and the University of Port Elizabeth's Institute for Planning Research which produces figures for a Household Subsistence Level (HSL) and a Household Effective Level (HEL). These terms refer to a hypothetical 'average', household rather than individual households, and have been referred to as practical guidelines for determining wage levels (Potgieter). Potgieter states:

> The household subsistence level may be defined as an estimate of the theoretical income needed by an individual household if it is to maintain a defined minimum level of health and decency in the short term. It is calculated at the lowest retail cost of a budget of necessities of adequate quality, comprising the total food, clothing, fuel, lighting and washing and cleansing materials required for each person, together with the fuel, lighting and cleansing materials needed by the household as a whole, the cost of rent and of workers, transport. (p 4)

He points out that the HSL is made on assumptions of rational expenditure and the short term satisfaction of basic physiological needs, and that it indicates only a theoretical budget of necessities rather than an adequate income. The HEL is seen as a more realistic document for determining income levels, being the

> level of income . . . after one third of it has been allocated to other items, which is equal to the cost of the HSL requirements for that household [i.e. 150 % of HSL].

Criticisms of minimum living levels

Trade unions have rejected these measures as racist (could a poor white family live on the defined levels?), and inappropriate. Budlender (1985), in a scorching critique of PDLs raised the following points:

- ❑ the incorrect assumption of *Homo economus* which postulates rational buyers, with perfect knowledge, making best use of market conditions;
- ❑ the use of a descriptive poverty measure for purposes of wage prescription;
- ❑ the adherence to different measures of poverty based on race;
- ❑ the lag between measures and ongoing inflation;
- ❑ the inability of most workers to buy in bulk at cheap shops owing to full-time employment, transport problems, cash shortages, and a lack of refrigeration facilities for the preservation of perishables bought in bulk;

TABLE C1
The components of the HSL

HSL Components	Items and Measures
Food	• Cost of theoretical minimum required to maintain health. • Cheapest prices sought (excluding temporary 'special offers'). • Minimum food requirements based on food ration scales adapted from the USA's food and Nutrition Board which has assessed minimum protein, vitamin and calorific requirements of the 'average' adult and child. The department of health (RSA) has adopted these measures for use in assessing the minimum requirements of South African blacks and coloureds, proposing 'culturally' different eating habits and assuming their requirements to be lower as they are generally shorter and lighter than Americans. Included in the component for blacks are: skimmed milk powder, meat, fish, eggs, cheese, dried beans/peas, fresh vegetables and fruit, margarine, oil, brown bread, mealie-meal, samp, sugar, jam, coffee, tea, salt, spices and condiments.
Clothing	• Potgieter notes that 'the clothing components is perhaps the most subjective of all the cost components' as it attempts to find not only the cheapest lines but those which provide good value. • As with the food component, departmental stores were the cheapest sources. • Children's requirements are assessed as a proportion of an adult woman's requirements: 0–4 years (25 %) 5–9 years (50 %), 1–15 years (75 %). • Yearly requirements for men comprise: 1/3 overcoat, 1 sports jackets, 2 pairs trousers, 2 pairs shoes, 4 shirts, 2 pairs underpants, 2 vests, 1 pullover, 3 pairs socks, 1 pair pyjamas.

HSL Components	Items and Measures
	• Yearly requirements for women comprise: 1/3 coat, 3 dresses, 1 skirt, 1 blouse, 2 pairs shoes, 2 pairs panties, 2 vests, 2 bras, 1 petticoat, 1 nightie, 1 jersey, 3 pairs stockings, 2 head squares.
Fuel, lighting, washing cleansing materials	• Again cheapest prices are used following scrutiny of local chain stores. • Monthly requirements comprise: 4 bars blue soap, 1 large double sunlight soap, 2 large packets soap powder, 2 tins floor polish, 1 small tin shoe polish, 1 small tin stove polish, 3 bags coal, 1 bag wood, 9 litres paraffin, 4–1/3 packets candles, 4 boxes matches and electricity and water.
Rent	• Figures represent 'what the bulk of the population is committed to for housing cost purposes'.
Transport	• Organisations providing public transport are consulted to obtain transport costs. • Only the cost of transporting the breadwinner to and from work is computed - it does not include transport costs of other family members or non-commuting costs incurred by the family head.

❑ inappropriate nutritional scales for those involved in heavy physical work;
❑ an exceptionally mean clothing estimate;
❑ inadequate rent estimates;
❑ a personal hygiene section which precludes even toothpaste or a toothbrush, confining itself to sunlight soap;
❑ no provision for education, even in the SLL;
❑ limited transportation estimates, in the case of the HSL making provision for only public transport to and from work;
❑ no recreational allowances;
❑ inadequate or no medical and dental provision:
❑ inadequate or unrealistic provision for household equipment.

Budlender (1985) highlights the derogation of the terms 'maintenance of health and decency' in these measures, stating:

> 'Living' necessitates the requirements for full psychological and mental, as well as physical existence. We also need to acknowledge the very real difference between the long term and short term, even when speaking of mere survival. In the long term we also cannot expect that the lives of all household members will run smoothly. A long term survival budget must allow for contingencies. People fall ill, are injured and die. Goods are damaged, stolen, lost and broken. In all these cases the family must outlay amounts of money. Transport costs are involved in most contingencies. In others there are the costs of hospitals, lawyers, replacement, repair . . . there is no provision for contingencies in the PDLs. (p 21)

Other measures

Two other measures of a living wage are worth mention. SPA Consultants investigate income requirements for low income families in South Africa's townships. Newall (1989) notes that figures from this source are 'of the order of 80 % higher than the MLL'. (p 33)

The Labour Research Service (LRS), a trade union service organisation in Cape Town, estimates a living wage based on housing needs. Assuming that housing should never use up more than 25 % of a family's income, the LRS estimates the cost of paying off a modest home and multiplies this by four for a living wage estimate. This figure runs to about 100 % higher than MLL or HSL figures, standing at R850 per month in 1987. (SALB 12 (4) 1987)

Criticisms of the concept of a living wage

Sloane and Whitney (1977) point out that the following problems may arise in attempting to implement a living wage concept:

- ❑ Wages may lose touch with economic reality.
- ❑ Employer sympathy may not be related to economic capacity.
- ❑ Raised wage levels may have the consequence of job reduction.
- ❑ Families may have more than one breadwinner.
- ❑ Disagreements inevitably arise between protagonists in the debate raising problems of standardisation.

THE CAPACITY TO PAY AND DISCLOSURE OF INFORMATION

Sloane and Whitney (1977) state that the level of profits is an indicator of the wage paying capacity of an enterprise involved in negotiations, but add that no clear formula has been devised to assess fairness in this regard.

These authors propose that bargaining which centres around the capacity to pay argument gives rise to the following problems:

- ❑ Further conflicts arise over disclosure of information, accounting procedures and interpretation, and managerial 'rights to manage'.
- ❑ It raises the debate as to whether wage bargaining is a future-based issue or an historical catch-up process.
- ❑ A wide variety of economic, social and political events may preclude an enterprise from continued high performance rendering wage levels bargained under those conditions inappropriate.
- ❑ Profits are only one factor in determining ability to pay -others include fringe benefits, demand for product, productivity and ratio of labour costs to total costs. Where ratio of labour costs to overall costs is low, then an employer is generally better placed to pay larger increases. An additional factor is the ease with which a company can pass on increased costs in the form of higher prices (an inflationary move).

Disclosure of information

An issue which raises heated debate between labour and management is that of demands for disclosure of information. It is argued that if bargaining is to be a rational process, then all parties require relevant information to inform their demands and offers, maintain realistic expectations of the process, and limit brinkmanship. Employers who refuse unions relevant information have little room for complaint about ignorance or lack of realism in demands. Those who plead poverty, and then, after negotiation has been completed, release news of improved profits to the media, destroy trust in labour relations. Employers often respond emotionally to disclosure demands, fearing an invasion of their accounts and being unsure what the boundaries of such a request are. They fear union competence and responsibility in dealing with data, erosion of managerial prerogatives and a shift in power relations. Having said this, however, some companies have offered to disclose information to the union during bargaining. In my experience these are companies with their backs to the wall financially — not unsurprisingly, unions sometimes turn down such offers, knowing that if the offer is made, an investigation is unlikely to strengthen their case. Of course disclosure during bad times may well establish practice precedents which would demand follow through during profitable periods.

In South Africa there are no legal duties to disclose information at company level bargaining, although section 30 of the Labour Relations Act makes provision for industrial councils to subpoena information it considers necessary for achieving settlement in an enquiry. It is not clear whether this refers to wage bargaining, and if it does, what use an individual company's information would be to a sectoral wage negotiation. In the case of public companies, unions can obtain published financial reports to assist in their preparations for bargaining, and they can also apply to the registrar of companies for information on wholly owned subsidiaries of publicly owned companies.

In the USA a failure to disclose relevant information to a union could be an unfair labour practice, and once the argument of inability to pay has been advanced, there is an expectation that proof be provided to this effect (see also good faith bargaining). In the UK legal provision is made for disclosure of information without which a union would be impeded in bargaining. The Advisory, Conciliation and Arbitration Service (ACAS) has published guidelines to assist employers in establishing policy on such matters.

Generally employers do not have to disclose information which:

- ❑ adversely affects national security;
- ❑ relates to an individual, without that person's permission;

- ❑ includes information given to an employer in confidence;
- ❑ would, if disclosed, cause substantial injury to the employer's undertaking for reasons other than its effect on collective bargaining;
- ❑ has been obtained for purposes of legal proceedings;
- ❑ would demand the compilation of information which would involve work or expenditure out of reasonable proportion to the value of that information for bargaining purposes. It must be relevant to the issue under negotiation. (Nel 1984)

AECI has published guidelines for managers with regard to disclosure to promote compromise and agreement in collective bargaining, protect the business interests of the company and to ensure fair labour practice. Essentially these guidelines state that:

- ❑ A union requesting information should justify its reasons for doing so and indicate its relevance to the collective bargaining process.
- ❑ The company should advise the union of its obligations not to prejudice its position with regard to competitors, customers and suppliers.
- ❑ The company should consider whether the absence of information requested would impede collective bargaining, and consider whether it would be an unfair labour practice not to disclose such information.
- ❑ The union could be supplied with published information which a public company must prepare for shareholders under the Company's Act including data relating to the company's organisational structure, finance, profit-ability and competitive situation, pay and conditions, IR policies and procedures and manpower details.
- ❑ Except in certain cases relating to pension fund trustees or committees, no individual information should be disclosed without written permission from the person concerned.
- ❑ Other categories of information which demand greater caution in disclosure are identified and include matters relating to technological developments, contributions per product, details of proposed investments, price quotas, tenders applied for, cost per unit to manufacture, technical agreements.
- ❑ The union should guarantee that disclosed information will be used responsibly.

❑ Certain information disclosure should be a regular and ongoing process, including not only unions but all employees, supervisors and managers directed not only toward improving collective bargaining but a imparting a wider understanding of the business, its objectives and performance.

THE COMPARATIVE WAGE DEBATE

Employers and trade unions both use comparative wage arguments in negotiations — usually with the former citing examples of poorer payers, and the latter cases of more advantageous conditions. Sloane and Whitney (1977) observe that the basic idea behind comparative arguments

> is the presumption that the economics of a particular collective bargaining relationship should neither fall substantially behind nor be greatly superior to other employer relationships.

They suggest that this has the following advantages:
❑ it standardises wage costs in competitive industries;
❑ uniform conditions allow for greater membership contentment for unions;
❑ it allows for the emergence of 'market rates; and
❑ it indicates what is acceptable to labour and management in an industry.

However, such arguments also have limitations:
❑ The capacity of firms to pay varies according to technology, markets, location, stage of development, and financial resources.
❑ Comparisons may be superficial.
❑ Actual jobs may differ in comparing wages across industries and companies.
❑ Variations in fringe benefits may distort comparisons.

Unions have criticised salary surveys as prescribing wage levels rather than indicating rates across industries, and cite them as weapons for wage restraint on the part of employers. Employers use supply and demand arguments to back their case for paying comparable (market rates) for jobs, and indicate that wage increases will raise risks of capital substitution and workforce reductions.

TERMINATION OF CONTRACT

A hierarchy of rules governs the termination of contracts of employment:

- ❏ the common law,
- ❏ regulatory legislation, and
- ❏ fair labour practice guidelines.

The common law

The common law allows for termination of contract under the following circumstances:

- ❏ expiration of an agreed period,
- ❏ by due notice,
- ❏ by mutual agreement,
- ❏ on completion of a specified task,
- ❏ by repudiation of the terms of employment,
- ❏ on the death of either party,
- ❏ on insolvency, or
- ❏ by virtue of impossibility of performance.

Generally, the notice period would be a week for weekly paid employees, and a month for monthly paid personnel. However, the common law recognises the right of an employer to dismiss summarily (without notice) under the following circumstances:

- ❏ failure to place labour at the disposal of an employer;
- ❏ disrespect, disobedience, or insubordination;
- ❏ impediment of an employer's business (dishonesty/disloyalty); and
- ❏ gross misconduct.

(Riekert 1984)

In terms of the law of contract the employer acquires the right to summarily cancel the contract if the employee breaches a vital term of the contract. This cancellation amounts to lawful summary dismissal.

Regulatory legislation

The exercise of common-law rights is constrained by various laws. The Basic Conditions of Employment Act constrains the employer's power to link discipline and remuneration, provides for minimum notice periods in cases of termination of contract and obliges certain duties on an employer such as provision of a certificate of service. The Labour Relations Act limits the exercise of employer's powers through the definition of the unfair labour practice. In effect an employer must now act not only lawfully in terminating an employee's contract, but also fairly. Dismissals can now be challenged not only in terms of legal technicalities, but also considerations of equity. The industrial court has referred to British and American law in making determinations but its core reference is conventions and recommendations of the International Labour Organisation.

General principles

Convention 158 of 1982 and Recommendation 166 of 1982 are the key points of reference in cases of termination of contract.

Article 4 of Convention 158 states that employment shall not be terminated unless there is a valid reason connected with the capacity of conduct of a worker, or by virtue of operational requirements of an organisation. The Convention (*Articles 5 and 6*) further states that union membership or participation (with the consent of an employer during working hours); the filing of a complaint against an employer or participation in proceedings against an employer involving alleged violation of laws; race, colour, sex, marital status, family responsibilities, pregnancy, religion, political opinion, national extraction or social origin; and absence owing to illness or injury are not valid reasons for termination of a contract. *Article 7* states that employment shall not be terminated for reasons of conduct or performance before a worker has had an opportunity to defend himself, unless an employer cannot reasonably be expected to provide this opportunity. *Article 8* states that an employee who feels that his or her employment has been unjustifiably terminated should have a right of appeal to an impartial court, tribunal or arbitration process, which is waived if not exercised within a reasonable time. *Article 10* states that such an appeal body should have the right to order or propose reinstatement, order payment of adequate compensation or other appropriate relief. Unless there has been serious misconduct, reasonable notice shall be given to employees whose contracts are to be terminated (*Article 11*). *Article 12* states that where employment has been terminated, a worker shall be entitled to some form of severance allowance or benefit to be the responsibility of either the employer, an employer fund or the state, according to national law and practice.

In *MAWU* v *Barlows Manufacturing Co* (1983) 4 ILJ 283 IC the industrial court determined that an *employer should justify or give reasons for termination contracts of employment*. If this were not an

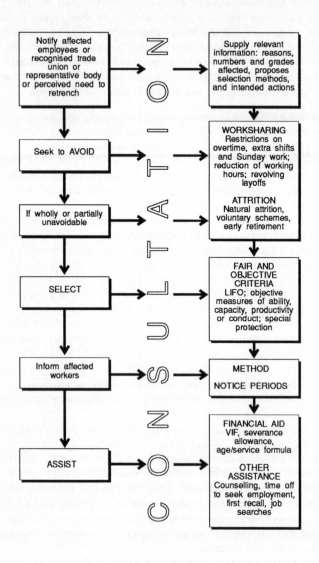

Figure C.2
Guidelines for fair retrenchment practice

obligation employers could exercise their power to dismiss employees quite unchecked, simply by issuance of lawfully defined notice, i.e. lawful rather than equitable behaviour.

Like the ILO Convention, South African labour law recognises three basic reasons for termination of contract: *operational necessity, incapacity and misconduct.*

Operational requirements: retrenchment and redundancy

The industrial court has made a large number of determinations relating to retrenchment situations. These can be summarised in the form of Figure C.2. Retrenchment and redundancy fall into the category of terminations of contract owing to operational requirements. Generally retrenchment refers to situations where a temporary decrease in jobs occurs as a consequence of economic circumstances, while redundancy refers to the permanent disappearance of jobs owing to advances in technology or changes in the production process or markets. The following guidelines apply.

Consultation is the basic requirement for fair retrenchment practices. Cameron et al (1989) suggest four basic reasons for this process:

- ❑ to explain reasons for the proposed retrenchment and consider alternatives to its implementation;
- ❑ to endeavour to agree on criteria for selection of employees;
- ❑ to endeavour to agree on a timetable for the retrenchment; and
- ❑ to consider special cases where retrenchment might cause particular hardship (exclusions).

The employer should consult with representative trade unions, or worker bodies and individual employees in the absence of a trade union. Recognition does not imply a formal recognition agreement. In *Hadebe and Others* v *Romatex Industrials* (1986) 7 ILJ 726 IC the company argued there was no need to consult with the union as no formal recognition agreement had been accorded the union. The court rejected this, reinstating the employees, and pointing out that a formal agreement was 'in gestation', the company had given access to the plant to the union and instituted stoporder facilities, and allowed the election of shopstewards, indicating that 'a form of recognition, was in place. The paramount consideration was industrial peace in such circumstances. In *Gonya* v *Besterecta* (1986) 7 ILJ 39 IC the court found that the employer should have initiated the formation of a workers, committee for consultative purposes in the absence of a representative union. The court has then placed considerable onus on the employer to consult with a representative body of some sort, and certainly a union where it has a presence.

Avoidance of workforce reductions is usually the primary objective of trade union, and a central issue to the consultative process. Avoidance measures fall into two main groupings:

❑ *work sharing.* Available work is spread among existing staff by reducing the number of hours worked, usually through measures as overtime restrictions, restrictions on extra shifts, reduction of normal working days in a week, or revolving lay offs wherein employees might take turns in periods of unpaid leave as a form of worksharing.

❑ *Other measures.* These include natural attrition, volunteer schemes (usually an attractive severance package), early retirement (with compensation for any disadvantageous consequences in terms of benefits), and internal training and transfers.

Notice of the intention to retrench should not be confused with notice of termination of contract given to affected employees. Notice of intention to retrench should be provided to a representative body before notice to affected employees in order to allow a fair consultation process wherein alternatives to retrenchment might be discussed. The yardstick for the court is whether a notice period allowed reasonable time for consultation weighed against the demand imposed by the employer's economic predicament (Riekert 1987). For instance, in *NUTW and Others* v *Sea Gift Surfware Manufacturers* (1985) 6 ILJ 101 IC the court held that notice given on the day of the intended retrenchment was inadequate and ordered the reinstatement of workers. At the same time a union must respond timeously to such notice. In *Liebenbergh and Others* v *Franz Falke Textiles (Pty) Ltd* (1986) 7 ILJ 513 IC the union's continued postponement of meetings to discuss retrenchment was deemed vindication of the company's decision to proceed without further reference to it. In countries such as Britain, West Germany, France and Canada statutory notice periods to consult are provided for in cases of workforce reduction (Yemin 1984). As already indicated such notice should be given to a representative union or where no such union exists to an elected employee body or the employees themselves.

The notice should contain information as to the reason for the proposed retrenchment, numbers and types of workers envisaged to be at risk, proposed methods of selection, and proposed timing.

Selection

Yemin (1984) states that there are two kinds of criteria used internationally in considering how to select workers for retrenchment:

❑ those aimed at maintaining work for those who might suffer most hardship from job loss such as length of service, age, family and health circumstances (usually emphasised by worker representatives); and

❑ those aimed at protecting the interests of the enterprise in retaining qualified personnel, such as ability, qualifications, efficiency, and adaptability.

South Africa's industrial court has made several determinations obliging employers to adopt objective or fair criteria in selection. In *Shezi and others* v *Consolidated Frame Cotton Corp Ltd* (1984) 5 ILJ 3 IC the court stated that criteria should as far as possible not depend solely on the opinion of a person making a selection, but be objectively based in such measures as attendance records, work efficiency, experience or length of service. Similarly in *Mwasa* v *SA Broadcasting Service* (1986) 7 ILJ 754 IC the court stated that the more vague and subjective the criteria to be used in selection, the more opportunity an employee should be afforded to contest them and their application (consultation).

Special protection may be afforded to certain groups such as worker representatives, pregnant women and women on maternity leave (Yemin 1984). In South Africa apprentices and persons doing military service are afforded special protection by statute in cases of workforce reductions.

Assistance for retrenched workers is provided for in two ways:

❑ *state benefits* through the Unemployment Insurance Act (30/66 and 89/82) amounting to 45 % of weekly earnings received at the last date of being a contributor, receivable for 26 weeks in any consecutive 52 week period (subject to various conditions such as earnings level, employment for 13 of the previous 52 weeks, and capability and availability to work); and

❑ *company level* assistance in the form of severance benefits usually worked out on a service based formula. The industrial court has not set any specific sum, but has (somewhat controversially) made mention of the desirability of severance pay in retrenchment situations (see *Masondo & Others* v *Bestform (SA)* (1986) 7 ILJ 448 IC. In *MAWU and Others* v *G&H Erectors* (1985) ICD (1) 28 the court reinstated workers to an insolvent company returning their status as preferant creditors — thus presumably improving their chances of some level of remunerative benefit. Other forms of assistance might include guarantees of first recall, time of to seek new employment, job searches by the company, and counselling. (Anstey 1989)

Misconduct

Terminations of contract for reasons of misconduct are essentially concerned with issues of discipline. In recent times the emphasis in matters of discipline has shifted from a punitive to a corrective character. Generally employers are required to behave in a manner which meets criteria of *substantive and procedural fairness*. Standards of conduct and performance are usually governed by disciplinary or substantive rules, the application of which are regulated by fair procedures.

Generally an employer is expected to abide by its own or agreed rules, but this alone will not ensure fairness. Standards are required to be fair and fairly applied, demanding a balance between consistency and flexibility in consideration of the merits of each individual case. (Rycroft and Jordaan 1990). Various disciplinary measures are available to an employer including verbal and written warnings, suspension with or without pay, demotion and dismissal. Warnings are generally issued on a progressive scale according to seriousness of offence or repeated infractions of company rules. Usually provision is made for such warnings to be removed from an employee's file after a period (often about six months) — they do not remain in effect indefinitely. Suspension without pay requires the agreement of the employee concerned, and in certain instances may be prohibited in terms of an industrial agreement. Similarly demotion requires agreement from the employee unless it is permitted in terms of legislation.

Dismissal is a remedy of last recourse and should only be used in serious offences, particularly in the light of South Africa's high levels of unemployment which render such a decision akin to 'an industrial death sentence'. The court requires a *valid and fair reason* for a dismissal. In other words there must be a reasonable belief on the balance of probabilities (vs beyond reasonable doubt) that an employee committed an offence, and once that has been decided, the offence should be sufficiently serious to warrant dismissal (sufficiency of reason). The circumstances of the offence are important in determining sufficiency of reason, but the court has found theft, dishonesty, unprovoked assault, gross insubordination, and intimidation to warrant dismissal in certain instances. Where misconduct is so serious that it renders the continued employment relationship impossible, or is a continually repeated offence in circumstances where the employee knows that dismissal could be the consequence (the importance of warnings) then dismissal may be warranted. In exercising discipline it is important that the employer apply rules consistently and impartially, and gives appropriate consideration to extenuating circumstances in determining a penalty or corrective measure. Extenuating circumstances might include length of service, disciplinary record, work performance, personal circumstances and circumstances of the case in question.

Procedural fairness basically demands the conduct of a *hearing* in which an employee has the opportunity to state his case in response to charges, and to bring mitigating circumstances to the attention of the employer. A fair hearing would generally accord an employee the following: advice of the alleged offence, timeous disciplinary action but adequate notice to allow for preparation, impartial adjudication to the extent possible, representation, the opportunity to state a case and defend oneself, the right to call own witnesses and cross examine, an interpreter of own choice, notification of a finding, consideration of extenuating circumstances, advice of penalty and finally the right to appeal the matter within and beyond the organisation, i.e. via arbitration or the industrial court. An employer may be excused from holding a hearing in cases of overriding or extreme crisis, or where the employee waives a right to a hearing through abuse or desertion.(Rycroft and Jordaan 1990).

Poor work performance

Incompetence may arise from a lack of skill or training, or incompatibility or owing to medical reasons. In the last case the term incapacity is generally preferred and this is dealt with below. In cases where there are skills deficiencies an employer should attempt to raise performance levels through training or counselling.

Rycroft and Jordaan (1990) propose several factors which might be considered in determining *substantive fairness* of dismissal for poor performance: extent or degree of inability to perform properly, possible prejudice to the safety of others, effects on the morale of other employees, likelihood of future improvements, the availability of other work which may suit the employee's capabilities, and the seniority and experience of the employee. Dismissal will only be fair if it is indicated that the incompetence or incompatibility is irreparable.

Procedurally, the employer should inform an employee of shortcomings in performance, allow a reasonable opportunity for improvement, warn of the consequences of a failure to improve, and assist with appropriate training. A final opportunity to state a case should be provided before a dismissal. (Rycroft and Jordaan 1990).

Incapacity

In cases of incapacity to perform, a different approach is required to that of misconduct or skills deficiencies. Where the problem is of a permanent nature or of indefinite duration, Rycroft and Jordaan (1990) suggest following the redundancy procedure on the basis of operational requirements. In other instances they suggest that the following criteria can be used to determine whether the employer can be fairly expected to continue the relationship *(substantive fairness)*: nature of incapacity, likelihood of recovery period of absence, effect on employer's operation, effects of problem on welfare of others, employee's status, work record and length of service, cause of incapacity. The employer can legitimately expect the employee to submit to independent medical examination. For purposes of *procedural fairness* the employer should consult with the employee, try to find a solution to the problem, and possibly even locate alternative placement or medical assistance.

INDEX

INDUSTRIAL RELATIONS TITLES FROM JUTA

)USTRIAL RELATIONS HANDBOOK
licies, Procedures and Practices for South African Managers
DREW PONS

s loose-leaf publication assists the management team to promote successful relation-
es with employees in order to continue to develop in the medium to long term. It has
en designed to take cognizance of developments both in labour law and the current
ctice of industrial relations in South Africa. Practical guidelines are set out in detail
uring the value of this book as a 'hands-on' text suitable for all levels of management.
ludes Revision Service 1 (July 1991)

)USTRIAL RELATIONS IN SOUTH AFRICA
NIA BENDIX

ome 600 concise and informative pages, frequently punctuated by tables, figures and
rts, Sonia Bendix skillfully analyses international industrial relations principles and spe-
ally gives in-depth insight into our own. It includes the 1988 amendments to the Labour
ations Act and a chapter is devoted solely to dispute settlement machinery in South
ca, dealing with the question of fairness, unfair labour practice and the Industrial Court.
cond edition October 1991.

RSONNEL MANAGEMENT
e Business Owner's Handbook for Small and Medium-sized Companies
LIA HOLDEN

tten specifically for any business that is operating without in-house personnel manage-
nt staff, this easy-to-read subscription publication provides a working system that is quick
mplement and provides the procedural 'knowledge' required to deal with employees. It
he only publication available that provides vital working documents that the subscriber
ee to copy and to use. The only entrepreneur who can afford to be without this handbook
he specialist who consults and works alone.

)RKER PARTICIPATION
uth African Options and Experiences
RK ANSTEY (EDITOR)

iture South Africa will demand industrial relations that operate beyond the adversarialism
strikes and stayaways, dismissals and litigation. This text comprises a unique collection
apers by South African and international industrial relations practitioners and academics
all experts in their field. The book contains not only theoretical insights, but practical
delines for implementing various approaches, and helpful South African initiatives.

'GOTIATION
eory, Strategies and Skills
OFESSORS H I J SPOELSTRA & W E PIENAAR

nough various approaches and theories of negotiation are acknowledged, the authors of
text clearly view negotiation as a process wherein the development of alternatives is
ongly emphasized. Verbal and non-verbal strategies and skills in negotiation receive
ailed attention. The book explains how power can be deployed during negotiation and
v attitudes and behaviours can be changed through the use of a few step-by-step recipes.
blication September 1991

)NFLICT MANAGEMENT
OFESSOR D DE VILLIERS

s is a pathbreaking text on one of the most important aspects of industrial relations
tten by one of South Africa's leading academics from the School of Business Leadership
JNISA. It is of value to anyone affected in any way by employer-employee relationships
d, indeed, interpersonal relationships in every sphere of their lives.
blication September 1991

COACHING AND THE BLACK MANAGER
Dr J A E CHAROUX

Dr Charoux provides an easy to read book which also turns out to be easy to use and eas
to keep using. It is a manual for managers who strive for the best results from, and th
best results for, their subordinates. The context is South African. Current changes ar
stresses are taken into account and this book might well prove to be a valuable buildir
block for a new South Africa.

INTEGRATION OF BLACK MANAGERS INTO SOUTH AFRICAN ORGANISATION
Dr J A E CHAROUX

This book addresses commerce and industry, the academic and the black manager himse
providing a practical, reliable method of advancing and integrating the black manager in
the higher levels of South African organisations. It is based on wide-ranging case histori
and discusses the latest research in this area of industrial relations.

BLACK MANAGERS IN SOUTH AFRICAN ORGANISTIONS
L HUMAN & K HOFMEYR

This work will enable readers to formulate a strategy for black advancement within the
company and it will help in the selection of potential managers. It will assist in motivatir
and training employees and enable employers to relate more meaningfully to the aspiration
of the members of their new management teams, thereby harnessing the considerab
economic resource of a vast talent pool.

INDUSTRIAL RELATIONS AND ORGANISATIONAL DYNAMICS
Cases & Text
SONIA BENDIX & FRED JACOBS

The cases contained in this publication reflect real situations through which readers ar
trainees can engage in pro-active, preventive learning experiences. Although a number
cases reflect traditional industrial relations situations and problems, the text reaches muc
further, examining the underlying dynamics of organisational and management-worker i
teractions which so often lie at the root of major conflicts. This title is published in tw
editions - one for students, the other for practitioners.
Publication September 1991

RETRENCHMENT AND REDUNDANCY
Some Practical Guidelines
A W DU PLESSIS & C DE W VAN WYK

The current economic situation in South Africa has ensured that retrenchment and redu
dancies have moved to the forefront of the list of contentious issues confronted by trac
unions, employers, and employees. This book is an essentially practical tool for use I
industrial relations specialists and legal practitioners. Its immediate relevance is ensur
by the inclusion of the latest relevant Industrial Court cases concerning retrenchment a
redundancies in South Africa.
Publication September 1991

PRACTICAL EMPLOYMENT GUIDELINES
A Handbook
P D GERBER

The fragmentary nature of the legislation regulating the practice of employment (and
attendant conditions of service) highlighted a need for a concise and practical handbo
suitable for use in the employment process. It was inevitable and necessary that this bo
which details the application of employment practice in the South African business en
ronment, should see the light of day.
Publication August 1991: ENGLISH AND AFRIKAANS EDITIONS